"During an era when people were boasting about the power of that little red book by chairman Mao Tse-tung, Rev. Cecil Williams took the Bible into the bars and the hangouts of some underground people and said read this little book; it will guide you to lead a fuller, blessed, and kinder life. Rev. Williams and his wife, the poet laureate Janice Mirikitani, welcomed the underground characters, criminals, prostitutes, drug dealers, and everyone into the church. They said that Jesus Christ made wine out of water, and spoke to publicans and walked with sinners. Williams taught us Jesus came to bring us joy and bring it in abundance. As students and followers of Christ, it offered joy to all of us, to the pretty and plain, the rich and poor, the fat and thin, the gay and straight, and we accept it. We learned and we grew and I am one of one thousand to join tens of thousands to say thank you to Cecil and Jan."

—Joy! Maya Angelou

"Glide Memorial has been the soul of San Francisco and the model for what the church ought to be for more than fifty years, and at its heart has been Cecil Williams. Cecil has always led the way when it comes to putting flesh and bones on the saying 'God Loves you.' He has shown the broken down nature of the conventional church and conventional church people even to the point of incarceration and threats to his own life while pointing us forever in a different, real direction. Thankfully for all of us, he now shares his wisdom earned over a lifetime of saying and doing right against all odds. Blessed are we!"

—Archbishop Desmond Tutu

"The Glide community with Cecil and Janice at the helm has been a beacon in San Francisco and something for which we can all be proud. And now they share their many stories and lessons of wisdom, courage, and leadership through the years so we all can benefit. Thank the heavens for Cecil, Janice, and Glide!"

—Jeremy Affeldt, World Series–winning pitcher for the
San Francisco Giants

"Cecil and Janice took a dying church and turned it into one of the most important social institutions that I've seen in this country."

—Warren Buffett

"It's a radical Christ that Cecil Williams follows. Social justice is a next door neighbor to redemption, in Williams' wisdom . . . no faith without actions is his doctrinal certitude. Glide is the only parish I know where you can get an HIV test during the service . . . and everyone, I mean *everyone* is welcome as they are. If I lived closer, I'd go to church every day."

—Bono, cofounder of ONE and (RED)

BEYOND THE POSSIBLE

Also by Cecil Williams

*No Hiding Place: Empowerment and Recovery
for Our Troubled Communities*

I'm Alive! An Autobiography

Also by Janice Mirikitani

Out of the Dust: New and Selected Poems

Love Works (San Francisco Poet Laureate Series)

We, the Dangerous: New and Selected Poems

Shedding Silence: Poetry and Prose

Awake in the River: Poetry and Prose

BEYOND THE POSSIBLE

50 Years of Creating Radical Change at a Community Called Glide

Cecil Williams
and
Janice Mirikitani

HarperOne
An Imprint of HarperCollinsPublishers

HarperOne

HarperCollins website: http://www.harpercollins.com

HarperCollins®, ®, and HarperOne™
are trademarks of HarperCollins Publishers.

FIRST HARPERCOLLINS PAPERBACK EDITION PUBLISHED IN 2013

Designed by Level C

Library of Congress Cataloging-in-Publication Data

Williams, Cecil.
Beyond the possible : 50 years of creating radical change in a community called Glide / Cecil Williams and Janice Mirikitani. — First edition.
pages cm
ISBN 978–0–06–210506–6
1. Williams, Cecil. 2. Mirikitani, Janice. 3. Methodist Church—California—San Francisco—Clergy—Biography. 4. Church work.
I. Mirikitani, Janice, author. II. Title.
BX8495.W638A3   2013
287'.679461—dc23   2012033636

HB 03.30.2020

To the people of the beloved community at Glide—you
demonstrate what it is to go beyond the possible every day

To our children, Kim, Albert, and Tianne; and our
grandchildren, Kaya, Albert, Zachary, and Nicolas

CONTENTS

FOREWORD

Unconditional Love

THERE ARE A lot of things to talk about when we talk about Cecil Williams and Janice Mirikitani and Glide, but Unconditional Love—and it's right that we capitalize it—is the most crucial. This is the most radical of Glide's many trailblazing ideas, and it's the one from which we can learn the most.

The love and marriage of Cecil and Janice is built on this concept: Unconditional Love. Clearly the union of a black Texas minister from a solid upbringing and a Japanese American agnostic from a broken home required Unconditional Love. Surely the changes to Glide detailed within this incredible book, where the church went from staid and empty Methodist also-ran to the always-growing center of hope for the downtrodden and uplifter of the recovering required Unconditional Love. The people who come to Glide's Sunday Celebrations come with this same thing in their hearts—Unconditional Love—and if they don't, the incredible, explosive joy of those services, even for the most cynical, will mean that they most assuredly will leave with it. Everyone Glide inspires, serves, or employs either brings Unconditional Love with them or will soon learn and act on the concept. Glide welcomes all, accepts all, serves all, and inspires all. And in that, Glide is pretty rare.

The unacceptable fact of most churches and most organizations that seek to do good work is that no matter how much they might preach openness and social justice and a level playing field, there is almost always someone being left out. There is always a group considered apart or beneath, some group, at the very least, that is being treated with some level of skepticism. An overarching theme of nearly all groups, all well-meaning organizations and assemblies, including the very United States of America, is *Equality for All—Just Not All at Once.*

Even here in progressive San Francisco, we suffer from the same sort of everyone-but-this-one-group thinking. I heard an unsettling story the other day that illustrates this. There was a conversation recently between two staff members working at an extremely progressive nonprofit that provides people with opportunities for self-expression. One day, noticing that a large portion of a certain workshop's attendees were gay, one staffer wondered aloud if having so many gay members would "scare off" straight people.

Now, it's important to note that the staffer who said this was a young person of color himself, and that he'd grown up in the city, too. He was intimately aware of being marginalized, and knew well the feeling of looking at membership—and possibility—from outside a closed door. But here he was, himself closing a door based on the assumption that some would-be attendees might be made uncomfortable by, or would simply avoid, a workshop where a certain (unacceptable) number of the attendees were gay.

If there's one thing that people in San Francisco know, it's that progressives will find a new way, every day, to shoot themselves in the foot. They will sow divisions among themselves, they will split political hairs, they will endlessly let their hang-ups get in the way of real action. What is left, after all the hand-wringing about how many white people should be allowed on this board of directors or how many gays should be allowed in that workshop, is inaction. Too often, what is left after everyone has argued about whether more Asian students should be allowed in this school or whether there are enough African Americans on that advisory committee, is nothing. No results. Lots of talk, nothing achieved. Lots of identity exploration, lots of one-upsmanship about who is most progressive or most radical, but in the end, no actual progress. Lots of cataloguing of motive and power and intent, but no movement. It's driven by conditional love, not Unconditional Love.

But then there is Glide.

Whenever you need some reminder that there is a place that's above these squabbles, this hyperpolitical tail-chasing, this stasis, you should go to Glide. As a matter of fact, I recently did just that. I went at a time that I was very frustrated with the ability of progressives, with nonprofit idealists, to fight among themselves and prevent anything worthwhile from getting done. So on a particular autumn Sunday, I went down to Glide.

That Sunday morning was bright, clear, and sunny, but cold, so cold. Winter cold, just over 40 degrees, and the residents of San Francisco were walking around, baffled and looking warily to the rising sun, as if to say, "You *will* be solving this soon, yes?"

I went into Glide about half an hour before the 9:00 A.M. Celebration and sat near the entranceway as the parishioners filed in. In front of me there was an usher, whose nametag said Mark, and I began watching him as he did his work.

Mark was a white man in his midfifties, wearing a big round button that said, in purple letters, WELCOME TO GLIDE! And he meant what his button said. Every person that entered that morning was personally welcomed by Mark. "Good morning!" "Welcome," he said to everyone, and to everyone his greeting was as bright and sincere as if he'd just invented the very idea of welcome. Of the people entering, he knew some of the people personally, maybe half of them, these people got hugs and kisses and there were discussions about past services, other work they or he was doing at Glide.

An older woman, her silver hair cut stylishly, arrived, and Mark said, "There she is! Now we can tell Cecil we can start this show." She took Mark's hand. "So warm!" she said, still chilled from the morning air.

The Change band began warming up. The drummer thumped a few times on the bass drum, and it was as if the building's heartbeat was starting up.

The pews filled up with a seemingly impossible cross-section of the city—black, white, Asian, Latino, old, young, gay, straight, wealthy, poor, healthy, and less so. Handicapped parishioners sat in the aisles. There were tourists from all over the world. Always at Glide's Sunday services there are Europeans, South Americans, people from everywhere who have heard about what happens there.

A man entered and asked Mark if he could bring coffee inside. "No, unfortunately," Mark said. "People get in the spirit, and the coffee flies."

As if on cue, the band's drummer thumped again, and the horns began tuning up. The room was getting fuller and warmer. It was like a plane getting ready for liftoff.

A man who might have slept outside the night before walked in, his eyes scanning the room. The cuffs of his pants were caked with dirt five inches up. His face was unshaven and his hair was a wild nest of grey. He walked in, and down the main aisle, his eyes still searching.

Just afterward, a tall and glamorous woman swooped in, her hair an expensive shade of red, her black coat long and immaculate. She seemed to be a regular at Glide. She took her place in a pew, next to a tired-seeming man in a thin tank top, his clavicles protruding from beneath, a man who had seen hard days and sleepless nights.

A group of teenagers, twenty or so members of a youth group from another church in another city—their faces mostly white—rushed down the aisle and walked up to the balcony.

As the church continued to fill, it seemed that someone, somewhere, was curating the attendees of this service to perfectly and completely encompass every single sort of person who might be in San Francisco that day. The Thai American couple leaning on each other, deeply in love. The man in a

Twilight: New Moon sweatshirt, his shoes as old as the earth. Was there any church, any gathering, that day or any other, so rich with everyone who shared the city? Unlikely. And unlikely, in part, by design. Do all churches welcome the homeless and ragged the same way Glide does, or at all? No, they don't. Do any churches at all welcome the gay community as Glide does? Not at all. In fact, on that November Sunday, the Catholic Church, the church of my youth, had just issued a new and stringent statement against gay marriage, and with it they stated that they—the Vatican, the world's billion Catholics—were the faith of conditional love. Or worse, conditional acceptance. But who needs that? Who wants to be accepted when they can be loved?

At Glide, we were repeatedly urged to take the hand of the person next to us, to offer greeting, or a hug, or another greeting, or another hug. And we did, and everyone was happy. It was cold outside, but we were inside. Outside there were suspicions, and people looking askance at each other on the street, people stepping over each other to get wherever they were going, but inside Glide we all stood together, shoulder to shoulder. It was stunning how happy everyone seemed to be, and throughout the service, we were all reminded why. This was the first service after the reelection of President Obama. There was much talk of his recent triumph, as it was a victory not just over a Republican challenger but over a campaign that sought to divide and villainized all kinds of Americans, from immigrants to veterans to union members to, for good measure, anyone who had ever been down on their luck and in need of assistance, government-provided or not.

But that battle over, the Celebration seemed powered by relief and joy. The Glide chorus sang, swaying left and right, and as they sang, Cecil Williams slowly walked onto the stage, smiling, with Janice, in a black suit and high heels, just beside him. The picture seemed very complete. The music picked up, and Cecil took the microphone and complimented the band and the Glide Ensemble. "Aren't they great?" he asked, and the crowd roared its affirmation. "We have to have a great band because we want great music!" he said, and the crowd cheered and the band and chorus got louder.

Next to me, in my pew, there was an African American woman of about seventy, missing all her teeth, wearing a 49ers baseball cap, and looking so energetic that she might jump out of the pew and onto the stage. When the ministers onstage asked us to embrace, we did, at least three times. In front of me, an African American couple, about sixty, dressed nattily, turned to shake my hand and offer a hug; they were longtime members of Glide and were determined to welcome and guide the newer attendees around them. Behind me, alone in the last pew, there was a white man of about thirty, wearing a hoodie and looking very tired and troubled, and when the ministers onstage asked us to shake hands and send warm greetings, we did, many times.

The service was, as always, full of incredible visuals and music. There was an explosive version of "Lean on Me." There was a definitive version of "People Get Ready." There were slides projected on the nave that said, "Love Is Never Wrong," slides that celebrated gay marriage, slides that memorialized a parishioner, Michael Cooper, who had recently passed on,

slides from Obama's victory night, slides urging organ dona-
tion. There were announcements about the church's upcoming
holiday toy drive, about Glide's need for donations to fund
their daily meals, the lines for which were getting ever-longer
during these lean economic times.

And finally there was the sermon, delivered by a young
man, the associate pastor named Theon Johnson III. (Glide
Celebrations are overseen by a ministry team, which con-
sists of cofounders Cecil and Janice, and also Glide's pastor,
Karen Oliveto.) Theon, delivering the message this Sunday,
is handsome, charming, very funny, and seamlessly moved
from secular and the spiritual, the language of the street and
the language of scripture. He talked about the unity possible
in diversity. He talked about how the presidential race barely
mentioned poverty. He talked about Jesus Christ's caring for
people on the margins, the outcasts, and how they are too
often forgotten in a political contest and on any other day.
And then he told a story that seemed to encompass everything
that is core about Glide.

It concerned a woman he met who had come to San Francisco from elsewhere, and who was on the streets, and who in
a troubled time saw the lights of Glide in the wee hours. She
said, "Why are the lights in that church on at 4:00 A.M.?" And
because Glide had its lights on at 4:00 A.M., she entered, and
found shelter and help and warmth and acceptance. What she
found there was Unconditional Love. And this Unconditional
Love was expressed by these lights always on. At any time of
day or night, the lights are on and all are welcome.

Theon went on to explore what it would mean if we all, as
humans, kept our lights on at all times. What would that be

like? If a church can keep its doors open and lights on, accepting all at all times, could we? Could an individual person keep his or her own lights on, their arms and doors open, at all times?

It's hard, that's for sure. It's really damned hard. There's always someone who annoys us. For some, there are Republicans. There are white people, brown people, black people, Asians. There is always someone who is in our way or whose ancestors oppressed our ancestors, or stands for something we don't like, or seems to be standing in the path of progress. The wealthy. The homeless. Tourists. Industrialists. Real estate developers. Hippies. It doesn't matter, but you know what I mean. Wherever you are, there is someone who is unwelcome.

But then there is Glide, with its dozens of empowerment programs, its doors open and lights on. There is Glide, built by Cecil and Janice and nurtured into the future by the Marks and the pastors, by the staff, by the young people, and by the thousands of members who are poor and rich, black and white and brown, well-fed and hungry, clean and unclean, on their way up and on their way down, devout or full of doubt—all welcome, all equally necessary, all equally valid, all offered Unconditional Love. It's a radical idea, but the only one that makes any sense at all.

—Dave Eggers

Imagination

Cecil

IMAGINATION IS ONE of the most penetrating and incendiary forces I've ever experienced. It's plagued me and it's freed me.

I grew up imagining what the world could be like in our segregated town of San Angelo in west Texas during the 1930s. The African American section was cut off from the white section by railroad tracks that ran near my family's house. My sister, five brothers, and I went to an African American school, attended an African American church, and shopped at African American stores. My father was a janitor for the white church in town, and we lived in a ghetto, so our future was limited.

Crossing the railroad tracks in San Angelo could be dangerous. The risk was worth it if my mother saved enough money to walk a half mile to the white grocery store that stocked better food and had a wider selection. One day, when I was eight years old, my sister, brothers, and I went with her. The presence of a black family was allowed in the white part of town as long as we kept our heads down and understood the unwritten rules. There were no formal laws stating that blacks had to get off the sidewalk to make way for whites, but enough white people got angry if you didn't defer to them that we learned to move aside. We always pretended that we didn't notice the difference.

My mother, a very attractive, light-skinned woman, carried my baby brother Reedy, who had bright blue eyes and a fair complexion. Just seeing this "high yellow" mother and child angered some white customers. One woman walked up to Mother in the store and hissed, "Who you been foolin' with, nigger?"

Later in life I would realize that light-skinned African Americans caused many white people to question the sexual practices of white men. The woman who spoke so hatefully wasn't so concerned that my mother was "foolin' around"— she worried that somebody white had been "foolin' around" with somebody black. My mother said nothing. She knew that to answer back would invite trouble, just as her children knew they had to stand aside at the cash register counter until all the white customers were served.

On the way out of the store, we were surprised to find two white police officers waiting for us in the street. They told my mother to open her grocery bags and take out all the purchases, which they checked against the store receipt to make sure we weren't stealing. A crowd gathered around.

Soon people were laughing at the "little nigger children" on their knees trying to stop the groceries from rolling all over the street. When Mother told one of the cops that none of us would ever steal, he called her a "nigger bitch" with such loathing that I looked at the gun in his holster and suddenly wanted a .45 of my own more than anything. It was the only time in my life I wanted to shoot a white person.

That day, I learned that imagination comes not when you're happiest but when you're floundering. It starts deep inside the cracks of life—the places that pull you apart, that make you feel like a failure, that tell you over and over that something's wrong. Often without knowing it, you look for a better way, and that's where imagination starts to grow. I had known something wasn't right about segregation as long as I could remember, but until those cops tried to humiliate my mother, I didn't think I could do anything about it. Now, here, suddenly, was the power of that gun. Imagining it in my hands and thinking about revenge took me out of myself, if only for that moment. I knew that violence only made things worse, but the next thought, though just a glimmer, was inescapable. Somehow, some day, I would imagine our way out of this kind of injustice.

What I remember most about that episode is my mother's dignity in the face of police intimidation. She was angry and dared to speak sharply to the cops, and they indeed lashed out, but she demonstrated to her children that if you know who you are inside, nothing can break you on the outside. I vividly remember Mother's square shoulders and straight back as she calmly led us away.

Later, my parents would use this incident as an example of racial conflict that we children would have to face in life. We could end segregation, even change the nature of racism, but only if we were informed and had the credentials to show it. "Get that diploma," my mother said. "That's what the people in power will want to see." No door would open for us without that piece of paper. For me, having simple goals—get good grades, finish school, go on to college—helped me survive a system that felt oppressive and smothering in small, day-by-day incidents such as trying to shop at a white grocery store.

In our community, the reverend who spoke at services on Sunday was more important than any political leader, just as the black church was the center of activity in most African American communities. Many black families as large as ours hoped the oldest boy would go into the ministry, and most parents waited to see if the calling "took" on the first son. Not my mother. Of all the kids in my family, I had been nick-named "Rev" by Mother from birth, despite the fact that I was the fourth of five boys.

"Someone's going to be the reverend in this family, and you're it," she'd say with a knowing smile. My fate might have been sealed at birth, but there was no doubt that I grew up wanting it and picturing myself in front of a congregation too. Perhaps I inherited the imagination gene from her.

Our church, Wesley Methodist, was a classic black church—a place of safety and comfort, very much like an extended family, where inspiring sermons and soaring choral voices nearly blew the roof off every Sunday. We attended services and events there almost every other day of the week and regarded the pastor as our direct connection to God.

There was only one problem, as far as I was concerned. The black church offered an environment of love and peace, but it could never grant us redemption on earth. We were told to avoid temptation and live a moral life because this was the way to earn our way to heaven. When we died, Jesus would grant us salvation. Only then would we be free.

These promises sounded okay, I guessed, but each Sunday I gazed out the window knowing that across the railroad tracks, white people were having their freedom *right now.* They had the power to run things during their lifetime here on earth, and they seemed to be getting Jesus's salvation in the bargain. This reality felt as out of sync as when I watched Negro adults crossing the tracks to go to work every morning as janitors, stewards, domestics, and cooks. Those were the jobs all of us were destined to have. But our real role in life, I knew, was to appear grateful to whites for giving us any paid work at all. Any hint that we didn't feel that way—that we were, in fact, angry at the injustice of it all—put our jobs at risk.

So like many African Americans, I grew up in a sea of contradictions. Whites ran everything, so I wanted to be white, but I hated white people and everything they did to keep us down. As I got older, I felt that being black was bad. With my kinky hair and big lips, I'd never be accepted in white society, which meant that my whole appearance was one giant negative, and every time I thought that, I couldn't accept myself. I was proud of my strong and loving African American family, but I was ashamed that we lived on the "wrong" side of the tracks.

Soon the nickname Rev became a source of anxiety as well as pride. What happened, I asked myself, when leaders led? Abraham Lincoln might have freed the slaves—my grandfather, Papa Jack, had been one of them—but here in San Angelo, "We're still oppressed as a people," my parents said, so we had to be patient. "It's going to take time, but things will get better," they'd say and, as always, remind us how important it was to get that diploma. Papa Jack himself encouraged us to make a better life. "I'm an ex-slave," he would say. "Now all of you be ex-slaves." That sounded good, but none of us could imagine how we were going to do it.

Then at the age of twelve, I was struck by what felt like a bolt of lightning. It was as though all the pressures in the world punched a hole in my mind, and I was left with nothing but terror. It happened one moonlit night when I sat on the porch with my family. Suddenly everything seemed to turn pitch-black except for the moon, which appeared to melt into itself with fat drops of hot lava falling on my skin. Then I heard a roaring engine and looked up to see a giant train barreling right at us. The smell of hot metal and the sensation of scalding wax from the moon made me scream. Snarling voices came out of the darkness, which overcame light. I felt this darkness sucking out my life. Nobody saw or heard any of this but me. My screaming caused the family to leap up and try to help, but my body jerked and bucked as if some kind of monster were pulling me away. Nobody could do anything but hold me tight. My mother was sure I was having a seizure.

Word spread quickly of my attack, if that's what it was. Within minutes, neighbors arrived, doctors visited (we had two on our side of the tracks), our minister came, and relatives raced over to the house offering help. I couldn't hear or see them, but I did hear alien voices screaming at me. *We will kill you*, they yelled. *There is no escape.*

I thought the only way to fight the voices off was to walk around, and I did, yelling. My parents must have thought I had turned into a madman, but they spoke to me soothingly through the night until I fell into a fitful sleep. By morning, I was calmer, but I knew that melting moon, that big train, and those terrifying voices were just waiting for the sun to go away. I was right. That night the aliens' message was even worse—*We are coming to kill you*, they said—and from then on, night after night for many months, the horror returned. My imagination seemed to be strangling me.

Our family doctor diagnosed my problem as a "nervous breakdown," a nice way of describing a madness that nobody could do anything about. You'd think these ugly, wild fits would have made me a pariah, the kind of crazy person children run away from and adults pity, but not in our section of town. Throughout my time in hell, no one ever judged me, stigmatized me, or shied away. Instead, coming through the house was a steady flow of folks who didn't let up. They comforted me, cooked meals for our family, took turns walking all night with me, sang with me, prayed for me, and waited for some kind of healing to take effect.

Yet as the months went by, the voices only got scarier. They hissed and snapped and growled as though they lived in my ear. I missed school, stayed in bed, feared the darkness, exhausted my parents, and drove everyone to distraction.

No one knew why it was happening, but there was much conjecture. Our beloved but tormented neighbor, JB, had committed suicide a month before, and we all heard him screaming as he slit his own throat. Grief consumed me over the death of my grandfather Papa Jack, the ex-slave who refused to buckle under white control and waved his cane whenever white bill collectors came around ("Ain't we give you enough?" he would yell), but after his death, I seemed to recover along with the rest of the family. The birth of my youngest brother, Reedy, took the family spotlight away from me, but could that have triggered my fall into this living hell?

I believed there was a different reason. The contrast between my family telling me I was the Rev—the future minister who was going to "make it for this family" and pave the way for desegregation—had clashed in my mind with incident after incident in the white world that confirmed I was powerless. All I had to do was look in the mirror when the madness and the voices overtook me: that face, that blackness that the white power structure dismissed as nothing, looked back at me as a nobody who deserved to die.

As I stayed home from school day after day, my parents knew only that I couldn't shake this thing and wasn't growing out of it. In fact, the voices grew worse. They told me that my mother and father were out to murder me, not out of hatred but simply because they had to. Hearing that, I started to scream and yell even more than before. "Don't kill me!" I shouted to my mother. "Don't kill me!"

Everyone in the community prayed for God to help me. Folks were certain that our pastor with his direct line to heaven would surely get the channels open. But there would be no divine intervention for me. Every night, my parents, my brothers, and my sister took turns walking, talking, even joking with me in that way family has, conveying by their presence, *It's all right, Cecil. Hang in there, Rev—we're not giving up on you*. Friends in the community continued to stay all night with me too. Then I started thinking about what this meant. Here were my family and neighbors sticking by me no matter what, yet God was nowhere to be found.

Perhaps that did it. "I'm turning you loose, Lord," I said one night. "You keep gettin' in the way." At this point I had nothing to lose. Maybe that act—not defiance but an insistence that I had to go my own way—jarred something loose, because soon, out of the cracks where it had been simmering, my imagination started to boil.

I pictured myself as the Rev I could be, wanted to be— someone more loving and strong, even ferocious, than anything these voices could harm. Instead of trying to run from the aliens, I turned toward them. If there was no escape, then I wanted to face them. "I know you," I said when they visited me that night, astounded that this was true. "I can hear you." I was more curious than afraid. "I ain't goin' with you tonight," I said, actually sounding steady and firm. Soon it hit me; these voices were not the enemy. Whatever their threats, they could not really bring me harm. In fact, they had something to give me. It was a message. *You're more powerful than you've ever imagined*.

This release of fear came over me gradually, but I began to

fall into the soundest sleep I had experienced in a year. Eventually I woke up to a sunlight so sweet and the sound of birds so loving that I felt my life had started again. My mother was sitting on the edge of the bed.

"Is it over?" she asked with a smile.

I nodded. "It's over."

"Well, you look like a new person."

That's the way I felt. My terror was over. My hell was over. I was ready for whatever life would bring.

The voices never went away entirely. The next night—in fact, intermittently for the rest of my life—the train came at me, the voices shrieked, and darkness hovered like death. But never again would I be so riddled with fear. Because this was the message they brought to me: *Our demons are your alarm system.* In tense situations, they rose up out of nowhere to tell me, *Here comes your anger. Here comes your fear. Here comes your depression.* Just knowing this calmed me down, gave me some clarity and control, so much so that one morning, when I woke up after facing the monsters and not getting killed, everyone saw the difference. "Yes, Lawd!" my sister Titter cried, laughing through tears, "I can feel it!"

She was right to cry out to the very God I had sent away. As I look back on the breakdown today, I realize it wasn't that God finally listened to me, but that I finally listened to God. His message to me—to all of us facing personal crisis—was *I can't help you overcome your demons. That's your job. You have to stand up to your own feelings of powerlessness.* Just as black people allowed white people to define who they were, so I had been allowing the aliens to destroy me. *Embrace your power,* God was saying. *Use this breakdown to come back strong; define yourself.*

A while after that, once I had truly healed and was back in school, my imagination seemed to explode. Great ideas appeared everywhere as the world opened up to me.

Every so often I got the kids in my family and neighborhood to come together for a game of Church. It started whenever we'd find a dead bird or lizard and decide to bury it. As the Rev, I would locate the gravesite and make up the funeral ceremony, but first we would set out chairs around an improvised altar with room for a choir and seats for laypeople. Then I'd do the designating.

My church was not going to be a black church or a white church. It was going to have every color I knew. I'd say to my brother Dusty, "You be black," and to Jack, "You be brown," and to our neighbor Donnell, "You be yellow." My sister, Titter, always complained, "Shoot, why do I always have to be the white person?" But they all got the idea. Our church had room for everybody—not just all colors, but all ages, all kinds of people, and beliefs.

As the minister, I got pretty good at modeling myself after our impassioned pastor at Wesley Methodist, but in my church, the message was different. I talked about freedom for blacks in the everyday world. I talked about Jesus helping us desegregate white schools. The laws and traditions of San Angelo might give white people all the power, but my "flock," at least for the moment, had the freedom to imagine the end of segregation.

Playing Church was the first time I felt my nickname meant something that I could put in practice *now*. Once I imagined a church of all colors, I would never believe that white people themselves could be free until black people, and brown and yellow and red people, found equal freedom *before* they died. Now when I crossed the tracks and saw the hatred of some whites (not all) for people of color, I saw that racial inequality was a sickness of the mind, and that white people were enslaved by it too.

My imagination kept soaring. Didn't we all want to be free, to be equal? Couldn't each one of us quietly desegregate parts of our hometown? I decided to test this idea. Having never been comfortable sitting in the colored section at the back of the bus—the whole practice was humiliating and unnecessary, I thought, even though it was law—I imagined a way to change it. Every day when I got on the bus, I lingered up front so I could start up a conversation with the white driver. He was responsible for enforcing segregation and was always glancing back to make sure black people sat in the back section and white people sat in the front. By distracting him with a question or two as he pulled away from my stop, I stayed in the white section and found out a lot of things—how hard it was to drive in heavy traffic, which routes were boring and which routes were interesting, where accidents were likely to happen. My biggest discovery was that white bus drivers were lonely. Sometimes they got bored and sometimes they felt unappreciated, but most of the time they craved conversation, and it was worth it to bend the rules a bit if an inquisitive Negro kid happened by.

A similar event took place at the big downtown hotel. Like my brothers, I had a talent for singing, and by the time I was thirteen, a white piano teacher named Marie Watkins believed I could turn professional one day. She trained me to sing everything from classical pieces to popular songs, and together she and I were invited to perform for groups like the Kiwanis, Lions, and Rotary clubs on the white side of town.

One recital took place in a hotel where African Americans were supposed to enter through the back door. Before our performance, the president of the club caught up with Mrs. Watkins and me in the parking lot and reminded her that she could come in through the main entrance, but that I should use the kitchen door. He was just stating hotel policy, he said, knowing the subject could be touchy, even in the 1940s.

Mrs. Watkins said she would talk to me about it, but by the time they finished talking I had already walked through the front door of the hotel and was standing in the outer lobby. Technically I hadn't breached hotel policy, although people were staring at me as though I didn't belong in this part of the hotel. Then Mrs. Watkins found me and explained what the president had said. She remarked that I still had time to go out the front door and reenter via the kitchen. But why? I said to her. We were the *paid* entertainment. It didn't make sense to get out of the sight of white people in one place and on the stage in front of everybody in another.

Nevertheless, my training and experience as a young African American told me to avoid making a fuss. It was not my place to put any white person through the "embarrassment" of changing the status quo. If I hoped segregation would end one day, I should humbly enter through the kitchen, knowing that I was contributing to the quiet assimilation of Negro people among gradually tolerant white folks. Thus would history change.

Here was that sea of contradictions again. Oh, how I wanted to *not* make a fuss. But I looked at Mrs. Watkins's kind face as she told me what the president had said, and I couldn't do it. Sneak out the way I came in so I could sneak in through the kitchen? The whole thing scared me to death, but no, I *wouldn't* do it.

"I won't come in the back way," I said. "Let's just walk to the stage from here." Mrs. Watkins looked at me for a long moment. She knew that if people objected, we would have to leave right now, and the service club would never invite a black performer again.

But perhaps this was my moment to learn that imagination is nothing without risk. If you can imagine how to make things better—to stop a war, get out the vote, deter racism, end police brutality—there's going to be resistance, and it won't be easy. But if you know that risk is worth it, following your imagination will always take precedence.

I wasn't all that relieved when Mrs. Watkins told me that the club president had decided I could walk through the front door after all, and that the hotel manager had not stopped him. I only thought, as Mrs. Watkins and I walked into the hall together, *Well, finally.*

There's a photo of me standing by the piano in my very

sharp suede suit with my hands tented together. I did this to relieve the tension and to show people I had power in my voice and my hands. We wowed them with our recital that day, so it's the performance, not the entrance to it, that I like to remember.

As I got older, imagining a better world impelled me forward, without either thinking or worrying. In my late teens, I took a job cleaning offices for two white dentists in San Angelo. On the third day, the local newspaper ran a front-page story about a group of young African American men who had been caught with a white woman, a prostitute, and arrested. People all over town were talking about what would happen to them. On our lunch break, we did the same.

"What were those niggers doing with that white woman?" one of the dentists said to me. "They know better than that."

I had never heard either dentist speak this way. "What did you say?" I asked. It wasn't as though I hadn't heard the word *nigger* before. I just hadn't heard this respected white man say it in his office.

He felt no compunction about repeating the question. "What could those niggers have been thinking of?" he said. There it was again, not just "nigger" but that sense of entitlement, that ring of superiority. He sounded like he owned us.

"Here," I said, getting up. "I'm giving you my broom right now. No matter what these men did, or what you think they did, they're not niggers."

He looked like I had thrown a bucket of water in his face. "Wait a minute," he started to say.

"And I'm not one either," I said on the way out. I needed the money, but I couldn't imagine getting it that way. I was so mad, I walked all the way home.

Most of the time, though, segregation clamped down on us as law. There was no flexibility and no escape. When I was seventeen, my father took ill and couldn't go to work in the downtown bank where he was a janitor. I went down to take his place and was sweeping the front entryway when the president of the bank, a tall white man in a three-piece suit, walked through the front door with a newspaper under his arm. "Good morning," I said. He walked past me without saying a word. After a few minutes, he came back into the hallway and stood directly in front of me.

"I want you to know," he said, "that your father says, 'Good morning, *sir*' to me every day. You didn't say 'sir,' so I'm letting you go. Your father, too." And he walked away.

I stood there not knowing what to think or do. My father had worked at this bank for two years. He was one of the few Negroes allowed inside, and he had earned the respect of every white person there, including the president, however tentatively. Now his son, having worked at the bank for less than a day, had lost the job for him. The shame and rage hit so hard that I stomped out without knowing where I was going. My feet led me straight home to break the news to my father. I was hurt, too, but like most black people I had learned to stack up the hurts and put them aside, waiting for that day in the future when I could do something about them.

My father was a very sweet man who guessed what had happened the moment I walked in the door. "I can get another job," he said when I told him, "but not another son." He patted my shoulder proudly. "You stood up," he said. I hadn't stood up to the president, actually—my father imagined it that way—but I took that look in his eyes and stacked it away in memory too.

And then as often happened with my family, we started to sing. Music had always filled the room spontaneously because we were all very good at harmony and loved to sing together. This time we sang to ease my hurt, because that's what all gospel songs and spirituals are about, the pain of living under the control of somebody else. My parents knew I needed a safe place where I could let that hurt out and let it go. Before I knew it, we sang our blues away.

2

Acceptance

Cecil

IN WHAT WOULD become one of the most infamous photographs of 2012, the Republican governor of Arizona, Jan Brewer, was seen angrily shaking her finger in Barack Obama's face when he arrived at the Phoenix-Mesa airport.

The cause of the conflict didn't matter so much to me as the image of a white woman dressing down a black man who happened to be the president of the United States. It struck me that journalists played down her blast at the president as a "tiff" and a "dustup." It was much more than that.

Racism is embedded in American culture, unseen and unnoticed by many. Instead of an uproar taking the governor to task for her display of racist superiority, the general reaction was a mild rebuke for her "bad manners." We see this so often that pretending racism doesn't exist has become commonplace. How easily Newt Gingrich got away with referring to Obama as "the food stamp president," a cheap shot that played into negative stereotypes of African Americans being dependent upon welfare. Gingrich was not called to account for what was deemed at most a "racially tinged" charge. Then there were the political analysts who admired the strategy of Governor Mitt Romney, who they said was trying to be "the whitest white man" to run for president. A Romney adviser bolstered that image by stating that Romney's "Anglo-Saxon heritage" was too "special" for Obama to appreciate.

People of color have known for years that with the many victories of the civil rights movement, racism moved under the radar—hidden from view but insidious and institutionalized all the same. If we're aware of that, my question is, what are we to *do* with this information? How can people of all backgrounds work toward an equal and just society when we know that racist policies, stereotypes, humor, and profiling are still entrenched?

I have worked all my life in the civil rights movement to change the status quo, but after seeing the "finger-shaking" photo, I began wondering if it's even possible to challenge the established power system today. It occurs to me that perhaps there's something to learn from a time past, when acts of blatant racism were common. How did we deal with them then, without turning bitter or vindictive or beaten down? Was it easier to fight back when white people hated you openly, not to mention legally? Were there lessons from my own struggle that could be applied today?

One episode stands out as a lesson. It took place during a very hot spring in 1945, when I was a junior in high school. My brothers had just been discharged from serving in the military during World War II. I was sixteen and eager to get out of San Angelo, Texas, to see the postwar world on my own. When the chance came up to compete in an all-black, all-high-school track meet in Tuskegee, Alabama, I went for it.

Tuskegee is about seven hundred miles across three states from San Angelo, so you'd think it would have been an ordeal for six sweating bodies (four athletes and two coaches) crammed in the head coach's car to make the drive in a single day. But it wasn't.

Just the thought of Tuskegee—already famous for training the first black pilots in U.S. history—was a thrill for any Negro kid, regardless of the long, hot, dust-filled drive. Not only did the four of us sprinters get to compete, we won our relays and both the 100- and 220-yard dash. Feeling triumphant, we then piled back in the coach's car.

On the way home, the head coach decided to stop at a food store next to a gas station about fifty miles out of Selma. He had been a famous football star at Tuskegee some years before and was always talking about Alabama catfish. Here was our chance, he said, to get some very fine victory takeout.

The assistant coach, who was driving, pulled the car into a slot near the store. We all settled back to wait while the car idled, but after less than a minute, *BAM!* The door flew open and the head coach came charging back out, running toward us like a man on fire.

"Get away! Get away!" he shouted, jumping into the passenger side only seconds before three white men with clubs raced out of the store after him. The assistant coach slammed the car in reverse, but too late. A big white guy smashed a blackjack through the driver's-side window and hit him full force in the head. Glass flew, blood spurted, everybody shouted as he reversed gears and hit the accelerator. The big white guy raised his club again, but the car spun away from him and out of the lot in a blizzard of rock and gravel. I looked back to see more enraged white men running out of the store behind us.

"Go left!" the coach yelled. "Left! *Left!* Now!" The assistant coach wiped blood away from his eyes with one hand and gunned the car onto the highway with the other. He had no time to look for oncoming traffic and jerked the steering wheel left as sharply as he could, the car weaving crazily on two wheels for a terrifying moment. From the rear window the three of us in the backseat counted *ten* white men with blackjacks and pipes jumping into three different cars and starting to race after us. *This is it,* we were all thinking. If we didn't get away in the next seconds, these men would beat us to death and hide our bodies in the swamps of Alabama.

"What's the matter with them?" I shouted over the screaming engine. "Why are they chasing us?"

"I went in the front door!" the coach yelled. "They want to teach us a lesson!" Behind us the white men were actually waving their weapons in fury outside the car windows. It was like a cops-and-robbers movie, I thought, except they were insane with rage. The coach kept yelling, "Don't let up! Go faster!" and from the backseat, we kept yelling, "They're gaining!" The assistant coach, still bleeding in rivulets down his ear and jaw as we careened around every bend in the highway, got the car up to ninety miles per hour. I braced for the bullets these crazy white men were sure to start shooting through the car windows at any moment . . . but then, nothing. A WELCOME TO MISSISSIPPI sign flew by, clouds of dust behind us cleared, and the three cars with all the white men vanished. Just like that.

"What happened?" somebody said.

"I think we're in Mississippi," the coach said. "I guess they're not crossing the state line." The assistant coach slowed the wheezing car over to the side and stopped, so the coach could look at the gash on his temple. We sat there flooded with relief in the hot Mississippi sun while the coach told us what happened at the food store. When he walked in, he said, every white man in the place looked up and yelled at him, "Nigger, use the back door!"

"I told them I didn't see the separate entrance for coloreds. I guess I thought they might show some respect for us if I told them I had some hungry young athletes waiting in the car who had just competed at Tuskegee. Hell, they might hate us, but aren't they proud of Tuskegee?"

The white men didn't seem to hear any of that. All they heard was an uppity Negro refusing to obey. "I should've known to back out of there the instant I saw those blackjacks," the coach said, shaking his head. "They were just waiting for an excuse to beat up the next colored man."

Hearing the coach's story changed the mood in the car completely. If we had been flooded with relief for just surviving the chase before, now we felt rage welling up. Trying to push it away, I got out of the car and kissed the ground. "I don't care what state you are," I said to the asphalt, "but I sure am happy to be in it."

Then I turned around and looked at the Alabama side. Those white men were probably still laughing at us on the drive back—probably still waving their weapons out the windows. I was angry and humiliated enough to feel like crying, but I wasn't going to let myself feel hopeless. My mother's advice came back to me. *When you're down, that's when you rise. No matter what they do to you, remember—they cannot determine your life for you.* I straightened a little taller, remembering her proud defiance, and made a silent vow. *I'm coming back,* I said to those men. *You nearly killed us this time, but one day when conditions are different, you'll have to deal with me.*

I wasn't thinking of taking them on in a fight—that would be suicide. And I had an inkling that hate was not what I should foster, but love. There were no words for this—at sixteen, I felt like a big piece of unshaped dough—but I felt the spirit inside me flowing into my fingers and hands, not to make fists but to give that dough some form and direction. Love was so, so hard. I might have wanted to get in the car and race right back across the border, to find them and hit them as hard as I could, right now. But the spirit I believed in required patience and time. At every step I would have to say, *That's all I can do right now, but I'm coming back.*

I was a young black man who believed in the America my brothers fought for in the war, an America that promised everyone would one day be equal to everyone else—not just tolerated, not just given a modicum of respect, but accepted as fully equal. The white attackers were clinging to racist hatred that had its roots in slavery, but the day would come when we would meet again, and when that happened, this grandson of a slave would choose the terms.

I thought often about that vow as I went through high school and enrolled in the all-black Samuel Huston College (later Huston-Tillotson University) in Austin, joining my brothers who were starting out at the same time as freshman on the GI bill. Soon the four of us, who had long billed ourselves as an a cappella quartet called the Williams Brothers, were paying our tuition and expenses by picking up gigs at receptions and church events. We got our break when the Methodist Church began encouraging white parishes to help "separate but equal" Negro education. At the time, financial contributions were the only way that liberal whites could give support to black colleges, so Methodist churches throughout the West invited the president of Samuel Huston and his wife to attend fund-raisers and talk about the college. He asked my brothers and me to travel with them and sing Negro spirituals such as "Go Down, Moses" and "There Is a Balm in Gilead" at the end of his presentations.

One evening during a long trip from Texas to California, we stopped for dinner outside Los Angeles. The restaurant was busy but not very crowded, so we were surprised that after fifteen minutes or so, no one waited on us. The president hailed the manager.

"We'd like to order," he said. "Could you send our waiter over?"

"Just a minute," the man said.

Time passed, waiters rushed by, and finally an African American man in a dirty white apron—apparently the dishwasher—came out of the kitchen and walked over to our table. We knew something was wrong when he wouldn't look at us.

"Y'all can't eat here," he said.

"What do you mean?" asked the president.

"They won't serve you. Read that sign," the dishwasher said, pointing to a flyer on the wall that read, WE RESERVE THE RIGHT TO REFUSE SERVICE TO ANYONE.

"Do you mean you're not going to serve us because we're colored?" the president asked.

The dishwasher nodded and walked back to the kitchen.

"But that's . . . They can't do this," the president stammered. "Why, if they don't serve us. I'm going to take something!" Out of frustration and a need to act boldly, he grabbed a stack of cloth napkins and stormed out of the restaurant. The rest of us followed him outside, our anger growing as we walked into the parking lot. This was *California,* not Texas, we told each other. We had driven without incident from Dallas to Los Angeles, and now this? Refused service in a restaurant on the West Coast? And what about the dishwasher? The only black man in the place, and they made *him* tell us we weren't welcome? And he did it?

When we got to the car, the president said, "Look at this automobile. We're as respectable as anyone." My brothers shook their heads. Being middle class made no difference. The problem was racism. What an irony! We were visiting *white* churches; *white* people were donating money to Negro education; this man (with the napkins still clutched in his hand) was the *president* of a *respected college*.

As they continued talking, their voices faded into the background, and a familiar feeling of dread overcame me. *Oh, no*, I thought. It felt like the aliens that had driven me to madness during my breakdown at age twelve. They were screaming at me with the same awful, frightening message. *You are nothing. You are worthless. No one wants you here.* I thought, *No, not now. Go away.* I tried to stuff the alien voices down, but they were too powerful.

In the car as distant voices buzzed, I realized that my feeling in the restaurant was similar to what I had felt before the breakdown. It was humiliation—of rejection, of being told we were nobody—and it was shame. Shame for being dismissed and despised because of the color of our skin. And yet I learned that very day that the aliens who had so vividly taken over my life were now becoming the source of a new kind of courage. They were warning me, like an alarm system in my head, to stop being a victim, to stand up to fear and vulnerability and most of all, to remember who I was—a black American whose family and community, themselves maligned by white people, had never judged me, never resented me, never stopped loving me no matter how long those horrible nights of my breakdown went on. Once again the power of community saved me—it was like a lesson I had to remember again and again, especially when I felt rejected by white people.

Then I thought about the dishwasher. In our anger, my brothers and I had blamed him, the messenger, and called him an Uncle Tom. The fact was that more than any of us, he was the powerless one. A black man abused by his employers, knowing his job was on the line, had no choice but to comply with their order. I kept thinking there was something more I could have done.

Instead of angrily walking out and leaving the dishwasher to his plight, I could have made a connection and said to the man, "Brother, this is not on you. I know how hard it must be to bring a message like that to us. I feel it, and I'm with you." Just to say he wasn't alone, at least for that moment. Just to say, *I embrace you. I take you with me.* A few sentences like that might have spoken of something larger than what had just happened. Something like love. But I was nineteen and remained silent.

These are the kinds of memories—my as-yet-unfulfilled vow at the Alabama border; my missed opportunity with the dishwasher—that tend to follow us as we move ahead in life. We learn from them and go on. But I didn't think either experience would come back to haunt me, until nearly twenty years later, in 1965, when I watched the TV news from my office at Glide and could not believe what I saw: hundreds of demonstrators in Selma, Alabama, beaten back and trampled by sheriff's deputies on horseback at the beginning of an attempted voting rights march from Selma to Montgomery, the state capital. Hearing the cries of terror and pain from the marchers and watching helmeted troops use clubs on children as well as adults amid clouds of tear gas—all this was so shocking that

I raced to the phone to make a plane reservation and the next day flew to Selma by myself to see if there was any way I could contribute.

I didn't know anyone in Selma, but I felt that surge of solidarity that comes when you meet people who are responding to a crisis as a single mind—in this case with love and strength rather than violence and hate. Martin Luther King Jr. had flown in with lawyers from the Southern Christian Leadership Conference to argue against the State of Alabama's attempts to stop the march. Since his court appearance would take a few days (it turned out to be a few weeks), I used part of my time in Selma to speak with clergy, teachers, health-care workers, food vendors, and organizers working out of dilapidated buildings and with few supplies to help sustain the effort until the march got started again.

Armed with new information, I flew back to San Francisco and called a press conference with other community leaders to put out a plea: *The people in Selma need our bodies, our supplies, our money, and our help. If you can't come back with me and other folks from the Bay Area who are flying to Selma next week, give what you can.* Hundreds if not thousands of people responded as Glide hurriedly organized the trip.

The following week I remember sitting in that packed airplane listening to the pilot announce that we had just crossed the border from Mississippi to Alabama and would be starting our descent soon. People strained to look out the window for evidence of the crowds gathering below. In a few hours we'd be in the thick of preparations for the next attempt at a voting rights march from Selma to Montgomery. This time it wouldn't be a few hundred but at least several thousand people marching, or so observers predicted.

For me, of course, that state line represented a life-or-death border I had known very well at age sixteen. I remembered standing there vowing to return one day and face racism on my own terms. Thinking of this filled me with new resolve, because I wasn't coming back alone to do this. I was bringing two planeloads of volunteers, along with cash donations amounting to $45,000 to help shore up preparations for the march. After we arrived in Selma, I distributed three packages of $15,000 each to three organizers whom I had met earlier and who I knew would put the money to good use for the march effort. At the same time, the sheriff of Selma was deputizing civilians right and left and assigning them places on the Edmund Pettus Bridge, where the horrible conflagration I had seen on TV had occurred a few weeks before.

Even now, the organizers of the march from Selma would need all the help they could get. When a call went out for volunteers to distract the deputies from the main part of town, I joined a group of marchers taking buses to the mayor's home to demonstrate for voting rights. This nonviolent act would probably be interpreted by law enforcement as a threat to life and property and would thus draw a number of deputies away from the city. About six hundred of us arrived at the house, but just as we assembled on the sidewalk and started our demonstration, the mayor's wife ran out the front door with a gun in her hand. It was a little silver pistol.

"I've got six bullets!" she yelled. "I can take six of you niggers out!" We stood there facing her with our arms linked and were careful not to step on the mayor's property. She appeared just wild enough to shoot but didn't seem to know how to unlock the safety. It was a lethal yet humorous scene that got even more comical when the sheriff's deputies arrived, each one carrying a baton, a cigar, a gut, and at least one gun. Collectively they looked like a classic image of the big, hulking, Southern white cop with everything sticking out. Trying to line us up for arrest, the officers realized there were too many of us to fit in the overcrowded jail, so the deputy chief made an announcement.

"You niggers think you can come here and share a cell with Martin Luther King? Well, he's the last person you're gonna see."

They commandeered our buses and loaded everybody back on to take us to a large high school gymnasium with two big basketball courts that would act as makeshift holding cells—one for women and one for men. Finding ways to affirm our presence through nonviolent action, we sang freedom songs that had emerged from the many marches of the civil rights movement, and we even made up new lyrics. Soon our voices, our clapping, and our cheering for justice resounded with a kind of spirit that nearly lifted the gym off the ground.

The police hated guarding us when we were having such a good time but didn't dare turn violent after the debacle of "Bloody Sunday," as the attack on the Edmund Pettus Bridge was now called, so they decided to appear generous by letting us go.

"Y'all can git," said the deputy chief, standing next to the open doors. "No one will be cited."

We had no leader or spokesperson, no time to huddle or vote or make sure everybody agreed on what to do. And yet, all the people in both gyms just quietly shook their heads as if we had planned for this moment all along. To me, this was the potential of community at its rawest, most instinctive core. It proved as never before that when African Americans got together, a power they thought they never had emerged as a uniting force. It spoke of independence, of deciding for ourselves, and it spoke of unconditional acceptance—we trusted one another as deeply as we trusted our own families, and the deputies knew it. They were furious.

"Why, you niggers are crazy to stay here," the chief deputy said.

"Book us, then!" people called out. "We're not moving." As long as our six hundred remained, dozens of deputies had to guard us, or (so they thought) we'd tear the place up. Quite the contrary—our message was nonviolent. It said, *We're not going to fight you. We're going to confront you with our love and with our goodness, because that's who we are, in the face of who you are. Even if you choose to use violence, we will bring about change. Against your violent inhumanity, we will match you with our nonviolent humanity, so that even you will be changed.*

With this message, I experienced the incredible "power of soul force," as Dr. King phrased it. This was nonviolence as a way of life.

The sheriff's men walked out, slamming and locking the doors again. That was fine with us. All night long we harmonized and talked and sang to one another, basking in this new strength. By 6:00 A.M., when the deputies opened the doors, we kept on singing as we walked through Selma to the church where Martin Luther King Jr. held a rousing spiritual celebration.

I remembered the March on Washington of two years before when I stood on the steps of the Lincoln Memorial watching Dr. King deliver his "I Have a Dream" speech. Not only the power of his words but his fearless confrontations against destructive and inhumane power systems galvanized my commitment to the entire civil rights movement, to fight for acceptance on every front, whether for gender, sexual orientation, nationality, race, or class.

And now the Selma march was more than inspiring. We accomplished our goal—pressuring Congress to pass the national Voting Rights Act of 1965, which prohibited the poll taxes, rigged literacy tests, and selective registration requirements that had kept blacks from registering to vote for many generations. But the meaning of the march—the huge, beating heart of it—would become a landmark in the way change can happen in America. The six hundred people who'd been stopped on the Edmund Pettus Bridge on Bloody Sunday increased to three thousand the following week and to twenty-five thousand when the march finally made it to Montgomery on March 22, 1965.

In the three months that followed passage of the Voting Rights Act, the number of African Americans registered to vote in Dallas County, Alabama, soared from 363 to 8,000.

I couldn't have imagined such changes taking place twenty

years before, when as a sixteen-year-old, I kissed the asphalt on the Mississippi side of the border, vowing to return. Perhaps that's why "We Shall Overcome" brings up enormous emotion in me. It's not only the belief that adverse circumstances will change someday, but a certainty that the oppressed of every kind *already have* the integrity, the will, and the love to rise up again and again and stand our ground.

What can we do about embedded racism today? Our first step is to stop pretending the problem has ceased to exist because it isn't as obvious as it was in the past. Intolerance is still the biggest hornet's nest in society, and until each of us deals with it honestly, America will continue to shake its finger in blame at people of color, at the poor, at women, at immigrants, and at people of different sexual orientations.

The second step is to recognize, as Governor Brewer did (one hopes), that when you shake your finger at someone else, you need to point it first at yourself. Since the era of protests and marches has passed, the responsibility is on each of us to acknowledge our own prejudices and stretch beyond present inequalities to create a just society, and to tell the truth when we see racist acts happen in front of even the president's nose.

The lessons we learn from our reaction to racism can be very powerful. The incident at the restaurant in Los Angeles taught me something I have remembered all my life: *the more painful the rejection, the more powerful the revelation*. The dishwasher in that restaurant was a source of humiliation and shame because he represented a sense of powerlessness I would come to fight against every day of my life. His action revealed to me my own determination, my life's calling.

And there was a second lesson: *rejection inspires action*. Remembering the chase across that border in Mississippi and the dishwasher's order to leave the restaurant in Los Angeles took the words right out of me. I was headed for the day when no more talk, no more complaining, no more planning would be necessary. As I saw in Selma, and later at Glide, putting your body out there and standing up for what you believe make rejection irrelevant.

None of us exists today because we were born this way. What we see as our character has been forged by painful experience. We've been tempered by every episode in our past, and for me the episodes at the Alabama border and the L.A. restaurant helped fire up the determination I felt when I went to Selma and stood without fear and without hate along with twenty-five thousand people demanding not only that black people be tolerated, but that we be accepted unconditionally as fully equal and fully different—fully welcomed, fully received, fully appreciated, and fully celebrated. Just like everybody else.

Today when racism is not as visible and has been shoved under the table, it's doubly hard work to understand unconditional acceptance. How much easier it would be if everybody in the room looked like you, came from the same place as you, and made the same jokes as you. How much harder it is when difference invades the room, and you have to be sensitive to everybody's culture/color/gender/nationality/ability and sexual orientation, let alone religious belief. You have to not only accept each person, you have to remove all conditions that might limit your acceptance. That's hard work, yes, but look what diversity gives back: when that room is filled with diversity, we are enriched by each other's differences; we are as complicated and as joyous and as wise as the whole world.

I say this practically every Sunday: the reason Glide aggressively celebrates diversity is because experiencing difference humanizes us. We may never completely achieve unconditional acceptance, but along the way, we can learn how to be more human.

3

Integrity

Cecil

I WAS JUST about to graduate from college in 1952 when a group of Methodist seminarians led by Bob Brian invited me to apply to the all-white Perkins School of Theology at Southern Methodist University. At twenty-one, I had never heard of Perkins and planned to attend an all-black seminary, since at that time all the white schools were segregated.

But Bob explained that because students at Perkins had made a formal request aimed at desegregation, which had been passed by the faculty, I had the chance to be part of a unique experiment. Five African Americans had been preselected to cross the color line on a campus of white seminarians (Perkins), which itself was surrounded by thousands of white undergraduates (SMU). If the experiment worked, it would be "the first voluntary desegregation of a major educational institution in the South," as Merrimon Cuninggim, dean of Perkins, put it. The students were proud of that word *voluntary*, and in those Jim Crow years, I felt its magnetism also. Instead of waiting years for civil rights lawsuits to force everyone's hand, Perkins wanted to begin the integration process now. It was a daring step for this conservative bastion of theological scholarship, and oh, how I wanted to be part of it.

At a time when many white people in Texas still believed they would contract a disease if they got too close to a Negro, Perkins was going to open its dorms, cafeterias, bathrooms, gyms, and locker rooms to five African Americans because its students believed (or were told to believe) that integration was a God-given right. The very idea stirred my soul.

A few months before enrolling at Perkins, I heard that word of the experiment had leaked out, and hostile white groups were already organizing to stop it. African American ministers in Texas, on the other hand, took so much pride in my enrollment at Perkins that they referred to me as "our son in the ministry," a high honor. My own ambition, which I kept secret because it was too outlandish for its time, was to become the first black pastor in Texas of a large white Methodist church—or I should say a *formerly* white church. I imagined myself welcoming people of all colors to a congregation that would celebrate differences rather than reject every color but one.

On our first day at Perkins, Dean Cuninggim called the five of us into his office to say he was not going to rule "by fiat." If a race-related problem cropped up, he wanted us to talk to him about it, then make up our own minds. There were going to be a number of "historic firsts," not the least of which was rooming with white students in the dorms and participating in extracurricular events where no black student had been allowed before. No matter how sensitive the issue, he knew we would make "the right decision." Something sounded a bit too amiable about this wording, but of course we agreed. The dean promised that no overt acts of racism would interfere with the experiment, and in return he hoped we five would promise not to "upset the process" of Perkins's way of teaching, which went all the way back to the school's founding in 1915.

We weren't surprised when many students snubbed us in classrooms and meeting places, but otherwise, people made a point of welcoming us and drawing us into conversations. My white roommate and I got along very well. On the academic side, we worked hard to become serious scholars in the Perkins mode. It was not an easy mode. The professors emphasized theological theory, root words, and analytical attack, rather than storytelling, emotional inspiration, and—heaven knows—soul. If sometimes the teachings seemed cold and remote to me, perhaps that was the point: when I based a term paper about Exodus on theological derivatives, I didn't think I was succumbing to an exclusive white academy at the expense of my black roots. I believed that getting an A in this class would help show the world that Negroes were equal to every task that whites could place before them.

And when it came to making the "right decision," we knew enough to defer to the white experience when necessary. Since African Americans had never participated in intramural sports at Perkins and SMU, it was a big step for any of the teams to choose one of us. When Larry Meredith, a prominent white pitcher, asked me to play catcher on a softball team, I knew that aggressively tagging out a white player could stir up hostility. Whenever there was a play at home, I would block the plate with my body and let the player sliding home choose how to come into contact. In his old-fashioned way, Dean Cuninggim was thrilled to see a potentially antagonistic collision of black and white bodies turn into what he called a "racially neutral rhubarb."

True to his promise, Dean Cuninggim kept overt hostility to a minimum. Ushers at SMU football games were told in advance that our student IDs allowed us to sit midfield in the whites-only section. This made us stick out like a big black dot, so the dean filled several rows of seats around us with liberal-minded students and security guards who were there to shield us from any bottles and refuse that might rain down on our row from unsympathetic whites. (This never happened.)

Throughout the campus, we searched for areas where a black presence might actually be welcome. When auditions were held for a student production of *Cry, the Beloved Country*, a play based on the bestselling novel about South Africa, I raced over to the theater, thinking a number of parts for black people would be perfect for me. I was a good actor with experience from college, but the director made it clear that the last thing in the world people wanted to see was a Negro actor playing a Negro role. As if to prove it, he and the white actors tried to pretend I was not there. It was a snub, although one person did mention that if I had gotten permission from Dean Cuninggim, they might have given me a try. *"Permis-*

sion," indeed, I thought. The idea of running to the dean for permission to do anything so angered me that I forgot to feel ashamed.

Students on campus did know that I was a good singer, or at least that was the reason, I thought, that organizers of the student spring show, *Panorama,* asked me to perform. I'll never know if it started out as a prank or an insult, but as I got onstage, word passed from row to row that everyone should withhold applause. Much to my surprise, when I finished singing, the hall went silent. It took me a moment to realize what happened, so I said, "Aw, come on. You know you loved it," and the audience burst out laughing. That was about as close to equal participation as I ever got.

We five did keep one secret. When the dean said he believed we would "make the right decision," he left unstated that we were not to befriend or date white women on or off campus. Of course, we knew that from the start. There was nothing white men hated more than seeing "their" women pursued by black men. What the dean could not foresee, however, was that some white female students on campus would aggressively come on to us. The suggestive looks, inappropriate touching, flirtatious overtures, and requests for dates happened often enough to keep us on guard wherever we went. Even in chapel, when everyone joined hands to recite the Lord's Prayer, the girl next to me tickled the palm of my hand salaciously as if we could soon run out for a quickie. Casual friendships with white girls turned into potential scandal when they wrote home to say, "Dear Mother, I had lunch today with a wonderful Negro student from

Perkins. . . ." The president of Perkins received so many angry letters from mothers "protesting the indignity" they had suffered from the news of such lunchtime encounters that we five promised to stay out of the student union and confine ourselves to a table at the Perkins cafeteria.

I found myself walking around campus in a state of surprise and disappointment about this. My mother had died of cancer a few years before, and I was still too filled with grief to conjure up her encouragement about "getting that piece of paper" no matter how difficult the process. I could not get over my bewilderment and my anger at God for taking away a woman who was so good, who had treated everyone with love, who believed in the church and its potential to change the world. How ironic it was that I, the one child whom Mother had chosen as the Rev in our family, should be toyed with or banished or treated like a sexual pet or threat.

The five of us often met in the black section of Dallas where we could have a meal and blow off steam at how bizarre life at Perkins was turning out to be. The popular pastor of St. Paul Methodist Church, I. B. Loud, invited us all to intern as student ministers at his church and see what it was like to be embraced by the black community every Sunday. With its capacity of sixteen hundred, St. Paul stunned us with giant waves of love and acceptance from the moment we walked in. People welcomed and cheered us as part of one big family. We dated African American women from the church—that's where I met my future wife, Evelyn—and Reverend Loud often took us aside like a father to talk about the importance of stepping up to life's challenges, especially those at Perkins.

"Remember what's ahead of you," he would say. "You're going to open doors to the people behind you. You're going to be somebody in the church because of this. So hang on."

His warning was far more timely than I realized. On my own, I had been participating in civil rights demonstrations and didn't think that would be a problem since they took place off campus. But after one demonstration against a movie theater in Dallas that allowed admission to African Americans only one night a week, a news photo identified me as a student at Perkins. Complaints to the administration poured in. Dean Cuninggim said at a meeting in his office that he knew I would make "the right decision" (meaning I'd stop participating in demonstrations), but by the end of the second year, I wasn't sure what that right decision was anymore.

To me, school was fine for studying and preparing, but injustice took place in our lives *now*. Activist ministers and seminarians needed to act *now*. The dean, on the other hand, believed that the experiment at Perkins had to be protected above all else. Embarrassing Perkins by carrying placards and getting arrested could only "stir things up" and get us all into trouble. I felt the old rage building. The dean knew that racism existed all over the campus and that it would have been easy to "stir things up" when it came to baseball games or theater auditions or fraternizing with white women. But stopping me from civil rights work that I felt would benefit the nation because it would lead to the end of segregation (a lot faster than compromised experiments) seemed to me a deal breaker. By that time I was offered a summer internship at a church out of state. Dean Cuninggim and I decided it was probably best for me to leave Perkins for a few months while I figured things out. The other four remained.

Matters got worse while I was gone. The board of trustees received a visit from the school's ultraconservative benefactor, Joe J. Perkins, who had known about the experiment but apparently missed the part about interracial living conditions in campus dorms. Mr. Perkins's name was on the school, so when he objected, the board usually obliged. He ordered Dean Cuninggim to "get rid of the Negroes as soon as possible," but this time too much was at stake, and suddenly everyone was taking sides. Dean Cuninggim himself refused Mr. Perkins and threatened to resign, which would have led as much to the collapse of the experiment as to "getting rid of the Negroes" altogether. Thinking they would break this stalemate, the four African Americans remaining on campus announced they would voluntarily leave the dorms and live off campus. That way, they figured, nobody would have to accept black people as part of the student body, so their presence would be easier all around, especially to Mr. Perkins.

This idea of hiding ourselves until we got through the third year was so completely at odds with what we were *doing* at Perkins that when they told me the news (I was still working out of town), I said absolutely not—I would resign from Perkins if they went through with it. To me, the good intentions of starting a quiet and gradual desegregation had turned into political gamesmanship, and what would happen to our integrity if we continued playing that game? If we said the experiment succeeded while black people were shunned from white dorms, what were we proving?

Just when it looked as though all was lost, Mr. Perkins's wife surprised everyone at a trustees' meeting by openly disagreeing with her husband and throwing her weight behind a vote to table forever the matter of "getting rid of the Negroes." With this simple act, the dean's job was saved, and the dorms opened up for us again, with one proviso: we had to volunteer not to room with whites.

I still didn't know if I would come back. Civil rights work was so essential to me that if the church refused to support it, maybe I wasn't a candidate for the ministry after all. Word of my indecision reached Reverend Loud, who took pains to set me straight. "Don't let them jockey you around like this," he said. "Figure out what it's going to take to finish your third year and get that diploma. Then, I promise you, the world is yours. You want to make changes in the church? You have to graduate with credentials." I remembered my mother saying so often to all her kids, "Get an education first. *Then* fight segregation."

Reverend Loud asked his interns to preach at Sunday vespers and encouraged me to deliver the message I was burning to bring out. It was there that I began to talk about how much the Methodist church needed to tell the truth about itself as a divided church. I referred to the fact that none of us black folks at St. Paul's could walk into a white church and be welcome. "You know what I'm talkin' about," I would say as people nodded. Reverend Loud never stopped me from broaching this uncomfortable topic. He regarded me as part of a new breed of ministers introducing ideas about civil rights that had been unthinkable in his day.

As word spread about that sermon, young Methodist pastors, black and white, asked me to speak at their churches also. At first the invitations were for "safe" days, such as during Brotherhood Month or on Race Relations Sunday, but later I was invited to be part of their regular service. At that level, being the preacher and walking up and down the aisles and talking to regular folks, I found that no topic was too controversial. But behind the scenes, where decisions were made, the game of politics continued.

Our tiny African American contingent graduated with the rest of the class at a balmy out-of-doors ceremony in 1955. I remember feeling a surge of energy as I received my degree. Instead of returning to my seat, I walked off the stage and kept on going. With my mortarboard tucked under an arm and my gown flowing in the breeze, I broke into a run. For the first time in three years I felt free.

Of course I was grateful that Perkins proved to other academic institutions in the South that desegregation worked. It wasn't integration by any means, but the door had opened. And, too, the advice of my parents to "get that paper" had helped immeasurably. Many years later at Glide, Janice and I would pass along that same advice to students in our youth programs who were struggling in school. No matter how hard it is, we would say, no matter how ridiculous you think the rules have become, or how alienated you feel from the teachers or other students, get that diploma or GED. As I ran down the path with the rolled-up paper in hand, thinking of my mother saying those very words to the six of us, I felt proud. You can't fight segregation without your diploma, she would say. Well, here it was, I said to the heavens. *Mother, I want you to see this! I got it.*

I think I was most grateful for graduating from Perkins because of a particular lesson I would forever apply in politically murky circumstances. The powers that be will always want to control if not undermine a black person's attempt to be accepted in white society. If you are that person, you know: you're going to be asked to play the game, to cut corners, to shortcut your principles. There is no easy answer when that happens, and at times you may have to compromise, but remember this: your charge as a human being is to stick with your integrity—to remain loyal to the authentic you.

The experiment at Perkins seemed so straightforward at the beginning. Here was a school that wanted to be the first big college (with SMU) in the South to open its doors to African American students. That was a courageous intention no matter how you looked at it. The problem began when both faculty and students depended on the notion that we five black students would always "make the right decision" and not embarrass the school. Our job was to be such almost-white students that our color meant nothing. Joining in the fight for civil rights; standing up for our identity, our heritage, our pride as black people; dressing or acting in any nonwhite way; even auditioning for black roles reserved for white students— all that would make the experiment too risky, too blatant, too incendiary for this very staid, very conservative campus.

This was another lesson I would carry with me forever:

when you're afraid of taking risks because of a decision you've made, you risk losing your integrity. The meaning behind your intention begins to turn hollow. Since I had no power at Perkins, I had to learn where I personally needed to draw the line. I wouldn't make a fuss about the theater group banning black actors, for example, but I would insist on joining civil rights demonstrations off campus. I wouldn't leave the dorms just to smooth Mr. Perkins's white feathers, but I would as a gesture give up my white roommate the third year and room with an African American. Looking back, I was encouraged that Dean Cuninggim also had to learn where to draw the line. He seemed to go along with the status quo at first by hoping we five would downplay our presence as African Americans, but when his own integrity was at issue, Dean Cuninggim risked his job.

The final lesson I learned from Perkins was that when things get complicated, which they always do with racial issues, look for an ally. How lucky I was to find a friend in Reverend Loud, who showed me the difference between getting "shoved around" like a pawn in a chess game and making each decision on my own. These were not always the "right decisions" according to the Perkins way of doing things, but in terms of the stand-up life my mother had always hoped would guide and protect me, they were the right decisions by my measure.

4

Community

Cecil

PEOPLE CALLED THE Tenderloin District in San Francisco "the last circle of hell," because no matter how quickly you drove through it, you couldn't help seeing the poor, the addicted, the sick, the homeless, and the mentally ill, many of them lying if not dying in the streets. You couldn't look away from wildly dressed sex workers of all genders (there were more than two) getting clubbed by the police. You'd see flophouses, whorehouses, drug and porno houses, runaway teenagers selling their bodies, cruising johns, and ex-cons. By reputation, the Tenderloin was a filthy, seedy, crime-ridden hellhole that nobody wanted to visit.

Yet the first time I walked through the Tenderloin on my way to Glide Memorial Methodist Church in 1963, I saw something else, too. I saw the most blessed place on earth.

Eight years had passed since my graduation from Perkins, and by most standards I was doing well as an up-and-coming Methodist pastor. I ministered to a small but growing congregation in a very poor, mostly African American section of Kansas City, where I cochaired the local CORE (Congress of Racial Equality) chapter and led protests against segregation at lunch counters and department stores downtown. Young, mostly white seminarians came by to work with the incredibly organized black women who helped revitalize the church, and over time we built Sunday attendance from fifty or so to more than eight hundred. I was proud of my work there and loved the congregation, but I knew it would always be a black church with a few white members. It was not the diverse congregation committed to radical change that I had dreamed of since childhood.

So when Donald Tippett, the Methodist bishop of San Francisco, invited me to the Tenderloin to visit Glide Church with the idea of becoming its minister, I was more than intrigued. Glide was named after a deceased millionaire cattleman whose wife, Lizzie Glide, had purchased the coveted corner property at the lower end of Nob Hill in 1929. For a time, well-to-do congregants followed Lizzie's vision for a traditional Sunday church where people dressed up, sang hymns, and read scripture. However, their attendance slowed as Prohibition set in, the Tenderloin filled with speakeasies and gambling parlors, and the wealthy moved away, most of them up Nob Hill.

By the time I arrived in 1963, Glide still had a sizable endowment, but its congregation had dwindled to about thirty-five white people. They were intent on keeping services as conservative and starchy as Lizzie Glide had intended.

"There's no way to soft-pedal this," the bishop had said on the phone. "Glide is dying, and unless somebody comes in with some major changes, we'll have to close it down."

I thought about the bishop's words as I walked through the garbage-strewn streets. The Tenderloin was a rectangle of about thirty blocks that backed up against San Francisco's glitzy hotel and shopping district known as Union Square. Only minutes away from the city's famous St. Francis Hotel and City of Paris department store, I passed panhandlers, muggers, and pickpockets who stared at me as though I were prey. Alcoholics yelled comments at nobody in particular or slid to the pavement in a stupor. I walked by people I guessed were illegal immigrants from Central America and Asia, and teenaged prostitutes male and female who slept at the Greyhound bus station at night.

The Tenderloin was also the "meat rack district" with its "ALL NUDE" strip clubs, gay bars, adult bookstores, hardcore movie theaters, roaming prostitutes, and oddly quaint peep shows. It was an urban ghetto filled with exhausted and broken homeless people shuffling from one corner to the next. They were every city's visible poor—sick, addicted, desperate, hopeless—and they could not be "fixed" by charities, flophouses, or soup kitchens. People in cars sped up and passed by, trying not to see.

And where was God in all of this? The spirit we call God dwelled in each of us, I knew, but was so tamped down and packed away for these folks as to be irrelevant. Poor people had said to me before, *Don't talk to me about God. I'm starving, I'm addicted, I'm homeless, I can't feed my kids or get a job. God left us a long time ago.* Who could blame them? I thought. Under oppressed conditions, when you're told you're unworthy by the church and society, you can't be fully human in your spirituality. You can't see how the spirit around you affirms your humanity, wants you to be free.

But here was the surprise. I had expected the Tenderloin to be another skid row district, and in many ways it did have that down-and-out sense of futility. But something raw and energetic rose up from the streets as well. Perhaps it was the sight of entrepreneurial gay bar owners cleaning up after last night's police raid, or refugee families hanging laundry in the alleys, or children playing outside pawnshops, bars, parole offices, and pool halls. Or perhaps it was just so many poor people—old and young; gay and straight; native and foreign—making a life in wretched surroundings.

I remembered playing Church with my sister and brothers in San Angelo when we were kids. I had wanted a diverse congregation so much that I assigned them all the colors of the rainbow, and if I could have, I'd have given them all the roles and lifestyles and sexual preferences in the universe. Now here they were for real, these black, brown, yellow, red, and white people in the Tenderloin, as poor and disenchanted as anyone could get. Society treated them like bugs under a rock, yet even in this wretchedness, they had become a teeming colony, refusing to die though right on the edge of death. What would happen, I wondered, if somebody picked up that rock and let the sun shine in? Maybe they would scatter. Maybe they would morph into something else.

One day, I thought, people in cars would slow down and really look. They'd see the poor making their own choices about their own healing. They'd see addicts, parolees, homeless, and the mentally ill managing their own apartment buildings, their own food distribution, their own job training, health care, and community organizing. All that, I believed, was going to take a revolution, not just of body but of soul.

Soon the corner of Ellis and Taylor came into view, and there it was: Glide Memorial Methodist Church, standing pink and fortresslike with its tall spire and golden cross. I looked at Glide and saw it moving somehow—just shaking on the street, as if to say: *Here's a church that's mostly empty. What are you going to do about it?*

The bishop met me at the entrance with a sympathetic look. "It's pretty rough out there, isn't it?" he asked, indicating the Tenderloin.

"It's magnificent," was all I could say.

Inside the church, I couldn't believe how spotless everything was. The interior of Glide had the hushed and elegant atmosphere of a wealthy men's club. Hardwood floors gleamed brightly as if they had never been scuffed. I had just left the smell of urine and grime in the streets. Here an aroma of pine-scented furniture polish filled the air.

As he locked the door, I noticed the bishop had a glass eye. He hadn't mentioned it during our phone conversations, but he saw me glance at it and explained with a shrug that many years ago, his eye had been "punched out by a gang member in New York."

I thought, *Well, here is a man who's been out there.* What the church could do in a wild neighborhood like the Tenderloin might be similar to what the bishop experienced in New York. He was as soft-spoken as his name—Donald Tippett—and, I learned, as tough-minded as the story behind that punched-out eye indicated. Supervising hundreds of churches throughout northern California, the bishop chose to keep his office at Glide, despite the dangers of the inner-city ghetto just outside the door. Other ministers from the national office of the United Methodist Church (UMC) also worked at Glide.

"Thought you'd like to see the latest," the bishop said, handing me a news magazine as we headed down the hallway. "The Tenderloin is now the 'smut capital of the world,' according to this, so we can expect a boost in tourism very soon. Maybe not in here, of course."

He opened the door to the church's awe-inspiring sanctuary, with its two-story-high beamed ceilings and stained-glass windows that sparkled down on enough pews to hold a congregation of eight hundred. An enormous white cross at the front of the church seemed to soar to the rafters, dominating every sight line and drawing the eye to the ornately carved altar, pipe organ, and choir risers. With that huge cross piercing the wall like a white sword, the whole design seemed to say: the minister of this church lords it over the people.

The bishop took me into the much smaller Chapel of Sacred Memories, which had another big cross at the front and was also sanitized and empty. "Do you have many weddings here?" I asked. The bishop shook his head. "Not so many—well, not any in several years." He showed me the Youth Center, which boasted modern attractions that would appeal to young people—radio, record player, TV, table tennis—but it looked as if no one had set foot in it for some time. The same was true of the nursery. A dining hall had been the site of teas and socials during World War II but had rarely been used since. Religious workshops and Bible study groups once met in the church's main hall, but now the remaining members of the Women's Society of Christian Service used it.

"There are three other ministers on staff," the bishop continued. "They're usually out doing community outreach and have stopped trying to build up the congregation. The thirty-five members of Glide's congregation are older, you see. They don't want to change very much about the church. There's a choir of about a dozen people, and they stick to traditional hymns, so we don't really have a choral director."

"When you say older," I asked, "how old do you mean?"

"Well, it wasn't so long ago that some of our hard-of-hearing members listened to sermons with ear trumpets," he said. "Today I'd say a few congregants are in their thirties, some are older, and many are *much* older. The few stalwarts left do love the church, but you might as well build a moat around it. They hate what the Tenderloin has become, so keeping the church pristine and ceremonious means a lot to them."

"I noticed that the cornerstone outside says Glide is 'A House of Prayer for All People,'" I said.

"Yes, well, Lizzie Glide meant 'all people' like her—old-fashioned evangelicals who read the Bible and believed in Jesus as their savior. Past ministers opened up the Youth Center for the military during World War II. That's what 'all people' meant to them—servicemen—and they also had monthly Family Nights."

I wondered if the bishop knew what I meant by the words *all people*. I meant the nobodies, the scrubs, the outcasts, the disenfranchised. I meant the lowest members of society who were the earliest Christians, people who came from everywhere to hear about a radical concept called unconditional love, people who formed a community around that concept. Like Jesus's following, every movement that changed the world began from the ground up—never the top down, and never so exclusively that "you had to build a moat around it."

As the bishop took me through the rest of Glide, I asked him why the UMC ministers still kept their offices here. "The Tenderloin may have turned into a slum," he said, "but Glide has been kept in mint condition. It's a quiet, meditative place to work."

I also noticed that every door we passed was locked, and all the windows were barred. "The church has to keep things closed up tight," he said. "Burglars are plentiful enough in the Tenderloin, and recently the police said that roving gangs have been breaking into stores and hotels all around us."

I paused at yet another lock. Did a beleaguered church, a dying church, have to lock out the community to preserve itself? Or could a new minister throw open the doors and invite in "all the people"?

"Bishop, there's one thing you should know," I said. "If I become minister here, I'm going to turn this church upside down."

"Brother Cecil," the bishop said quietly, "welcome to Glide Memorial."

5

Action

Cecil

NEWS OF MY arrival wasn't exactly greeted with acclaim by the thirty-five white stalwarts who remained in the congregation. From their point of view, anybody from the outside with "a civil rights agenda" was going to change Lizzie Glide's vision in a way they wouldn't like. Every morning, Anne, the church's receptionist, gave me a stack of messages she kindly labeled "silly calls," which ranged from "this used to be such a nice, white church" to "tell that nigger to go home." The calls were mostly hang-ups, but Anne seemed to be sympathetic to my arrival and said she recognized a number of voices from our remaining thirty-five congregants. I could see how painful this was for them—they wouldn't talk to me in person and thought the bishop had betrayed them—but Glide now had to be *my* vision, not Lizzie Glide's. If I could lead us together as a congregation, skin color and socioeconomic status wouldn't matter.

To that end, I began walking the streets of the Tenderloin and talking to people about a "new kind of church" that welcomed individuals no matter what they believed. The multitudes didn't exactly pour in at first, and I couldn't blame them. Glide had been padlocked to street people for as long as anyone could remember. It took courage to step into a place that appeared to be aloof to the realities of poverty and crime they knew.

Unfortunately, once people did venture in, they weren't made to feel welcome by the existing congregation or the staff. Nor was I. One Sunday a few months into my ministry, I walked into the staff cloakroom and realized that someone had just told a racist joke. The word *nigger* hung in the air, and everyone looked at the floor. I said nothing and began the prayer I usually gave at this time to bring us together before we stood before the congregation. On this day I mentioned that we were all God's children regardless of class or color, and that we weren't just mouthing the word *unconditional* when we spoke of accepting people of all races, creeds, and colors. We fervently hoped to follow Jesus's leadership by finding that very deep love, that *unconditional* love, in our hearts for congregants of all ages, nationalities, job descriptions, and colors. And I asked God to help us forgive those who hurt us, or talked behind our back, or told jokes about us; because if we could forgive, we could love. I turned and walked into the sanctuary without looking at any of them.

Of course I then faced our thirty-five white members who were gazing up at me from the front pews with an air of such righteous impatience that I wondered if the padlocks had gone back up again. But I was young and enthusiastic, and the early 1960s were already showing signs of great change and promise. I did not expect the congregants to join me in my dedication to serving the poor and disenfranchised. I did hope they would be intrigued enough to discover a new kind of spirituality through diversity—that they would at least acknowledge different people sitting next to them, different ideas about faith, different goals for a just society, and of course a different religious perspective than they were used to. Whereas Glide had been a "Sunday church" before without much community involvement, soon it would be a church of action, of movement, of declaration, of confrontation. If they had been bored by the stiff, formal rigidity of the same ritual repeated week after week, I hoped Glide's new watchcry—"Act now, reflect later"—would appeal to the members' belief in a church that had once been a formidable presence in the city's downtown scene.

So I thanked my tiny congregation for its dedication to Glide and said that I looked forward to creating with them a new beginning—to flinging open the doors so that all people would be welcome without judgment or discrimination. And in what I hoped would be a stunning metaphor of transition, I took off my clerical robe. "Just as I am removing this symbol of traditional clergy," I announced from the pulpit, "so may we all welcome the time of openness and change that is coming to Glide."

That did it. In a single move, the thirty-five stalwarts stood up as a united block and walked out of the church.

I stood there stunned for a moment. Blatant rejection by white people has always hit an exposed nerve with me, yet I had to admit it was kind of funny. The bishop appointed me to increase our numbers, and here we were now, minus thirty-five.

That week the group met with Bishop Tippett and demanded that I be replaced. The bishop refused. He reminded them that Glide would have to close its doors permanently if the membership didn't increase. Think about it, he said. If the thirty-five members worked with the new pastor, they could have a voice in saving Glide.

On another Sunday the same unhappy thirty-five took their place in the front two pews as before. I didn't want a repeat of what happened earlier, so I took them by surprise by standing in the back of the church and starting my sermon from there. In my enthusiasm I thought if they just listened for a moment, they'd come to appreciate and maybe even love the idea of Glide as an all-inclusive church that practiced unconditional acceptance. But if they decided to walk out, it wouldn't be in an easy huff this time—they would have to pass by my physical body on the way to the exit and look me in the eye.

So I began: "The world has more to say to the church than the church has to say to the world." I was going to add that together we could save Glide if we could listen to truths outside ourselves. But sure enough, every one of those backs stiffened, and the whole group rose as one and walked into the aisle. On the way out, they looked everywhere else but at my face. "You can leave this church," I called to them, "but you can't deny my role here, or my existence." The new Glide was not going to shut out the world.

Back they went to the bishop the next day to demand my ouster, and this time he was adamant, pointing out the dozens of other Methodist churches they could attend instead of Glide. It would have been easier for me if they took his advice, but no. They, too, were adamant. They thought of me as a rabble-rousing black preacher who wasn't going to wait for Lizzie Glide's evangelical church to die—I was going to kill it by letting the worst failures of society come streaming in with all the filth and addictions and homelessness and crimes of the streets. *And* I was going to let these outcasts ruin every sacred thing the thirty-five folks believed the traditional church stood for.

The odd thing was, they were right. I was here not only to turn this church upside down, I was here to put it out of its misery and start over. The longer this tight little congregation fought for control, the longer we would stand around the resuscitation machine agonizing over when to pull the plug. At the same time, I didn't want to give up on them. They loved the church and all its rituals, after all, so maybe they'd be more attentive to something more metaphorical, more demonstrative.

So on *another* Sunday when services began, I walked up to the lectern with a big photo of myself hanging around my neck. "Look what I found!" I said, holding up the frame and pointing to my image. "That's the phony, the person I've been trying to confront all my life. He's so heavy. Can you see I'm suffering? Help me. I don't know what to do."

The thirty-five white folks didn't move. Maybe they were intrigued enough to see where the sermon was going. Maybe they were struck by a fit of paralysis. I talked about the things people do to be accepted in the world—how each of us carries an illusion of ourselves that we haul out when our self-doubt crops up. The phony me was supposed to be "better" than the real me. The phony me was supposed to fit in, make things comfortable, change nothing, uphold the status quo. That would be the disguised me, and didn't we all sometimes get lost in disguises? Didn't we all try to be the person we thought other people wanted us to be?

"So I've got to be honest," I said. "I've been hauling this image around to impress people long enough." I took the photo off. "Ooooeee! That feels so much better. You can't deal honestly with folks when you're pretending to be somebody else." The sermon was going to be a way of saying we're all vulnerable to pressures to conform. "Let's be honest about the real reasons we—"

And up they rose again! Walking out more haughtily than before, they never looked back.

Our standoff would continue for months, and although most of the original thirty-five eventually gave up and left, two elderly women named Lillie Edsel and Francis Brown kept coming back. Francis was a firecracker of an activist, very vocal and a bit notorious for telling off politicians. She worked with a retired minister named Ed Peet, and together they formed political action groups that lobbied for the rights of senior citizens. I attended several of their demonstrations and was proud of Glide's contribution to Senior Power, a concept that was just beginning to take hold (a group called the Gray Panthers would come later).

Lillie was also a firebrand in her way. Nearing eighty, barely five feet, and always elegantly dressed in a little hat and gloves, Lillie could be just as demanding about regular meetings of her Cancer Sewing Group as she was about getting announcements for her Women's Society for Christian Service into Glide's weekly bulletin. The WSCS disbanded when Lillie died, and with her went an old-fashioned propriety about church values and commitment to action that I would miss.

There were two sides to Glide when I arrived: the Sunday church with its evaporating congregation, and the Urban Center, a separate division offering services and programs to help the needy. For my first year, I worked with the three other ministers at Glide who ran the Urban Center. They believed as I did that when people are in trouble, the church had a responsibility to help.

We differed widely, however, on *how* Glide could help.

The ministers worked with the center to create halfway houses, recovery programs, and shelters with names like Huckleberry, Baker House, and others. Glide provided seed money and administrative help to each group so it could establish its own nonprofit status. Gradually we stepped away and let the originating group operate independently.

I worked with several of these spin-offs during my first year and thought they were fine for what they tried to accomplish, but they were "not really my thing," as I told the other ministers.

To me, the programs did not alter the system that created the need for their services to begin with. Instead of empowering people who wanted to take charge of their lives, the spin-offs provided important services but did not really change the status quo. And, too, these programs tended to serve middle-class white people, which again was fine, but not for me. My mission was working with the poor and disenfranchised of all races.

One minister, Ted McIlvenna, believed a program he brought to Glide could be called radical. This was the National Forum on Sex and Drugs. A few years earlier, psychologists at the University of California at San Francisco realized that with the invention of the Pill, the subject of sexual freedom was exploding in the '60s and taking religious leaders by surprise. UCSF worked with filmmakers to develop a series of educational movies about sex that they needed to try out, so Ted cleared out a coffee room at Glide and invited representatives of all clergy who wanted to be more informed about the subject.

The UCSF movies showed how people masturbated, how the disabled had sex, what gay sex was all about, and what happened during S&M, bondage, auto asphyxiation, and other risky activities that had already found their way to the Tenderloin. As educational and helpful as it was, the sex forum became more notorious than radical. When the press ran stories about Glide Memorial Methodist Church showing "dirty movies" in the basement, half the public wrote in to say that Glide had no business being a church, while the other half asked if they could buy tickets.

It was fine, I thought, for Glide to house the forum, but again, it wasn't really my thing. I did support new spin-offs that helped the "outlaw fringe," like the Black Man's Free Store, but to me a truly radical program had more to do with an exchange of power than an exchange of clothes. Viewing the world through the lens of the poor, as Jesus did, the church had to help lead the fight.

This approach to social change was my interpretation of liberation theology, a South American movement led by nuns and priests in the 1950s. Liberation theology said that if you were an activist in the church, you did not lay out solutions for people in a top-down manner. You supported grassroots movements from the bottom up by learning what people wanted to do for themselves, and by offering help through your knowledge of organizing, planning, and funding. The strength of the church said to existing powers, *You can't bully these people anymore. We're watching you, we're supporting them, and we're bringing in the eyes of the world to watch, too.* Then you took action that could change that world.

In those early years, Glide had many opportunities to "muscle up," as it were, while working with people who started out with nothing and ended up as powerful activists for radical change. Two projects in particular set the tone for the ways that Glide would work to create this change in the future.

BUILDING A SCHOOL

In 1965, a group of parents gave me a tour of Bayview Elementary School—a filthy, broken-down, rat-infested school with roaches dropping out of the ceiling. Ill-designed bathrooms opened onto the street so that anybody could come in and

mess with the kids. Families had been complaining about Bayview to the Board of Education for years but with no results.

After several meetings with parents, Glide helped form the
Bayview–Hunters Point Parents Action Committee in 1966.
The parents started by writing polite, firm letters describing the terrible conditions and health code violations. Again
the Board of Education responded with do-nothing answers,
clearly waiting for protesters to give up. The parents, however,
had discovered that working together made them bolder, more
determined, and angrier. They picketed, they protested, and
they got the media involved. At one point the Board of Education promised a few renovations. But the parents maintained
their kids needed a brand-new school and nothing less.

My role in all this was both as an adviser and activist. I
helped the parents set goals, raise money, build coalitions, and
make connections with the press and government leaders. I
stood with them in picket lines and made the power of Glide
a magnet for the press and public when it appeared that the
board was intractable.

After the second year of protests, the parents decided to go
for broke by having a large rally and disrupting the Board of
Education's general meeting. Glide offered its help. On the day
of the meeting, I assembled three hundred folks—a mixture
of parents from the Bayview PAC and new members of Glide
who joined in solidarity—to march ten blocks to City Hall
with banners and drums, intending to storm the BOE. I had
one of the hottest speeches of my career ready to go, but in
a way, the joke was on me. Board members by now became
rattled every time the Bayview PAC was mentioned, so when
they realized that our march was already on television, they

quickly passed an allocation for $1.8 million to replace Bayview Elementary with a new school.

At that moment, we were charging up the stairs to the third floor, determined to force the board to face us, only to be met by the superintendent of schools who said, "Look, we passed the allocation. We just didn't quite understand what you wanted earlier." A magnificent celebration broke out on that stairway, but that was far from the end of it. To stop the BOE from commissioning another badly constructed school, the Bayview–Hunters Point Parents Action Committee insisted on having a voice in every decision. The parents spent their own money traveling across the state talking to architects who specialized in elementary-school design. They not only came back with a plan the board accepted, they were instrumental in choosing the architect, the contractor, the teachers, and the principal. And they continued to have a voice when it came to renaming the school. The BOE could not understand why this community wanted to name the school after Dr. Charles Drew, the African American surgeon whose research in blood transfusion led to the establishment of blood banks. The Bayview parents argued that it made a big difference for black children to walk into a black school named after a black leader. And they kept insisting on it until the board realized these parents would never back down. Finally, the board agreed not only to the parents' demands but to working with the community on elementary-school issues from then on.

And ten years later, when laws were passed advocating "mandatory busing" across the nation, Bayview–Hunters Point parents had to stand up for their children's rights again. Under mandatory busing, children in black neighborhoods were taken by bus to "better" schools in wealthier, whiter sections across town. Today we know that this quick-fix desegregation plan was a disaster from the start. It isolated and exhausted African American kids who had to meet the buses at 5:30 A.M., deal with white student bodies and faculty who did not want them in white schools, and get bused home so late in the afternoon that they had little time to do homework.

But mandatory busing became so entrenched that it drained school districts in African American neighborhoods, which then had to close the schools that were being emptied of students. At that point in San Francisco, parents from our old Bayview PAC reunited. They created an expanded group, the Bayview Hunters Point Coordinating Educational Committee and Coalition, and asked Glide to help them take up the fight. I agreed. With help from the press, teachers, elected officials, and the bus drivers' union, we picketed, we stopped buses, we confronted police, we got arrested, and like similar coalitions throughout the country, we brought our case to the courts. Finally, mandatory busing stopped.

To me, this was the lesson: it had been clear for a long time that everybody from the president of the United States to local mayors and police knew that busing was wrong and racist from the start. But it took a grassroots campaign of committed, organized, and indefatigable parents in neighborhoods like Bayview–Hunters Point to bring about the beginning of the end of busing across the nation. Today Drew Elementary is known as Dr. Charles Drew College Preparatory Academy. It is still an elementary school but with sights vastly higher.

From Glide's point of view, the Bayview activists were perfect examples of liberation theology in action. They learned that once we find our source of power and bring about change, we ourselves are altered profoundly. We ourselves feel stronger, more purposeful, and more capable. And we learn that because the system can easily drift back into stereotype, bias, and neglect, we must remain vigilant and ready to act.

CITIZENS ALERT

As an African American raised when segregation was legal, I was accustomed to seeing people of color fall victim to chronic poverty, homelessness, and addiction—all states of misery I was later to see in the Tenderloin. But the district was also the city's "meat rack" (or as the bishop noted, the "smut capital of the world"), and a big part of its lure was same-sex attraction. Homosexuality was considered illegal at the time, but gay bars, men in drag, lesbian clubs, and various forms of "rough trade" were both hidden and evident (thanks to bribes) in the streets near Glide. This trade attracted what we now call "rogue" police officers—the kind who liked to bash heads.

I knew that corrupt cops in large cities often migrated to crime-ridden sections of town where they could deal drugs, operate as pimps, and take bribes. In the Tenderloin, things were worse—the police had been getting away with abusive and humiliating tactics for years, and cops who hated homosexuals were having a heyday. Gay bar owners paid them off but still got raided. Closeted customers were hauled off in paddy wagons and named in the newspaper the next day. Throughout, gay humor reigned—one nightclub announced on its marquis, "Police Harassment Nightly!"

Some cops were known for raping prostitutes on the way to the police station, others for being particularly vicious with flamboyant gay men and cross-dressers. Drunks and addicts were not spared. Cops could be seen kicking people who had passed out in the gutter, just to see if life remained in the body. Refugee families were routinely abused.

I began to walk through the Tenderloin and speak to everyone who was at risk—people of color, club owners, parolees, gays, the homeless, prostitutes, addicts, and clerks and cashiers in pornographic bookstores and theaters. They told me that individual complaints about the police had gotten nowhere. But the more I walked the streets, the more people found out about one another, and the more a community formed. Soon folks were gathering at Glide to talk about a line of defense, and to create a plan of action.

Together we created Citizens Alert, a twenty-four-hour hotline operated by Glide for people who were harassed or just plain beaten bloody by police. Our first step was to print up and distribute thousands of cards under Glide's name with tips on what to do if you were confronted by police. "You must tell an officer your name and address ONLY," the cards advised. "Never resist or talk back." "Get the officer's badge number, and call us." Even this small bit of information empowered people.

Glide helped bring in a team of lawyers and medical professionals who taught the Citizens Alert team how to document every brutality. When people called the hotline, we asked them to come into the church for a taped interview. If they were already in jail, we contacted a bail bond agency to get them released quickly so we could photograph the bruises, swelling, broken bones, black eyes, stomped-on hands— anything that showed serious aggravation. We would send an investigator to find witnesses to confirm what happened. We would get the victims to a doctor, and the doctor would provide a medical report. We would take our victim's report before the Police Commission and insist on a hearing.

Many times our lawyers had to fight just to get us on the docket. When we won the complaint, stories appeared in the press about *why* we won. Then we started winning more. We got lucky when one of our lawyers, Herb Donaldson, became a judge and urged others on the bench to take Citizens Alert seriously. Soon city officials who had been blind to police brutality were aware of the surprisingly high number of complaints coming in from the Tenderloin.

One night a dozen police walked into Glide unannounced and surrounded the fifty people attending a meeting of Citizens Alert. Who was handing out these cards about police brutality? they wanted to know. Tempers flared immediately. I found the sergeant in charge and took him to the back of the hall for a private talk. At first he asked if we had all the "facts," but he knew that we did, since we documented everything. Then he said in a threatening voice, "Be careful where you meet," hinting that we could be arrested for inciting a riot.

"This is a church, Sergeant," I said. "It's free. We can always meet in the church."

In 2012, a group of parents and friends met at Glide to discuss the murder of Trayvon Martin, a seventeen-year-old African American in Florida who had been shot for looking "suspicious" in a sweatshirt with the hood pulled over his head. Trayvon had been walking unarmed through a gated community when he was spotted by George Zimmerman, a neighborhood watch coordinator who assumed he was an intruder (in fact he was a guest of one of the residents). George Zimmerman said he shot Trayvon in self-defense during the altercation that ensued.

We called this meeting our "Witness Group" because we thought if only the community had been there to witness what happened between Trayvon and George, the shooting might never have occurred. (I think of subway victim Oscar Grant, shown in cell-phone videos to have been shot in the back by police; of Rodney King and many instances where cell phones and video cameras were more powerful than weapons.) More than that, we wanted to address the ways that racism is still a reality in America and so embedded in fears over hoodies and gangs and intruders that the George Zimmermans of the world can't see it or pretend not to. Police in many cities use such fears to profile young African Americans and Latinos, and that puts everyone in jeopardy.

So the Witness Group met at Glide not just to vent feelings of outrage but to explore nonviolent actions they could take to protect the Trayvons in every community. Every presumption that George Zimmerman made about Trayvon was familiar to people of color at these meetings. They talked about the time they were eight or nine years old when clerks first started following them around stores with the assumption they were stealing; or the time when they were teens, and clerks went through their bags in fitting rooms to see what they had stolen; or the times when police stopped them in cars, in their own neighborhoods, and in whatever equivalent of a hoodie made them look "suspicious" to others.

If that was a familiar anger, the Trayvon Martin killing inflated it with new fear: Could it be that self-styled vigilantes like George Zimmerman were making the routine illegalities of police look more acceptable? At least George was (eventually) arrested and charged, but what was the present reality for people of color, especially teenagers, in places like the Tenderloin?

One African American teen said he had been stopped for jaywalking and was surrounded by cops from *six* police cars who searched him without a warrant.

A young woman said a police officer had taken her cell phone and copied all her phone and e-mail contacts looking for pimps and drug dealers. That had to be illegal, but what could she do?

A common truth was voiced by one preteen who said, "When I walk down the street alone, I'm a suspect to the cops. When I walk with a friend, we're a gang."

What did we learn from this witnessing? First, that some police officers were abusing people's rights and getting away with it, and second, that few of us knew our rights when stopped by the police. As long as we didn't know, we would be victims, and we would be out there alone.

What action could we take? With our Citizens Alert experience, Glide sat down with volunteers to design and print a thousand laminated business cards with the words I KNOW MY RIGHTS next to the Glide logo on one side and a list of those rights ("to refuse to consent to a search of myself, my car, or my home"; "to calmly leave if I am *not* under arrest," etc.) next to the local ACLU phone number on the other side. These cards made it clear to every person of color in or out of a hoodie that they were not alone, that the community was organizing on their behalf, and that together we could all work for a truly just America.

Then came the promise of a modern-day breakthrough that might correct the imbalance of power between the police and the people, especially in a dense inner-city environment like the Tenderloin. A subcommittee was formed to develop a cell-phone application that could be used by anyone who was stopped by police. This app would alert people from a contact list of those who might be nearby—say, within a radius of five hundred yards—to come quickly with their cell-phone camera held high. Since suspects being interrogated by police might look suspicious if they put a hand in their pocket to send a text message, volunteers discussed the idea of designing a special kind of hoodie with a cell-phone pocket that could text the emergency message by an unseen yet strategic shift of an arm or shoulder. Discussions are ongoing as of this writing, but the hope will always be the same: abuse that happens to one of us can be prevented by all of us.

Hundreds of groups like this have met at Glide over the years, and we never know which ones are going to realize their goals. Sometimes just having a place to express frustration and anger at having to face injustice every day makes a difference in people's lives. So does hearing the truth expressed by someone else. At the Trayvon Martin meetings, one white person after another has vehemently stood up to say, "That would never happen to me!" meaning the way police often treat people of color. Or "My kids have never gone through that kind of nonsense!" Because young people keep coming, we use the meeting for educational purposes, too, running movies about black history like *Slavery by Another Name* to remind us that no one is alone and to give us all a sense of solidarity over time.

Watching this mix at the Trayvon Martin meetings of parents and teens, computer experts and business card printers, people who could write and people who could sew, and anybody who could contribute new ideas, all leaning into that circle at Glide to find the truth of their experience and *act on it* for the good of the community, I have been filled with a mix of nostalgia and destiny. I remembered how expensive it was to keep Citizens Alert going fifty years ago and that thanks in large part to two determined gay people on our staff at the time, Phyllis Lyon and Del Martin, we were able to raise money for lawyers, doctors, photographers, private investigators—and one very shy, very young, and very cynical temporary typist named Janice Mirikitani.

And now what a thrill it was for me to watch Janice at seventy-one as she walked around the Witness Group encouraging people to form new committees, distribute the cards, and research apps and hoodie designs. She had become as much a founder of the new Glide as I was, and yet fifty years ago, nobody could have been as distrustful of churches—and of ministers, of the idea of community, or of any notion that justice was possible—as Janice was that first day she walked into Glide.

6

Compassion

Janice

I WAS A graduate student at San Francisco State College in 1964 when a friend told me about a temporary typing job at this odd new church. At first I said, "No way—churches and me do not mix." But I needed the money, so I applied for the job, and after funds were raised, I got it.

My role was to transcribe taped interviews for a new program at Glide Church called Citizens Alert. The people talking on the tapes were victims of police abuse, and from the first day I was in shock as one person after another described being stopped by police in the Tenderloin and beaten with nightsticks. They were yelled at, ridiculed, clubbed, and kicked routinely. Then they were either arrested or left in the street.

I didn't trust anyone in those days. Graduate school was not holding my interest, and I preferred to study on my own. Part of my surprise when I put on the headphones was that I often recognized myself in the stories that went through my typewriter. I was a powerless Asian American woman who lived on the edge. I had taught high school but found it limiting, so going back to graduate school had made sense for a while. Being a perennial student kept me nicely incomplete, with no commitment to a future and no sense of identity. But I could type.

My desk was located in a small office upstairs at "the new Glide," whatever that meant. At first I kept my head down and transcribed one ghastly tape after another, preferring to remain invisible. That lasted about a week.

I began to notice an odd assortment of young people coming into Glide because a new minister named Cecil Williams, whom I hadn't met yet, had invited everyone in. I was amazed to see gay runaways wandering around, many of them fledgling drag queens. These guys would spend the night on the streets in polished nails and makeup, sometimes in full drag, and walk into Glide scrubbed up and baby-faced, often sitting on my desk to talk to me between tapes. Sometimes the male voice in my earphones sounded like the sweet young man with cracked ribs sitting in front of me. I knew how it felt to be a victim of racism because of color. But for somebody to come up and attack you because you're in drag or openly gay—well, that astonished me.

A lot of sex workers, straight and gay, began volunteering at Glide during the day. They typed, answered phones, ran errands, and welcomed newcomers. There was one tall black woman named Chicago who brought in six or seven hookers to help us out in their free time. Then they, too, would go to work at night.

My typing job was the beginning of a weird, the-world-isn't-as-I-thought-it-was kind of existence. Sometimes I got into conversations with the gay guys about self-esteem and what nightmares our parents had been. A few had relatives who had raped them. Many, like me, had been victims of incest and never told anyone about it.

I wasn't much older than they were, but I thought of them as kids. At night and sometimes at Glide, they dressed and acted outrageously, as if to say, *Look at me. I'm here, in my feather boa. I'm visible. If my orange hair and body piercings are unacceptable or you laugh at me, at least you see me.*

At first I didn't know how to relate to them at all. I thought, *Okay, as long as I look glamorous and wear dramatically feminine clothing, these people will pay attention to me, and then straight white men will pay attention to me, too.* It wasn't about wanting sex with them—it was about needing to be visible myself.

Most of these young men had an acid sense of humor that cut through my self-destructive ideas of who and what I should be. Up to then, I had been trying to be white, which to me meant trying to be accepted, trying to get my college degree, and trying to find myself a respectable white husband.

I told them about hating my straight hair, and hating my Asian eyes. They said, "Honey, we would *kill* to have your hair! We make up our eyes to look like yours. We call ourselves Jasmine and Jade, all these exotic names. You hate to look like yourself? We *want* to look like you."

I was completely taken aback. These men were holding up a

mirror, insisting that I look at a positive self-image I had never seen before. Reversing the negative me I had grown up with was scary, yet this kind of thing seemed to happen at Glide. No matter how defeated or marginalized you felt, Glide accepted you, and affirmed you.

And how brave these victimized people were. Sometimes I laughed out loud as I typed up the interviews because the drag queens especially refused to get mad when the cops put them through sadistic strip searches. They ridiculed the system by doing imitations and making jokes, often sexual, about the police. I remembered that aside from the hilarious role playing, this was how my cousins used to talk about being in Japanese American internment camps during World War II. They, too, were familiar with abuse.

Juan, one of the gay men who became a good friend, turned out to be the most positive person I'd ever met. Everybody laughed about Juan's behavior when he saw Rev. Cecil Williams in the street from even a block away. Without hesitation he'd wave and yell, "Hello, sweetheart! Hello, baby!" In the office, Juan always made me feel better. "Oh, darling. You look *so good* today." I think his own life had been such a horror that he sensed what I was going through. Juan was a little heavy, so he joked about my skinny legs in his soft Hispanic accent, "Oh, *honey*, these net stockings make your legs look *better*. They hide your boniness." During the day, he wore a sweatshirt or a T-shirt with jeans and a bomber jacket. His hair was slicked back. After sunset he had a different life, but by midday, he'd be back. He stood up for me with his outlandish humor, and he would cap on everybody: "Oh, that *queen*, that minister. He just needs to come out and experience me!" But if somebody walked in, Juan would leave. He was open to those he cared for but very private personally.

Eventually, I realized it wasn't the level of police brutality that surprised me about Citizens Alert, bad as it was. It was the fact that somebody cared enough to listen to people who otherwise had no voice; to have these transcriptions made, to ask difficult questions, and to bring in teams of professionals who actually confronted the police. And all this compassion was being spread around in a *church*.

This revelation was probably why I started to feel a sense of propriety about the place. Over time I suspected the young gay guys were not only hooking and selling drugs on the streets; they seemed to be bringing clients into the church with them. When people complained that the men's bathroom was locked or that the stalls were always in use, I, the person who felt invisible, was compelled to knock on the door and say, "Hey, guys, you can't be turning tricks in the church!"

So here we were, all these people on the fringes of society working together, making a community from our shared brokenness. Even when you feel like a nobody living in the margins of society, as I did, seeing other people making a place for you can change your whole perspective.

That was the other thing that impressed me about this very odd place. You didn't have to believe in God or Jesus or church to feel a community forming around you and supporting you. I had tried not to care about anyone when I first came to Glide. Now these dear souls were taking an interest in me and wouldn't let go.

7

Creativity

Cecil

I THOUGHT I understood what Janice meant when she would say that religion was not "her thing." Many people in the 1960s felt betrayed by religion in the same way they distrusted government, corporations, and all the faceless institutions that made up what was called "the establishment" at the time.

Janice was tough. She called herself an atheist, thought of the church as a "pimp," and believed that ministers were power-hungry demigods. After our second meeting, she told people on our staff that I was the "most egotistical person" she had ever met.

Janice had grown up in the farmlands of Petaluma but was completely at home in the grit and grime of the inner-city ghetto where Glide was located. While others felt pity or superiority toward the chronically poor and mentally ill—street people who wandered into Glide talking to themselves and asking inappropriate questions—Janice treated everyone equally and respectfully. She felt pity for no one.

She was organized, tough-minded, flinty, and fiercely committed when it came to ethnic studies, gay rights, prison conditions, abortion rights, and draft evasion. The best writer among us, she didn't mind helping me compose letters, speeches, and church bulletins. She was fascinated by the contradictions of Glide as a Methodist church that gave out free condoms, performed gay marriages, and marched on the Board of Education, just for starters.

Janice herself was a walking contradiction. She dressed seductively but was shocked when men leered at her. She could swear like a sailor but covered her mouth when she laughed. I wasn't the only one who worried about this petite young Japanese American woman walking through the Tenderloin at night, but Janice would only laugh and say she could take care of herself. I didn't believe it until one day when Moses, a six foot three mentally unstable homeless man, was heard shouting, "Get her off of me! I didn't mean it!" I ran down the hall and found Janice yelling a string of profanities as she backed Moses into a corner for uttering a sexist remark.

Later on I learned that Janice not only forgave Moses, she took him out for a drink after work with his best friend, Larry, another tough guy nobody but Janice would stand up to. She was a born listener. The sullen teens who usually spoke to no one—young men and women who had been kicked out of their homes and were now working as prostitutes out of the bus station across the street—loved Janice and considered her family.

Janice and I bonded early on. I was an African American who grew up in a segregated town that kept black people poor and powerless. She was a Japanese American whose family lost everything in the internment camps of World War II. Both of us went through a phase of hating white people yet wanting to be white ourselves. Both of us believed in radical, not gradual, change. And both had a drive, a zeal, a passion—mine to build a church of love that would start a revolution; Janice to give voice to populations who had been silenced.

Our memories of childhood were quite different, however. My parents loved me, believed in me, and supported me, especially during my breakdown at age twelve. Janice's step-father beat and sexually molested her for eleven years while her mother apparently misunderstood what was going on and pleaded for them both to "stop arguing." The women in Janice's family stressed the importance of marrying a husband who would protect and take care of her. They believed women were too vulnerable to strike out on their own and would not be respectable without a man.

So my family loved me, but Janice's betrayed her. I turned my anger at racism into a force that would make me strong. Janice clung to her anger as a way to survive.

At work, she never seemed to run out of fresh ideas. When I told her the church bulletins were cluttered with religious sayings I thought nobody read, she suggested I throw out the old format and bring in provocative modern poetry (Lawrence

Ferlinghetti, T. S. Eliot) and rebellious show-tune lyrics (*Hair*). We brainstormed endlessly about how to spread the word about Glide as a new kind of church where Sunday services emphasized freedom of thought, not worship, and the energy was so high that I replaced the term *service* with *Celebration*. Janice loved the idea of celebrating life on earth and dispensing with the "myth" of an afterlife in heaven. For someone who scoffed at religion, she grasped the complexity of my vision for Glide more quickly and thoroughly than anyone. She got it that Glide was a politically active spiritual community; she admired my insistence on placing the word *unconditional* in front of *acceptance* and *love;* and no one was thrilled more than Janice that I wanted to bring a passion for fighting injustice into the heart of a church. Here was a way to put her anger to work.

So I was surprised at the self-doubt in her voice when Janice told me how much she resented the American press for the white establishment that ruled it, the inaccurate and sloppy "news" that filled it, and the lack of people of color on the masthead. I felt the opposite, I told her. I respected the power of the press and welcomed its potential as an ally for Glide. You're kidding, she told me. Take away the racism, and you still had an old boys' club that sat on its laurels and couldn't report the real news if it wanted to. And it silenced the rest of us.

"But what does that mean?" I asked her. "Should people of color be victimized by the press, or should a place like Glide learn how to use the media for our own ends?" This approach had never occurred to Janice. Working with jaded editors on your own terms for your own reasons? That would mean we had to stop being intimidated in the first place. It meant we had to get their attention with stories that would make them better journalists.

I had decided to transfer the choir and organ to the balcony to make way for blues, gospel, and jazz groups to play at Glide on Sunday mornings. This was a controversial move that the thirty-five stalwarts from Glide's long-standing congregation did not like, while folks in the Tenderloin were mesmerized by the sounds of contemporary music and gospel in the sanctuary. But getting the word out was slow going. When the popular John Handy Quintet agreed to play during the holidays, I told Janice, "Imagine: Haydn, Handel, and Handy on Christmas Day." She saw the news potential of this unexpected mix of the sacred and the hip and started work on the next press release immediately.

Before long, news stories about jazz in the sanctuary at Glide cropped up everywhere, and on that Christmas Day of 1966, the church was packed. The morning after, jazz critic Ralph J. Gleason devoted a full column in the *San Francisco Chronicle* to the concert, with the headline "Haydn, Handel, and Handy at Glide Church." I looked at Janice as if to say *You placed that headline;* she looked back at me to say *You placed that headline.* Thus our collaborative life began.

So this was the way, I realized, that Janice worked. When you hit that nerve of creativity, of passion, or of rage, she would detonate with ideas that made Glide a happenin' place.

She formed a theater group and invited members to write

original scripts. She organized a dance troupe that included the disabled and the addicted. She choreographed original pieces to reflect political messages of the day such as antiwar and anti-rape. And she plunged into radical politics, working energetically with the antiwar movement, the sanctuary movement, the American Indian Movement, and the women's movement. Her sense of humor began to emerge. She applauded me for judging a Tenderloin beauty contest and laughed when I confessed that I had no idea the contestants were male.

And while I brought in celebrities who were exploring their own spirituality and loved speaking to the congregation—Dick Gregory, Bill Cosby, Sammy Davis Jr., labor organizer Saul Alinsky, Marvin Gaye, African performer Letta Mbulu—it was Janice who saw the potential for getting Glide's mojo working: our Sunday Celebrations were crowded with musicians, speakers, sermons, performances, and a light show, but what the congregation felt, thanks to Janice's behind-the-scenes ability to keep things flowing, was a spontaneity and excitement about life that had a rhythm of its own. We never paid for a single celebrity to visit Glide, and just about everything in those days was accomplished on a bare-bones budget. Instead of worrying about money, Janice stressed the antiestablishment quality of Glide and wooed more volunteers in to help.

At some point people asked Janice why she, the maverick who didn't believe in religion, had such boundless energy for Glide Church. She laughed and said it was all due to her work ethic. Growing up on a chicken farm, she had been a machine of efficiency collecting, weighing, and candling eggs; hauling feed; and scraping manure off the roosts. It wouldn't come out until later that from the year she turned five, when Janice's mother remarried, her stepfather would not permit her to talk at the dinner table, threw things at her when she laughed, physically treated her roughly, and said she was stupid and ugly for having buckteeth. As she got older, he beat her when he was angry and sexually molested her in the chicken house where no one would hear her scream. The most painful part for Janice to talk about was the way her stepfather made it clear how "nice" he would be if she simply submitted, so she did. But being in collusion with her mother's husband this way made Janice turn on herself. She told me that one year when fleas infested the chicken house, her stepfather pushed her off balance, and when she reached out to the wall to steady herself, her hand turned black with fleas. That image summed up her disappearing life, she said. The only people she could trust were her grandmother, who loved Janice unconditionally, and her little brother, Layne, neither of whom knew what was going on in the chicken house.

I learned about the abuse bit by bit over a long period of time. Janice had never spoken of it to anyone, but because we talked about everything, including our personal fears and hopes, she ventured into this most dangerous ground. As painful as this was, she felt relieved of a weight that had become unbearable.

And I confided in Janice. My twenty-year marriage to my wife, Evelyn, had been unraveling for some time. We had met while I was still at Perkins seminary and married much too young. Evelyn was attractive and intelligent, far more socially active than I was, and conservative in her religious convictions. She had believed in me early on—or at least the "me" that the black church predicted I'd become, a charismatic minister and celebrated civil rights leader. Somewhere along the way we both realized that I really wanted to minister to the poor and disenfranchised, to live with them and learn from them, and to build a new kind of church with them. This dream didn't mean that Glide would become the little church of the lost, eking out an existence. Rather, I wanted Glide to become a powerful influence in the city, and I was already making connections with mayors, police chiefs, legislators, and philanthropists. But Evelyn pursued other interests. Working with high-end charities and attending the symphony and ballet, she began appearing in the society pages of the *San Francisco Chronicle* and gradually receded from her role as the minister's wife at Glide. We had two terrific children whom we loved deeply, but increasingly we found ourselves spending time with them separately, almost in alternating shifts.

I was deeply, desperately lonely. After a few years, as Janice and I became more of a team, we opened up to each other in ways that neither had done with anyone before. As the first and only African American minister at Glide (three other ministers served with me), I found myself isolated from the all-white board of trustees that had been in place when I was hired. This powerful group often demonstrated its "concern" over my belief in radical change by cutting or withholding financial support for programs (food, recovery, community organizing, protests) that I believed were essential. In one trustee meeting, the directors actually tried to convince Janice to stop me from being "too controversial." When Janice realized what they were asking, she shook her head and said simply, "I'm with him." They caught her meaning immediately. She believed in me and backed me no matter what happened, and her tone implied, *So should you.* It was the first time anyone stood up to the board on my behalf.

We discussed getting too close as boss and employee, and whether we were sexually attracted to each other. I had to confess that I was, while Janice had to confess that she could not be. Talking about her stepfather's incest made her feel so vulnerable that she thought she would fall apart if I "sexualized" the relationship—if I became anything other than a trusted counselor and mentor. I was not much more than a decade older, but it was clear to me that Janice needed a father figure, and I vowed that I would be that person. For the next decade at Glide, still very much the church's early years under my ministry, we avoided talking about attraction and focused on becoming the team we seemed destined to be—I the minister, the speaker, the firebrand, the galvanizer, the power broker; Janice the architect, the facilitator, the organizer, the orchestrator. Gradually, what I called the "screaming loneliness" that had made life so hard for each of us began to fade, replaced by a friendship that changed us both profoundly.

The strength of that relationship turned out to be important the more Glide worked with groups who came to us for help. Janice even saved my life one day.

Glide had been working for months with a group of low-income black women, many of them pregnant, while they lobbied City Hall to extend the city's bus line up a very steep hill to the federal housing project where they lived. The extension was not only necessary but inexpensive, yet it seemed pretty clear to me that because the women were poor and black, nothing got done.

Instead of giving up, this group learned about community organizing. It developed a strength and power the women had not thought possible before. When the time came for a very public and newsworthy confrontation, they decided to "help" media coverage by providing an irresistible photo opportunity—thirty very pregnant African American mothers-to-be surrounding a bus with arms linked and bellies out. As their adviser, I had to say I was a bit nervous about this strategy, but it was their decision and they were convinced it was safe. What cop would swing a baton at a pregnant woman? they reasoned. On the appointed morning, I accompanied them to the bus stop where they quickly approached a baffled bus driver and linked arms as they circled his vehicle so tightly that he couldn't move it. "We got ourselves a bus!" their spokesperson, Dorothy Tillman, told reporters and TV news crews who "happened" to show up, thanks to Janice. Even when police in riot gear arrived with orders to "use any means necessary to make that bus move," the women didn't bat an eye.

Janice had stationed herself at a nearby phone booth (no cell phones then) to monitor the situation with a roll of dimes in one hand and a list of Glide's connections at City Hall and the SFPD in the other. As soon as the cops appeared, she started calling. With so many photographers and TV news cameras recording the scene, she told representatives of the mayor, the district attorney, the chief of police, the district supervisor, and a congressional representative that she was sure no one would risk a violent confrontation. The folks on the other line were alarmed enough to hang up quickly and make their own calls.

At the last moment, when the riot cops had raised their batons and started to advance on the circle of women, the police captain's car radio blasted new orders from downtown. The cops pulled back but kept the bus and its protectors under guard. Meanwhile, the police captain arrested Dorothy and me and put us in a police cruiser headed downtown—not aware that Janice had left the phone booth and followed us to the Hall of Justice. At the city jail where I was incarcerated, she learned from a desk sergeant who was friendly to Glide (a founding member of Officers for Justice, an organization for minority cops that Janice and I helped organize) that I didn't look so good. An infirmary doctor had taken my blood pressure and announced that it was sky high.

Janice went directly to the sheriff: "You want a dead Cecil Williams in your jail cell?" she said. "How do you think that will look on tomorrow's front page?" The sheriff leaped out of his chair to make sure I hadn't died on his watch, and in a few minutes, I was released. In the end, the women got their bus line, all charges were dropped, and a stroke was averted, thanks to Janice.

In the late '60s, Janice decided to suspend graduate studies and work for Glide full-time. Apart from all her other qualities, she brought with her a rare sense of humor, even in violent situations. During the famous student strike for ethnic studies at San Francisco State College in 1968, police in riot gear waded into the melee. They were clubbing protesters all around Janice and me as we stood there with our protest signs in support of the students. It was a particularly bloody confrontation, but I noticed that the police were being careful not to hit me, a minister. They must have recognized me, because I wasn't wearing a clerical collar. When Janice realized that women with long hair were being beaten to the ground and dragged away by their hair, she turned to me and said, "Cecil, they know you, but I am too vain to have my hair pulled out," and disappeared. I couldn't blame her.

A big turnaround in Janice's life began when she opened up to me about the one thing in American society that made her most angry—the systematic manner by which American book and magazine publishers refused to acknowledge people of color, especially Asian Americans. In the late '60s, white male writers so dominated literary and academic worlds that to Janice, a genocide in print was taking place. Acting alone, she could do nothing but remain a victim. But Glide and the movements that emerged in the 1960s were showing that with a community as passionate about fighting back as she was, the world could change.

Janice plunged into the thick of the small press revolution, a grassroots movement that was overtaking the Bay Area thanks to a new technology called the Xerox machine. She joined the Asian American Political Alliance and helped to create *Aion,* the first magazine of its kind. She became a cofounding member of the collective Third World Communications, which published Latin, Asian, African, and Native American writers. She applied for and won grants for Third World anthologies, and she staged benefits in Glide's sanctuary with such writers as Lawrence Ferlinghetti, Gary Snyder, Ntozake Shange, Allen Ginsberg, Russell Leong, Alice Walker, Fernando Alegría, Isabel Allende, Al Robles, and Roberto Vargas.

Janice's own poetry was noticed and celebrated by the highly regarded poet and author Maya Angelou, a frequent speaker at Glide and soon a mentor and lifelong friend. Maya admired Janice for helping children and young adults write their own poetry and for encouraging them to read for the congregation at Sunday Celebrations. And both of us admired Maya's new bestseller, *I Know Why the Caged Bird Sings.* We often discussed the chapter in which Maya, age thirteen, moved with her family to the predominantly Japanese American district known as the Fillmore (not far from Glide) at the start of World War II. Even at that young age, Maya recognized a rare historical transformation—the sudden disappearance of Japanese Americans (who were being interned by the government) and the arrival of black shipyard workers from the South. "The Japanese area became San Francisco's Harlem in a matter of months," she wrote, and in that "air of collective displacement," Maya's own "sense of not belonging" began to fade. Janice and I well knew the complicated relationship between Asian Americans and African Americans and thought that Maya was more sensitive to the ironies and frictions of race and class than many. This may have been one reason that she warmed to Glide's celebration of diversity and our call for unconditional love. She applauded Janice's determination to bring unpublished writers to the page because of her own trauma after being raped as a young girl and remaining mute for five years. Having been silenced herself, Maya saw the power of giving voice and joined Janice in that effort.

It was perhaps inevitable that Janice, with her bent for creativity and her love for bringing diverse elements together, would, one day in 1966, recognize the stunning potential of Glide's parking lot. This was a grimy square of urban space, surrounded by buildings and garbage Dumpsters, with fifteen slots that were vacant on Saturdays—empty, available, and free. A group from the Haight-Ashbury called the Artists Liberation Front wanted a musical event outdoors. Janice and Larry Mamiya, a Glide intern at the time, thought the parking lot would be a perfect place for a music and poetry festival featuring local rock bands as well as poets whose poems would roll out of a mimeograph machine right on the premises.

I was at home when the police called that Saturday to say the amplified guitar music, and poets reading sexually explicit material on nearby street corners, had disturbed guests in the expensive hotels at the upscale shopping district of Union Square. "If you don't have a sound permit, you have to lower the volume or stop it entirely," the police captain said. By the time I got to the festival and realized that Janice and Larry had jammed the parking lot with radically political folks from the Artists Liberation Front, giant drums of all kinds, and even more explicitly avant-garde poetry, I had to say to myself, *Well! This is Glide at its finest!* Why would we "lower the volume" when we could ramp it up if possible and let Janice's festival do what it was supposed to do—inspire creativity?

Because that was when *I* got it. To me, creativity meant being *politically* innovative, fighting against injustice, and seeking radical change. But creativity to Janice meant *artistic* invention, literary freedom, and a revolutionary aestheticism that I had never thought possible.

Here was an example of my kind of political creativity: in the 1970s, Glide held a sit-in at the Standard Oil building downtown to force Chevron (and other large corporations) to give to nonprofit corporations a percentage of the money it received from the antitax measure Proposition 13. The building manager didn't know what to do with a lobby full of protesters, so he tried to freeze us out by turning on the air-conditioning full blast. We were so cold that you could hear teeth chattering. Janice brought in a "jacket brigade" of coats, scarves, gloves, and sweaters that helped us endure until finally, Chevron executives invited us upstairs to make a deal. In the end, more than twenty groups in California received sizable grants because of the protest.

But Janice brought more of an artistic creativity to Glide. She introduced poetry, dance, visual arts, fiction, and film. The Third World writers she helped organize refused to allow their work to be "siloed"—separated into racial categories and stored in inert bins—because the quest for art and the quest for justice were inseparable. Glide's famous "light show" began when Janice asked a group of young Asian American photographers and artists who called themselves the Red Lantern to take photographs and film of the amazing street life going on outside Glide all week. These images were then projected, along with excerpts of news articles, sermons, songs, and poetry, on the wall above the choir on Sundays. You couldn't look at that wall without feeling the vitality of the streets and the exuberance of political confrontation in one giant, ever-moving art installation.

But her own work as a poet was making a difference to Janice as a person, and to other writers as well. Maya Angelou in particular viewed Janice's poetry as original and important, and her work for Third World Communications as groundbreaking. Maya was an actor, producer, dancer, singer, and author who at six feet in height could be very imposing, and when she gazed down at five-foot-three Janice and said in no uncertain terms that the poetry of Janice Mirikitani was a "national treasure," Janice *had* to listen. She had to push her self-doubt away.

At poetry readings, Maya and I loved the way Janice changed from introverted novice to bold performer onstage. She would approach the microphone shyly, read a few lines, then begin pacing up and down the stage like a caged tiger. Her voice would rise and with eyes blazing, she'd allow that rage, that authority, that defiance from deep down to explode out of her like a geyser.

Some time later at a Glide benefit, Maya told the audience her impression of Janice at their first meeting. "I thought, 'Well, she's cute, and she's petite, but can she take it? Can she stay in there?' Believe me, this is a person who stays in there." Maya was talking about Janice the poet, but also Janice the organizer, the fighter, the friend, the force of nature.

But in the early years of Glide, every poem was about Janice opening up to a part of her own silenced history. Watching her was like seeing a drowning person break the surface for the first time. When Janice finished a poem, she seemed to go back into a shell, walking silently off the stage. The stunned audience would leap to its feet, clapping and cheering as though everyone in the room had also gone through something life-changing and unforgettable.

Later I would ask her how it felt when everybody clapped and cheered so heartily. The first time Janice said, "Did people applaud?" I thought she was kidding. It turned out she didn't hear people applauding because she was literally deaf to praise. It wasn't just that she had been abused so badly in her childhood that all self-esteem had been lost, although that was in part true. And it wasn't just that her mother had closed her ears by denying the incidents of abuse by Janice's stepfather and others. Instead, what I learned over many months as Janice let this last secret out, was that in the worst time of the incest, she had tried to fight back another way.

For two years, she said, between the ages of twelve and fourteen, Janice got her mother to drive her to a Christian church, which she attended with a vengeance. She was baptized and confirmed, took Communion every month, joined the choir, and tried to accept Jesus Christ as her personal savior. "Welcome Him into your heart, and He will save you," a brochure had said.

Janice was the only Asian in the congregation, but she was drawn to a painting above the altar of a white Jesus with his blue eyes and sandy hair gazing benevolently down at the viewer. Every Sunday, knowing that her mother would be at least an hour late to pick her up, Janice sat in front of that Jesus and prayed silently, *Please make him stop. Please make him stop. Please make him stop.* At the end of two years, she realized what a folly this had been. The abuse had never stopped, Jesus hadn't heard her, God had abandoned her, and the church, as far as she was concerned, was a lie.

Other girls her age with her history might have given up, and indeed, she said, thoughts of suicide did plague her for years. But also, Janice got mad. *God doesn't give a shit about you, kiddo,* she told herself, *so to hell with this* (stronger terms were used). By her early teens, she defended herself when her stepfather became abusive. She stood up to virtually every man who looked at her funny. And she finally got mad at her mother. If being meek and finding a man to protect you was what a good Japanese American girl was supposed to do, Janice did the opposite. In front of others, she lashed out at her stepfather, much to the dismay of her mother, and when he tried to hurt her later, she turned on him in rage.

I knew that it could not have been easy for a person with Janice's background to earn excellent grades in high school and win a scholarship to UCLA, but this, she said, was part of her plan to get out and on her own. She got her secondary school credential and found that teaching was bliss. This was no news to me, as I had watched her making dense and important literature accessible and fun to kids at Glide. As a teacher, Janice said, she had loved assigning controversial subjects for debate, but her contract was not renewed. She went back to graduate school, this time to study poetry, the only form of "expressing the unspeakable" that made sense to her. But she could not hear the praise that came back.

While working at Glide, Janice lived on and off, somewhat unhappily, with an associate professor at UC Berkeley who believed the answer to their problems as a couple would be solved if they got married. She asked my advice, and I advised against rushing into marriage. But I think she believed that as a white man he would bring stability and order in her life. When she asked me to conduct the wedding, I of course agreed. I respected her decision to marry and was delighted a year later when she gave birth to her daughter, Tianne, who was to become the love of Janice's life. When her work at Glide, her poetry, and her involvement in antiwar and student movements made Janice realize she had grown apart from her husband, they divorced.

She emerged from the marriage a different person. People used to kid her about it. This skeptic, nonbeliever, never-in-a-church-will-you-find-me rebel had discovered something larger than herself. Maybe it wasn't God—we could postpone that discussion for a moment or a decade—but surely it was Glide.

Who would have thought that Glide would make such a difference in Janice's belief in herself, in her reason for living, and one day in mine.

8

Love

Cecil

I WAS NOT the only minister appalled at the treatment of gay people in the early 1960s. When I spoke with other pastors, the talk often turned to the hypocrisy of San Francisco, which celebrated bohemian culture while turning a blind eye to the persecution and beatings of people in the gay community.

The more we talked, the more we realized how meaningful it would be for the traditional church to take a stand. In 1964, fifteen of us, representing nine Protestant churches, formed the Council on Religion and the Homosexual to speak out against religious disenfranchisement, to create a dialogue, and to welcome homosexuals.

At the time, the word *gay* had just started to replace *homosexual* as an accepted term, while *gay rights* didn't exist as a phrase. It was still a crime in San Francisco for people of the same gender to dance closely together. But gay advocacy groups were beginning to emerge, and the council made connections with any who were willing, such as SIR (Society for Individual Rights), the Mattachine Society, the League for Civil Education, and the Tavern Guild (gay bar owners). Our Citizens Alert director, Phyllis Lyon, and her partner, Del Martin, founded the Daughters of Bilitis, the first national lesbian advocacy organization.

The council started out as an information-gathering group with ministers acting as conduits so that one day we could gauge the size of the gay community and its needs. Instead we were soon on the defensive. The mere proximity of the words *religion* and *homosexual* caused an uproar in the city when it hit the news. Rather than give interviews explaining ourselves, we wanted to help gay advocacy groups take whatever steps they needed to change the world, or at least the world nearest them. True, many gay people hadn't come out publicly. Just being identified as homosexual often risked a person's job and reputation. But, we ministers thought, what if the council and gay organizations didn't worry about all that for now, and just did something big and splashy that told the world that *we* weren't worried about homosexuality, so why should *you* be?

The gay groups decided to go for broke with a Mardi Gras costume ball that would include colorful outfits, contests for the best this and silliest that, and "chaste dancing" for straight and gay couples alike. We would rent a ballroom, send out invitations, and use the profits for the gay groups and the council. And we would do all this knowing anything so very gay was going to attract the media and perhaps some hate groups and bring the cops out in full riot gear. Would people pay money to attend such a thing? The gay folks set the bar: we were going to do this and be a joyful people at the same time.

Established hotels on the edge of the Tenderloin, like the Hilton and the swank Jack Tar, would not rent us the space, but a much older structure called California Hall—a big barn of a building that was very much *in* the Tenderloin—opened up a ballroom-size space for the dance.

At that point, I went down to the Hall of Justice with my colleague Rev. Ted McIlvenna to talk to detectives in the SFPD vice squad, which officially handled the "problem" of homosexuality. We explained that the Mardi Gras Ball was sponsored by the Council on Religion and the Homosexual, and that it was going to be private, legal, and joyful. Members of the council would protect the privacy and safety of everyone inside California Hall, so the police wouldn't have to.

The detectives' eyes grew large as they sat there listening. A costume ball? For homosexuals? Sponsored by *churches*? When they realized we were serious, the question of security was batted away. They wanted to know what homosexuals were going to *do* at the ball.

"We'll be having a party," Ted said.

"Don't do it," the vice squad detectives said, almost in unison.

"We're gonna do it," I said.

"You know you cannot do this. There are a thousand reasons against—"

"We are doing it."

Once the detectives realized they could not stop us, they changed their tune. As long as we did our own policing and things didn't get out of hand, they said, the police wouldn't interfere. Ted and I looked at each other. That sounded too good to be true.

Then an officer said, "I don't understand why you ministers are so interested in sex."

"We're interested," I said, "because we want our brothers and sisters to fully participate in their rights as citizens. We're interested because they should not be arrested for something that anybody else would not be arrested for. It will be a very clean party. What are *you* bothered about?"

"We're really bothered that it's the homosexuals," they said. Then one of them asked, "Do you all engage in masturbation?"

I sighed, rather than laughed or winced. The police were as confused by the dawn of sexual freedom as everybody else, only they got to ask inane questions.

"Yes, we do," I said.

"Don't you believe that masturbation makes you blind?"

"Well, if that's the case, we should have gone blind a long time ago," I said.

We were about to leave when one of the detectives called out, "There's going to be trouble. If you don't uphold God's will, we will," he said.

On the way back to Glide, Ted and I agreed that without police interference, the Mardi Gras Ball was going to be fine. The gay organizations had sent out personal invitations so that nobody could crash the hall. Word had gone out among gay people to play it cool and not let the police draw them into a confrontation. The council's ministers and their spouses would be present, security would be provided by Glide, and our lawyers would be positioned at the entrance just in case.

However, the day after our meeting with the vice squad, the manager at California Hall tried to cancel the rental agreement. Figuring the police had pressured him, our lawyers threatened to sue, and he backed off. A few days later, two vice cops walked into a council meeting and said they would not tolerate "open homosexuality." We reminded them that this would be a private dance on private property. They left.

On the night of the getting-famous-before-it-even-began Mardi Gras Ball, I arrived early, expecting maybe twenty-five brave couples at the box office. Instead, several hundred invitation holders huddled in their coats against the fog. The line snaked around the block and kept going. *Why, this dance might be a hit,* I thought.

Very soon, a commotion started at the door. About fifty uniformed police arrived and set up cameras and banks of klieg lights with the intention of photographing everyone going in. So much for the SFPD's promise not to attend. Riot police stood on either side of the entrance with batons out. No press releases had been sent out, but the media arrived in force anyway, with TV cameras mounted on vans and reporters with cameras crowding police with cameras at the entrance. A paddy wagon across the street had its back door open and ready. Two squad cars with lights flashing cut off the intersections at either end of the street.

The whole scene was so bizarre that I wouldn't have blamed

people for leaving as soon as they saw what awaited them. But that was one of the joys of working with gay folks. Not only were they cool about the attention, but when they removed their coats, the costumes they had created were so hilarious, so exaggerated, and so beautiful—big hoop skirts, giant puffy sleeves, hair piled high, big shoulder-padded suits, uniforms of all kinds, many mocking the police—that they stole the show *back*.

Entering that gauntlet of police, the gay couples pretended the photographers had arrived at their suggestion and ordered sets of prints for their families. "I'll take six of these, honey!" they would say. It took even longer for the final count—an incredible six hundred guests—to register and come through.

Meanwhile plain-clothed detectives either sneaked in or had acquired invitations and marched in to look for reasons to shut us down. Del Martin and Phyllis Lyon were taking tickets and knew not to object. Our goal was to keep the dance peaceful and give the detectives whatever they were looking for, so we showed them unobstructed fire exits, the up-to-date liquor and health permits, and "chaste" dancing on the dance floor. It was a law-abiding party all around.

You would think the sight of ministers in clerical collars mingling with drag queens in stunning outfits and lesbian and gay couples having a good time would impress the authorities, but no.

The police went away and returned with ten more detectives who demanded to be allowed in without invitations.

"Goddamnit, that's enough," said Herb Donaldson, one of our lawyers. He told the door people not to let them in. "I don't need an invitation," one cop said. "I have this," and he held his badge up to Nancy, a ticket taker who worked as a secretary for the Teamsters. Nancy did not budge.

That was the standoff the police had been waiting for. More uniforms appeared at the back of the crowd and pushed, disrupting the orderly taking of invitations and opening a channel for police to stream through. They were stopped cold by a wall of ministers standing arm in arm, blocking the entrance. The cops started shouting. The guests shouted back. We ministers yelled, "Arrest us!" The police wanted to arrest guests, not clergy, so they did the next best thing. They arrested our lawyers and ticket takers.

Behind us, I was proud to see the Mardi Gras Ball going on both peacefully and flamboyantly inside the ballroom. The partygoers knew about the ruckus outside but insisted on enjoying this rare freedom to dance together openly and have fun. That's how the dance ended, and the next day that's what the media showed: a community exercising its constitutional rights and dazzling the cameras while doing so.

The council won its battles in court, and the gay coalition essentially never stopped meeting—never stopped growing, never stopped becoming more powerful—after that dance.

Today about 40 percent of Glide's congregation are proud lesbian, gay, bisexual, and transgender (LGBT) folks. Our newest member of the Ministry Team, Rev. Dr. Karen Oliveto, has been arrested on several counts in protest against antigay legislation on marriage. With her partner, Robin Ridenour, she embodies Glide's commitment to the principle of love empowered by justice. At the 2012 General Conference of Methodist Clergy in Florida, Karen was in the forefront of the battle to remove a line in the UMT's Book of Discipline that says, "We consider homosexual practice incompatible with Christian teaching." When the UMT voted against this change, Karen and pro-LGBT delegates disrupted the conference by singing the hymn, "What Does the Lord Require of You?"

I'm still asked to explain how it is that I, as an African American minister, could embrace gay rights when I must have grown up in the black church and must have been taught that Christianity, while acknowledging people as God's children, considered homosexuality as a sin.

This kind of assumption is the reason that gay people continue to be persecuted. It's my experience that black and white churches are full of gay people who remain closeted because the church doesn't want to see them. Why not welcome them, as you do everyone else, for the original creations they are? That's what my real training consisted of during childhood: my family was friendly with enough gay people (white and black) to know that sexual orientation meant little or nothing when it came to choosing trusted friends. A vision of a church for all the people began forming in my mind at age ten, when I saw how much everybody loses if conditions of acceptance are placed on any one of us.

And you don't have to guess the kind of African American pastor I have come to be, I tell these theologians. My commitment and my ministry began with the disenfranchised, the poor, the sick, the persecuted, and the oppressed. When I opened the doors of Glide to welcome people with unconditional love, that's what I meant—a love that included all. I know that for some folks, this is not an easy love. It is a love that practices acceptance of people as they are, not as others would like them to be.

And I think the way gay people have changed over the years offers a useful lesson about unconditional love. Fifty years ago at our first ever Mardi Gras Ball with its flamboyant costumes and police/press scrutiny, the humor was ironic and "in your face," because it had to be. Any of the participants could have been beaten up, outed in the newspaper, or fired the next day, so they stood up to the hostility before the hostility could get to them. They wagged their finger in the face of rejection and said, *Look at us, acknowledge us; we're equal to you and we deserve to be here.*

Today, even as traditional churches and conventional society move slowly to accept gay rights and gay marriage, the LGBT community seems to have swooped in to say: *We embrace you, whatever society you belong to.* You're part of us *whether you know it or not, because we are part of the world.*

Janice and I notice this every time we attend LGBT events, notably Springalicious!, a fantastic and elaborate drag show in San Francisco's Castro District. Here every gown, every poem, every lip-sync version of Donna Summer or Whitney Houston has become a minor art form. Hundreds of hours have gone into rehearsals and hairdos and the exact placement of a leg or an eyebrow with such dedication that the audience of straight and gay people goes wild. Original poetry is performed: Magnolia, a member of Glide who was fighting cancer and needed a wheelchair, brought the house down in 2011 with her insightful poem about street life in the city. And when Springalicious! is over, you come away with a feeling of joie de vivre that reaches out and embraces everyone.

This is how change occurs in society, I believe. Not by people in power reaching down to include those they've identified as lesser than. It's by the marginalized and disenfranchised who learn to love themselves and grow from within and become so expansive that *they include us* without self-consciousness. And they change the world in the process.

That's the attitude we feel at Glide when people from every possible walk of life get up on stage and say *I'm gay, I'm straight, I've survived AIDS, I'm black, I'm unemployed, I'm adopting, I'm alive, I'm in recovery, I've been married for twenty-five years,* and so forth. That is what the beloved community can be—a lot of different and very individual personalities emerging and morphing into one big community to take on issues that concern all of us. It's an explosion of voices, applauded from every corner, and the glue holding it all together is love.

9

Madness

Janice

A MONTH AFTER I started working at Glide, Cecil Williams walked into the office in his clerical collar. Without a word, he came over to my desk and waited for me to look up. I did not.

"Don't you know who I am?" he said.

"No," I said. He walked away.

I asked people on staff who was this man with the very large ego. They laughed and said, "So you met Cecil."

Of course I knew who he was. Only one black minister worked for Glide, the one who had walked the streets handing out his business cards to hookers and pimps and addicts in the hope they would come to church. Some of the hookers began passing his card around to their coworkers, but that became a concern when he was perceived as a "customer." Word had begun to spread that he replaced traditional Sunday services with "Celebrations," whatever that meant.

"You gotta come on Sunday," the prostitutes and runaway gay teens I worked with kept saying. "The uptight people are leaving, and Cecil's told everybody in the Tenderloin they're welcome." Then they'd say in unison, "And nobody's ever let *us* in church before!"

Cecil Williams challenged everything, they said, even the rules that had been drilled into us in childhood: *Be quiet in church. Don't speak out of turn. Don't show emotion.* They said Cecil believed that this way of thinking stifled the church, that people could say whatever they wanted at Glide.

Other than saying hello in the halls, Cecil and I hadn't talked very much since our first nonmeeting, and that was fine with me. It was this "new church" he was building that piqued my curiosity.

I decided to come in on a Sunday (my day off) and see for myself what this new minister was about. Attendance hadn't climbed very much by 1966—about a third of the pews were filled. My heart sank as eight untutored voices began singing dismal hymns from the balcony. *Here we go,* I thought. *Same old hierarchy.*

Cecil got up to speak. He looked conventional in his horn-rimmed glasses and close-cropped hair, but there was nothing severe or authoritative about him. He seemed excited about Glide and our potential as "a people," and he grew increasingly animated as the sermon progressed, waving his arms like an orchestra conductor and jumping up and down as if on springs. He said we were here to do prison work, which meant we could liberate all prisoners—those in jail, those in ghettos, and those of us in the prisons of our own minds. He rarely mentioned Jesus Christ, and spoke of God not as Our Father but as our means to freedom. "God wants us to be free," he said, gesturing around as if to say, *free especially of the church and of all religion.*

I still thought of him as egotistical, but for the first time I realized why having a big ego could be a good thing. He was so bold and so "out there" that maybe he needed that ego to propel his vision forward. His confidence and his conviction made people believe and trust him. And yet, I noticed, despite all he had to say, Cecil didn't mind being interrupted. When people called out questions or comments, he'd stop the sermon and answer them, even if the speakers were stoned or crazy. One man actually jumped up on the altar, which made everybody gasp. This was the Tenderloin, after all—you never knew what might erupt. Cecil, however, calmly handed him the microphone.

"Take it, brother," he said, and listened to the man speak as though he had been invited.

If the crowd got animated, Cecil would come down from the pulpit and walk around just as excitedly, sometimes disappearing in the back of the church, where he'd whisper dramatically in the microphone, "Can you dig it?" and everybody would laugh and applaud. Glide was like no church I had ever attended. No wonder Cecil called it a Celebration—we were all having too good a time to call it a Sunday service.

I went back to Glide as many Sundays as I could after that,

and as the years passed, I brought my baby, Tianne, with me. She loved the excitement and the music of the Celebrations. Cecil spotted us each time, and at work during the week we often discussed ways to get the audience involved. As my temp job expanded at Glide and I got into more administrative work assisting Cecil, I began writing church bulletins and press releases. At Glide there was no chain of command, so whenever I realized that something was needed, like making a list of press contacts for Glide events, I went ahead and did it. Graduate school had become a floating limbo for me, but at Glide I felt useful.

Others felt that way too. I noticed that even the young gay men who sat with me at my desk felt a need to take on something larger than themselves. They were still into their "behavior"—hooking, using, being outrageous—but instead of obsessing constantly about survival, they talked about wanting to *do* something with their lives. Maybe they could open a shelter or a center for marginalized gay men—runaways, prostitutes, addicts, drag queens. They'd call it Vanguard, and it could really make a difference in each other's lives, they felt. Just being part of something positive brought out a deep humanity in them. I, too, felt myself pulled enough out of my own problems to listen to their ideas.

By that time I knew enough about how things worked at Glide to suggest the name of Laird Sutton, a minister who worked with Glide spin-offs, as a contact to help them get started. Soon Vanguard began meeting at Glide as a sponsored center where high-risk gay men could create support groups, find shelter, and reconnect with the world. It was unfortunate that the "blue-haired contingent," as irreverent Vanguard members called the remaining thirty-five Glide congregants, created an uproar over "hustlers and sinners" befouling Glide's sacred ground. But Cecil was delighted. He used the controversy as a chance to discuss the importance of the church as a safe and nurturing environment for everyone.

Vanguard and Citizens Alert became my lens to the wildness of the Tenderloin and the tumult of Glide. Not a day went by that someone hadn't overdosed or been robbed, or been assaulted and left to die in the streets. Everybody seemed to be racing around rescuing everybody else, while I became so efficient and methodical at my work that people treated me as an authority. One day I walked into the children's playroom and saw a three-year-old girl masturbating in a crib. I turned to her mother and said, "She's stimulating herself because she needs more human contact." I don't know why I knew that—I wasn't married or a mother yet—but the woman went straight to the crib and picked up her child as if parenting had never occurred to her before.

I seemed to have a similar effect on Moses, my poetry-writing pal who wouldn't take his medications and sometimes lost control. Moses could be surprisingly perceptive and kind, but his infantile side came out when he was frustrated, and then he'd urinate in the hall. "That is *it*," I said finally, tired of cleaning up after him. "You do that one more time and you're out of here." He didn't do it again. Maybe I was drawn to people on the edge, I thought. Or maybe it was pure vehemence that attracted me.

"There's racism in this room!" Cecil would bellow furiously

from the pulpit on Sunday. "We have to face it! When we let racism happen, we're as guilty as if we enact it ourselves." I was shocked when Cecil showed his anger, having always tried to smother mine. I expected all the white liberals to get up and leave, but they never did. They were drawn to his bluntness just as I was because he wasn't just political; he was spiritual and he was loving. They knew his anger was directed not at them but at the kind of injustice that is rarely confronted or questioned.

"What are we going to *do* about this war in Vietnam?" he would say, the "we" meaning not just some but all of us—not just people in power but people who saw themselves as powerless. Down from the pulpit he would stride again, each time to roam the aisles like a talk-show host, cajoling people to tell their own stories.

This has *to be a gimmick,* I thought. The last thing any minister wanted was to appear to be equal to a person in the audience—or worse, to look as though he had something to *learn* from laypeople, especially street people. Then I realized that Cecil wanted us to hear each other speak. As we listened to the sometimes heartbreaking details of why an addict lost everything to heroin, or how it felt to be a sex worker in the Tenderloin, or how hard it was to sleep in the bus station if you were thirteen, the audience concentrated hard, as though they were hearing the sermon of sermons.

For some reason these stories weren't bleak and depressing. It was such a relief to hear somebody speak honestly—to admit they were screwed up on drugs or so lonely they wanted to kill themselves or so terrified of the draft they were abandoning everything to run away to Canada—that we felt at last, we're released from a life of hiding.

Several speakers were mentally ill or on the edge of being violent, and that was where Cecil differed the most from other ministers, I felt. He was like a kindly parent with the outcasts, the upstarts, the outlaws, the interrupters, the lost. It wasn't just the raw honesty of street people that affected those of us listening; it was their ability to remove every boundary between us. We didn't just listen or applaud or root for them; the longer they talked, the more we saw ourselves *in* them.

And, too, while other ministers sermonized about charity and tolerance, Cecil introduced us to *empathy,* that rare ability to understand and share the feelings of people unlike ourselves. Other ministers asked people to stand up and say hello to the person on either side. Cecil encouraged us to "embrace and smell and love each other" without judgment. Keeping this interaction to a friendly hug the first time was difficult for me because of my background (Japanese Americans are generally more formal) and because the man to my right had clearly been homeless and sick to his stomach for a long time. Yet to see a bedraggled soul who hadn't been touched or spoken to for months actually smile at this small gesture was a rare moment of human connection I would remember for a long time.

When Cecil first noticed that I was attending Celebrations regularly, he began talking to me on Monday mornings about the excitement of this diverse congregation. The crazier the behavior of "the folks" that Sunday, the more he smiled and chuckled like a happy dad who couldn't get enough of this big extended family. I was still cautious but had to admit that here was a minister who truly did not judge. He just got a kick out of everyone.

One regular I came to recognize was known only as Drummer Man. Every Sunday he waited patiently for Cecil to begin his sermon, and at that moment he would bang on an old snare drum he carried everywhere. No one could hear the reverend over that racket. The first time it happened, Cecil smiled and waited for the man to finish expressing himself. As soon as the sermon resumed, however, Drummer Man started pounding and drowned out every word. Sometimes he shouted wildly as though alien voices were telling him to "help" the preacher by assisting him with the drum.

You'd think someone in Cecil's position would have reassured the congregation by saying, *Don't worry, I've got it under control,* and calling security guards to oust the guy. But silencing someone wasn't Cecil's way. He did not want *anyone* to be in control, including himself. He wanted the congregation to see and feel the edge, the abyss where people like Drummer Man lived. Over time we learned that Cecil delighted in people like this; he was fed by them and created *with* them something authentic and inspiring that could only come from the spontaneity of the moment.

For Drummer Man, Cecil adjusted the rhythm of his sermon so the two of them got into a peculiar kind of sync. The audience was left to create its own moment with Drummer Man, because Cecil was not protecting us. He was not saying, *Just follow me. I have the word of God and will explain all.* He was saying that wisdom can be gained when people go to the edge of madness. That's where unexpected moments of humanity open us up. That's where God—the spirit inside you—makes your spirituality known.

One Sunday, just when Cecil said, "You never know when the spirit is going to knock on your door," a loud knock resounded from the back of the church. The audience applauded, thinking this was part of the program, but Cecil was as baffled as anyone and asked an usher to open the door. In walked Drummer Man, mad as hell because he thought he had been locked out. Everyone started cheering and clapping for him to come in, and Drummer Man got so excited that he started banging on the drum more loudly than before. No one was happier at all this than Cecil, whose message was loud and clear. When we can't predict what will happen in life, anything can happen.

That was the case with madness itself. After Cecil told the congregation about his breakdown in childhood, people realized that the brink of insanity, which kept Drummer Man teetering, was a brink that Cecil knew well. His demeanor seemed to say that sometimes you had to experience madness in order to pull yourself back from it. When you did, you were powerless no longer.

It dawned on me that in some indefinable way, madness saved Cecil's life every day. It gave him access to the message that some larger force (today I'd call it God or Spirit) intends us to see or hear—that to keep ourselves from falling into the abyss, we have to know our own edge. Because in those moments of utter absurdity and inexplicable craziness, the message of God is made manifest. Staying open to all that life offers, including the parts that scare or offend us, makes us free.

Cecil

Today the Celebrations at Glide are not as wild as they were in the '60s, and one reason is that a transformation has occurred among those who used to be written off as insane.

Our mentally ill population has learned to use prescription drugs that are effectively treating such disorders as schizophrenia, bipolar disease, borderline personality, chronic depression, and others. The overall effect has been to calm the need to act out, to experience a world that once was full of demons and danger.

At Glide we've become much more educated and experienced about all the drugs, legal and illegal, that come through the Tenderloin. We've also learned that most people can't be categorized or diagnosed only as crazy or homeless or addicted. Most people have multiple diagnoses of physical and mental conditions that can be treated with a combination of programs. With our health-care clinic operating daily from Glide, we are better able to bring together an ever-changing jigsaw puzzle of recovery, housing, medication, nutrition, education, Spirit, and love for every person.

So when we talk about madness today, it's not just somebody removing clothes or leaping on the stage or banging on a drum. It's somebody like the man who used to hear loud voices and could not make a personal connection with anyone. Today he's taking his medications and not only listens when he comes into Glide, he's developing his own curiosity about the world, and he's able to feel emotion. He comes back because he's on meds, and because the meds allow him to know he's loved.

The spiritual element adds inspiration to the mix. Another man, just out of the hospital for attempting suicide, burst into tears after church and said to Janice, "When you came over and said you missed me, and then you brought Reverend over and he hugged me, it changed my life." This man had not allowed anyone to talk to him or touch him for many years.

This is what a loving community can try to do. It tries to open doors for people so they can find their own way. It tries to acknowledge madness as both a condition and an opportunity. And it tries to celebrate the capacity in all of us to be loving and constant in the choices we make for ourselves.

10

Freedom

Cecil

GLIDE, I REALIZED, was not a logical or harmonious place where everyone felt comfortable. It had to reflect the struggle for justice that was going on in the streets, and it had to mirror the contradictions that made the mid-1960s in America so passionate and explosive.

The "Summer of Love" of 1967 lured tens of thousands of young people to the Haight-Ashbury and to the Tenderloin. They joined a hippie culture that embraced sex, drugs, and rock 'n' roll as a means of finding freedom. Against the establishment's push to conform came the counterculture's push back to be free.

Central to it all was the giant mobilization to stop the war in Vietnam. Alongside that were continued protests for civil rights, gay rights, women's rights, students' rights, immigrants' rights, and disability rights. So many PACs (political action committees) supporting those causes were coming to Glide for advice that Janice and I set up the Center for Self-Determination, a coalition that helped new advocacy groups learn how to define themselves and their goals. Small successes were important to the motivation and spirit of these groups, so we helped them draw up "agendas of attainable tasks." We were careful not to tell them what to do. The center provided training for advocacy, organizing, protesting, and funding, but each group needed to determine its own destiny.

Glide became a magnet inside a magnet. Every time I walked down the halls, I'd see members of the Black Panther Party, feminists, gays, hippies, transsexuals, Native Americans, Vietnam veterans, Latinos, the physically challenged, and Asians in feverish discussions. I'd think, *What a wonder this is.* Glide provided not only a place to talk, organize, and build but also a vision of what might come of it: justice, freedom, love, and spirituality.

Glide also provided free meeting rooms and cheap office space. We were a home base for AIM, the American Indian Movement that occupied Alcatraz Island; Officers for Justice, the first organization of police officers of color; the Vietnamese Youth Development Center; CUPP (Community United against Political Prisoners); and the first prostitutes' union, COYOTE (Call Off Your Old Tired Ethics). And we offered space to people without organizational names: draft evaders, conscientious objectors, and followers of the "Revolutionary Messages" delivered to the congregation by Glide's rabbi-in-residence, Abraham Feinberg.

Maya Angelou often visited the Sunday Celebrations and would bring us a new poem or read an excerpt from her bestseller *I Know Why the Caged Bird Sings*. Maya was a spellbinding storyteller who spoke with such force and elegance that people were mesmerized. I remember one Sunday feeling transported to her grandmother's store in Stamps, Arkansas, as Maya read her chapter about the African American boxer Joe Louis defending his heavyweight title against the white contender Primo Carnera in 1935. She described African Americans crowding in to listen to the broadcast on her grandmother's radio, and you didn't have to be black to know how it felt when the radio announcer described Joe Louis trapped against the ropes: "It was our people falling," Maya read. "It was another lynching, yet another Black man hanging on a tree. One more woman ambushed and raped. A Black boy whipped and maimed. It was hounds on the trail of a man running through slimy swamps. It was a white woman slapping her maid for being forgetful."

How moved we all were! How personally we took every word! Off the stage, Maya was equally impressive. She spoke six languages, and when she leaned down to talk with an immigrant family in their own language, she did that magical thing that is almost impossible to do from the outside—she made people proud from the inside. Audiences walked out of Celebrations feeling the significance of their heritage, whatever it was, because Maya Angelou had made the simple idea of difference so personal and profound.

Glide's slogan at the time was "Get Involved." Take a stand. I grew out my hair "Afro" style, wore an African dashiki instead of clerical robes, and shocked and delighted the congregation by pulling out my favorite book, *Quotations from Chairman Jesus.*

The only thing still holding Glide back, I felt, was that giant white cross at the front of the sanctuary. Backlit by dramatic spotlights, the cross was so imposing that despite my passionate sermons about getting our hands dirty fighting injustice, the cross seemed to say, *This church sanitizes the truth.*

Of course, Christ died for our sins on that cross. It was the central metaphor of all Christian teaching. Ministers liked to tell the story of a retired missionary who explained to his son, a famous preacher, how to retain modesty at the pulpit. "Son, there are two ways to preach," said the missionary. "One is to get the people to look at you. The other is to get them to look at the cross."

Well, at Glide, that was not our way. I wanted people to look at *each other* during Celebrations—to see themselves sharing acceptance and love, to feel the power of their own humanity, to know the importance of celebrating life. "To know God is to do justice," I would say, but behind me, the cross said the opposite. The cross told everyone, *Give up your power. Let God take over.*

But I had to speak the unsanitized truth, and the truth was that as long as we allowed racism, homophobia, and other kinds of bigotry to exist, we were still crucifying Jesus on that cross. We were still yelling, *Crucify him! Crucify him!* As long as we crucified Jesus, we did not have to understand why we crucified folks we really despised—any folks who were not like us.

Of course, preaching from the altar had an effect, but I kept thinking the most truthful and influential messenger needed to come from the poor. By this time (the late '60s), I had begun inviting folks from the street to speak at Celebrations. I felt their unvarnished experience carried more honesty and more weight than any of the homilies the church instructed its ministers to present.

One day I approached Bart, an outspoken white man who had set up an encampment of about fifteen winos, also white, with their boxes and shopping carts outside Glide's entrance. Bart had been kicked out of the army for reasons we would never know. He yelled at passersby about what was wrong with the world while trying to drink himself to death. He was so angry and sounded so threatening that people crossed the street to get away from him, which was exactly what Bart wanted.

"Get outta my sight, you motherfuckers," he yelled. "The world's falling apart and you walk away! It's your fault, you fuckin' piece of shit. You don't know nothing! Fuckin' cars all over the road. Fuckin' disease in the streets. . . ."

Crazy people are smart. It's their intelligence that drives them to the edge, and there they are, sounding unintelligible but making a lot of sense. They are everything we hate and everything we love. They are what Janice calls "the uncontrollable us."

Bart was mad at the world because he was a part of the world. "Nobody ever pays attention to us," he would say. "We're a bunch of drunk motherfuckers." He was right. Disease of many kinds *had* come to the streets, and Bart was part of it. Walking by Glide, you'd not only trip over homeless people and their rusty carts, you'd feel the lice jumping out of their blankets. Across the street you'd see children climbing piles of trash to pick out glass bottles. The squalor, the filth, the sickness, the desperation of the Tenderloin scared the world and pushed it away. But what was *our* view? Bart seemed to say. What could *humanity* do about it? That was the basis of Bart's railing. People who hurried by in cars seemed to be saying *Crucify him! Crucify him!* as they pretended not to look.

The only way to bring Bart's truth to the congregation was to walk *into* his path, to get *in the way* of his carts. No matter how drunk or angry he was, Bart made sense, and besides, he had a sense of humor. When he saw me walking into Glide, he'd growl, "My mother told me not to like niggers." Once in a while he'd add, "But you know what? They're *okay*." Sometimes he would instruct his men, "Now, we're not going to mess with the reverend today. Sure, he's black, and we know a lot of bad black guys who are drug dealers. But the Rev is not like that."

He was surprised when I walked up to him and said, "Bart, I want you to think about preaching."

"Rev, *no*," he said, shaking his head. "You got me all wrong. I can't preach." He looked scared at the thought. No way was he going to yell and shout in *there*.

"Bart, you've got to do it. You preach on this corner all the time. Bring what you believe inside the church. I think you're saying things the community needs to hear."

He resisted for a while, but then one Sunday, he wandered in with his troops, all of them more drunk than usual. I turned to the folks and said, "Bart has consented to preach this morning. I want you to know that I asked him to do this, and I hope that you will accept him. He may be in a stupor. He may lose the thread. But listen to him."

It was important that the congregation know I hadn't tried to change Bart or make him "acceptable." He represented what people sometimes chose to do with their lives—to destroy themselves, yes, but also to tell the truth about what they knew.

Bart staggered up, looking and smelling like the alcoholic street person he was, swaying at the mike and speaking incoherently. Then he said, "I didn't want to come in here. *Shhhh!* That big old cross up there says, *Shhhh!*" Bart spit this out with his index finger against his lips. He mocked the cross, but people laughed with him, not at him.

"I don't belong in here! Nobody cares a thing for homeless people, nobody. But the Rev here, he goes out in the streets and he never tells us, *Shhhh!* He listens." Bart was so emphatic that he almost fell forward. Then he swayed back and was done.

I remember whipping my head around at Bart saying, *Shhhh* in the name of "that big old cross" and thinking, *Why, that is exactly the problem.* To Bart and a lot of people, the cross wasn't just a symbol of oppression—it *was* the oppression. Instead of standing for the unconditional love that Jesus brought to a new community, the cross made people feel guilty because Jesus died for our sins. And what a crazy concept *that* was: Jesus was crucified for challenging the status quo, for being different, for showing the world how to be accepting and loving of all people. He was liberating people like the lepers and the blind and the poor. He was freeing the outcasts and the disenfranchised and the mentally unstable. And he was teaching people responsibility so that *they* could atone for their wrongdoings.

Out of nowhere I remembered the voices of rejection during my breakdown as a child, and I knew what Bart meant. Glide was a dying church, and yet, look what the cross was saying to the very congregation that could give it new life: *You are worthless; you count for nothing; the church will never accept you, let alone love you.*

All that week, thanks to Bart, I rethought my own assumptions about the cross. *How* had it become so enslaving, so removed from human experience? Because it had ceased to represent all of us. It had cut out the poor, the disenfranchised, the upstarts, and the lost. It had abandoned anybody who thought or acted differently.

The next Sunday I pointed to Glide's cross and asked: "Where is the sweat, the dirt, the imprint of the people's hands? If this is the church, the cross must show the presence of the people."

And since the people were not being served, I realized, the time had come to clear everything out and start anew. As sacrilegious as it sounded, we had to tear down the cross and all other examples of traditional church hierarchy—the pulpit, the chancel, the altar, the ministers' chairs, and anything that took away the people's freedom to act.

The following Sunday, I told the folks, "See this big cross up here? Well, it is not affirming what it should. The cross should be about giving life, not the taking of life. It should inspire, not belittle. It should reflect the love that Jesus's life brought us, not reject that love and keep us all quiet. The cross signifies suffering, yes, but it also means a new life coming out of that suffering. And renewing life is what we are about.

"So I want you to know that I am going to take this cross down. The cross needs to be among the people, in the streets where the Barts of the world suffer. The church keeps trying to tell us that the cross is here to save humanity. But the truth is, only humanity can save the cross.

"That means *you* are the cross. You bear responsibility for the suffering and the hope of new life, and you are the ones seeking transformation. The cross is all these things because Jesus brought unconditional love to the cross, and the cross is you. When you walk among the people, your unconditional love renews us. It frees us. It resurrects us."

There were some in the congregation who sat there stunned with their mouths open, but most people rose up shouting and clapping. True, a lot of folks were frightened and thought that God would reach down and smite 'em. In a way, I was frightened too. In the church I grew up in, nobody ever messed with the cross, nor had I ever seen a Christian church without a cross. My training at Perkins had made the cross inviolate. Even challenging its presence brought up voices that said, *If you do this, God's gonna strike you dead.* That's when I picked up the phone and called the contractors.

Janice

Word about Cecil's decision lit up the streets like electricity. "The reverend is going to tear down the cross!" people told each other. Nobody could believe it. Cecil Williams was a visionary, everyone agreed, but he might be a maniac too.

On my breaks, I walked into the sanctuary and watched the plaster falling down, the big pieces of wood clunking in front of me. For a long time the giant cross remained intact, illuminated with backlighting. Surrounded by the construction workers' scaffold, it took on a ghostlike effect.

I had to say I loved the look of it, this skeleton around the body of something that was dead until it got taken down, piece by piece, so it could come alive. Soon all the heavy woodwork in the sanctuary—the walnut-stained altar, chancel, pulpit, and giant Bible stand—was gone. Light from the stained-glass windows now streamed onto the cross, making the scaffold resemble a dinosaur, which to my mind couldn't have been more appropriate.

Seeing the cross about to come down, I thought, *Well, okay!* This minister was really out there, taking risks, going against tradition, opening up the church for his members. Then I thought the reverse. *This is way too nervy, even for Glide. People might stop coming.* After all my disclaiming of Christianity, I could not stop an old belief system: God punishes people who step out of line.

The deconstruction continued like a work of art in progress. With the backlights disconnected, shadows crept across the crippled cross, and for some reason, I remembered my mother saying when I was a child—as did all the women in my family—that my biggest goal in life should be to find a man. Even my beloved grandmother said it. I had to find a husband to shield me from the world, to validate me as a woman, to give my life purpose. Women achieved meaning through children and through nurturing, but most of all, through husbands. The whole system was geared this way. My mother and stepfather would pay for my younger brother's education, but I knew my only way out was a scholarship to college, perfect grades, and jobs on the side.

But now as I gazed at the remnants of Glide's cross, I wondered: Wait a minute. Was Christianity's message to humanity any different? Weren't men and women supposed to believe that God was our protector, that Jesus was our savior, that we shouldn't have to make our own decisions? All we had to do was attend church regularly, worship God, and believe that Jesus died on the cross to atone for our sins. In that way, the cross would shield us; it would give life purpose and meaning.

Most ministers still made that promise, and who knew how many of them actually believed it? Cecil called for an honesty that stripped the traditional church of hypocrisy and asked each of us to look for the power or the Spirit (he called it God) within. When we were independent of church mythology, we would know where God abides.

On these visits I'd see Cecil standing on a ladder, his sleeves rolled up, talking to the construction workers, kind of cheerleading them to work faster. On Sundays he preached in front of the scaffold, reminding us that the things that kept us oppressed—racism, homelessness, poverty—didn't mean we were enslaved. If the cross meant anything, it was that we could free ourselves and make our own decisions. If Jesus brought salvation, it was to make the cross a symbol of unconditional love.

Sometimes Cecil got so passionate about this message that

he climbed up the ladders while preaching and pulled out pieces of the cut-up cross to show people that transformation could really happen. It was scary to watch, because the scaffold wobbled a bit while he dangled from it or danced on it. The cross, he said, was not about Jesus's death; it was about life, about renewal. If Jesus died and was reborn, the lesson of the cross meant that no matter how far down you "fell" in your own or others' estimation, life was there to be discovered again.

Cecil never held back in his sermons, yet we could see a personal struggle going on inside him. He was "the Rev" who'd felt a calling from childhood to uphold the church's teachings, not tear them down. How could a minister who believed so deeply in the cross's message of unconditional love be the same minister who was ripping it down? Even Cecil wondered. "Can people do this?" he asked in his sermons. "Can a people take down the cross when it ceases to have meaning?"

Then he would answer his own question, with his hands reaching out to us like a sculptor's and the Glide Ensemble singing gospel music that seemed to soar to the rafters. Cecil refused to be our channel to God, but his hands were inviting us all the same, as if to say, *Come in! Come to a place that has always been there, but you didn't know was there. Make your own relationship with God, that spiritual force you have always sought in life.*

Then at a Celebration one Sunday, Bart did this incredible thing. He gave Cecil a cross hanging from a chain. "Since your cross is missing, Reverend, I want to give you this," he said. It was a touching gesture, complicated slightly by the fact that Bart had stolen the cross and chain. In any other church, the theft would have negated its value. Cecil didn't bat an eye. "This cross is important *because* it's stolen," he said, holding it up. "People in the margins can relate because they know what it means to have their lives stolen from them."

By the time construction ended, all that remained was a wall, a stage, and some stairs. If anybody else had taken down the cross, the sanctuary would have been empty. There would have been no living symbolism or meaning to that blank wall. But as Cecil knew, the absence of the cross meant the congregation now had to imagine what should replace it.

Cecil

And so we had this bare sanctuary. A religion writer at the *San Francisco Examiner* accused us of "defacing the church wall" by tearing down the cross. But we didn't deface it—we *effaced* it. We wiped the slate clean. We wanted that bare wall to reflect people's lives outside the church.

That happened almost immediately. A group of young Asian men called the Red Lantern worked with Janice photographing street life during the week and projecting images on the wall during Celebrations. So now we had a Sunday light show of images and movement representing our community. Here were people embracing, protesting, playing with kids, giving the '60s V-for-peace sign, talking to police—just everyday life, joyous and morose, gritty yet life-affirming, just because we saw these glimpses on that wall. If you were addicted or recently out of jail or chronically poor or homeless, and you thought, as Bart said, that nobody cared, seeing images of people like yourself living from one moment to the next could be profoundly moving. And to see humanity *visibly* flowing across the wall where the giant cross used to hang was to feel that God, or whatever spiritual force lived in all of us, became a living force in our lives because we had the eyes to see. We were the cross.

And since this was the 1960s, the Red Lantern added strobe lights and collages of flowing lava and bursting kaleidoscopes to give the wall a psychedelic feel. Janice used to say it was a "choreographer's dream"—take the cross away, and the walls themselves danced in delight.

Red Lantern also mixed in anti–Vietnam War and pro-Mao images, but Janice cautioned them about criticizing political figures in inflammatory ways—like putting Ronald Reagan's face on a fish's body, or projecting slogans like "OFF THE PIG!" on top of law enforcement symbols such as police badges and batons or weapons.

"If you show violence perpetrated by the police," she would say, "that's one thing. But to *advocate for violence* is another thing, and we can't do that. If you show factual images of Ronald Reagan, you've made your point. But putting his face on a fish is the same as Glide putting someone down, and that would be irresponsible of us. It would also advocate for a very negative response, and could easily get out of control."

Red Lantern got the message. Soon Janice introduced discussions about more artistic ways to express themselves. Glide was becoming a church that attracted visitors from all over the country and world, she told them. What opportunities existed to help educate people about our views involving the evils of war, empathy for others, and a spiritual connection to life? Red Lantern again got the point and ran with it. Glide would not skirt the hard truths, they showed, projecting newspaper headlines or hard-to-look-at images of war, such as children suffering from Agent Orange. And they loaded that wall with people's art—silkscreen prints, drawings, and photos of San Francisco's neighborhood festivals, multilingual storefronts, refugee children, pickup basketball games, and beautiful murals created by diverse ethnic groups all over the city.

We could not predict the future then, but when I think back on what we hoped for the people whose images were projected on the wall, I see the ninety-five programs that Glide offers today—from job training and recovery to food, shelter, medical care, computer coaching, legal advice, the children's center, and more. These programs embody the love and the hope that started out and still live on that wall.

And this was not the only part of the sanctuary we transformed. From the balcony and along the side walls we hung banners stating the values Glide stood for—*Justice, Peace, Freedom, Righteousness, Trust, Community.* Janice formed a dance troupe with an incredible spectrum of choreography including jazz, ballroom, and modern dancing and music that ranged from soul and rock to Eastern atonal and classical sounds. I had given the old Glide choir a vacation and frankly never asked them to return. In their place, the now-famous Glide Ensemble began to form, and a number of celebrities spoke and performed at Celebrations—Benjamin Spock, Jane Fonda, Joan Baez, Quincy Jones, Johnny Mathis. The congregation expanded to include a wild assortment of humanity each Sunday: hippies in thrift store finery (top hats, army boots, flapper dresses, beads and feathers), jazz aficionados, prostitutes, immigrants, drag queens, refugees, homeless people from the shelters, Vietnam veterans, performers from the Mitchell Brothers (the city's biggest porno theater), revolutionaries in army-navy gear, and lo and behold, traditional churchgoers in their Sunday best (none from our original thirty-five stalwarts).

Sometimes the pure, boisterous energy of the congregation struck a nerve of creativity. Leonard Bernstein attended a Celebration when he was struggling with writer's block while composing music for a concert for the Kennedy Center. Apparently the sight and sound of a packed church rocking to jazz and gospel music got to him. As I finished my sermon, he jumped out of his seat, ran up on the stage, and picked me up, yelling, "I've got it! I've got it!" as he swung me around. Then he took the microphone and told the audience, "You're doing it here! My finale for the concert will be the kiss of peace!" and explained his ideas about art and inspiration and discovering the spirit at Glide.

Over the years, theologians have asked if my real intention in taking down the cross was to secede from the Methodist church. Had we done so, they say, Glide could have independently explored radical ideas that the traditional church would never condone. I'm always surprised to hear this question, because the answer is emphatically no. Secession was never on my mind. In fact, I wish other churches would explore new ways to confront declining memberships across the country and turn to radical change as an answer. I was hardly the only pastor in America to face a dying church. Then as now I believed that the only option for Glide was to end the death throes and start anew.

Janice

Cecil's vision for the meaning of sanctuary without a cross hit home with Maya Angelou during a recent Easter sunrise service when she brought Oprah Winfrey to Glide. This was one of those occasions when someone from the audience had become so strung out on drugs that he stumbled onto the stage, trembling and shouting. The audience and our ushers leaned forward as if to stop him, but Cecil held up his hand and gave the microphone to the man as if he had been invited to speak all along. The effect of that gesture and its message of unconditional acceptance changed the man's state of being completely.

"I'm loaded and not in good shape," he told the audience. "But I tell y'all this—I'm not always going to be that way. I'm not!" He looked at Cecil with such trust and hope that people sat there with tears in their eyes. Maya and Oprah were moved by Cecil's openness with this man too. They said later they would have remembered the episode even if the same man, scrubbed up and clearly off drugs, had not stood up in the middle of the next Easter sunrise service and announced that he had been sober the entire year. Maya refers to this episode as "a true resurrection story."

11

Sexual Freedom

Cecil

I WASN'T AWARE that Glide's reputation had spread very far until 1969, when the organizers of a Methodist worship convocation in St. Louis invited me to speak. I was to be one of six ministers who would address a number of religious topics. Then we would split up to lead separate seminars.

None of the topics included sex, nor did any of the seminars—until the question-and-answer period began in my group.

"What about that topless choir you've put in your church?" someone called out to me.

"Glide doesn't have a topless—" I started to say.

"Don't people have sex in the aisles and the stairways at Glide?" another person asked.

"That was an event called the Invisible Circus," I said, "but it's more complicated than—"

"Do you allow people to masturbate during worship services?"

"Do you conduct weddings for homosexuals?"

"Do you give out free condoms after services on Sunday?"

"Do you sponsor conventions for prostitutes?"

I shouldn't have been surprised. Most mainstream churches either avoided the subject of sex or took the stance that pre-marital sex, gay sex, and masturbation were wrong. Glide, on the other hand, celebrated sex as a healthy bodily function that should be free of shame and guilt.

So yes, we gave away condoms to aid contraception and stop the spread of sexually transmitted diseases.

Yes, I was proud to officiate at any wedding that joined people who loved each other.

No, Glide did not have a topless choir. The fact that top-less bars and go-go dancers were popular in some parts of San Francisco, including the Tenderloin, didn't mean that Glide would objectify women's bodies.

And yes, we had a live-and-let-live attitude about consensual sex, I told the seminar audience. It did not bother me, for ex-ample, when I learned that a half-dozen couples had gone up to the roof to make love during an all-night event called the Invisible Circus. The only warning I gave them was not to fall off and to please come downstairs.

As to the Hookers' Convention, which did indeed take place on church premises, this meeting created a big sensation because it was the first of its kind and because it considered serious issues the country at large needed to discuss openly—legalizing prostitution, STD protection, women's rights, the pro-choice movement, domestic violence, and legal representation (why was it that sex workers were arrested by police but not the clients who created the demand?). I took pride in the fact that Glide was the host. Activist Margo St. James and other organizers had rented an office at Glide months before, and it was there that they created COYOTE (Call Off Your Old Tired Ethics), the first prostitutes' union in the United States.

It seemed to me that people were really asking whether Glide had become one of the crazy cults in the '60s that capitulated to the sexual revolution. Were we allowing parishioners to get so carried away that they ended up coupling in the aisles?

The answer was no, we did not, but the question was important. We wanted to help people break loose of myths and proscriptions about *all* forbidden subjects. We supported freedom of expression and the responsibilities that went along with it in terms of celebrating our sexuality, gender, race, age, class, and circumstance. During Sunday services, we certainly did encourage spontaneity, because we *wanted* people to get carried away. That was one reason I took down the cross—to clear out everything that stood in the way of people breaking free from the old constraints. With every change at Glide, I asked the congregation (and myself): *Can you let it all go? Can you throw out the old bulletins, the dreary hymns, the staid, stymied, hard-nosed theology? Can you live fully rather than guess at life?*

The Glide Ensemble had a song called "Breakin' Free," written by me and Janice, that revved everybody up. Our singers weren't topless when they sang it. Their voices soared during refrain after refrain that filled the church with spirituality and love, and in that heady atmosphere people became more accepting of change, of possibility, of diversity, of freedom.

In the midst of the sexual revolution, of course, we knew that pursuing this kind of emotional high had its own risks. People danced in the aisles, sometimes with so much frenzy that they threw off their clothes or embraced each other intimately or leaped onto the stage in an exhibitionist manner.

We dealt with each episode individually. When Janice took a nearly naked woman to the restroom, it wasn't to talk about why the woman came to church with no clothes on under her coat—that was no one's business. It was to talk instead about the effect of her beauty on the congregation when her coat fell open because folks wouldn't be able to pay full attention to the sermon.

I had the same talk with an actor-contortionist who performed sexually acrobatic acts on himself in the balcony. If he wanted to do this in movies that people paid to see, fine; but during the service, I required respect for all of us.

At the seminar in St. Louis, I explained that I was glad when people felt liberated because this meant that as a community we could learn something about freedom and the choices we made. At Glide we never said that sex was "bad" in its own right. We said that sex was good. It was a natural part of being human, and so were homosexuality and masturbation. And we said that decisions had consequences. We tried to approach each over-the-top action or situation with respect and good humor, no matter how bizarre it might be by conventional standards.

Janice

When you think about it, Cecil's career started with sex. Here was Glide Church, located in the middle of the Tenderloin in the '60s, home of sex shops, adult bookstores, strip clubs, porno theaters, peep shows, leather bars, dominatrix parlors, prostitutes, and pimps. In a location like that, a conscientious minister is not going to start with the virgin birth. He's not going to preach about righteous purity or Jesus Christ with his washed feet. He's going to start with the rawest, purest form of what some people would call sinful—sex, and then *same* sex, and then prostitution, and then forms of sex that people keep secret.

The acceptance of all this made Glide a place where people felt they could go for help without fear of being judged. On the one hand, Glide was an "unsafe" place because Cecil was always taking us out on the edge where the truth lay and challenging us to challenge ourselves, and that could be scary. And Glide was "dangerous" in the best sense of the word because it was exciting, spontaneous, and open. Anything could happen. People came because they knew that when you went to Glide, you left your comfort zone.

On the other hand, at a time of great sexual confusion in America, Glide opened the door to a new idea of "safe." Unlike any traditional church, Glide was truthful and educational about unsafe sexual practices. We passed out condoms. We talked about women and sexuality. We discussed sexual and domestic violence, and how women and men, and children, deserved a place that was safe from harm. We created a safe place for survivors of rape and incest, for young women who had been put out as prostitutes by parents and pimps, for young gay men who were selling their bodies in the street, and for ex-felons who had been raped in prison and didn't know what to think of themselves any longer. We welcomed all, and we embraced the reality of a spectrum of sexual behaviors without shame.

I thought of this while answering the phones and acting as receptionist at Glide. It astonished me how many people would describe their problems and ask advice from a stranger, but after a while I simply tried to help those who asked for immediate guidance and seemed to need it.

One day in 1967 when I was quite pregnant—about seven months along—a heavyset man came in for counseling. He seemed a bit shy until I asked him to sit down and tell me what kind of help he needed.

"I don't think my problem is anything like being gay," he said. "I'm married, and I love my wife, but I like wearing her underwear, particularly her panty hose."

"And you want the reverend to . . ."

"I don't think I'm a lesbian, either," he went on. "I'm more like a . . ."

"Like a cross-dresser?"

"No, I just, you know, get off wearing her underwear."

"Have you told your wife about this?"

"I don't think she would understand," he said. "In fact, she'd be shocked."

He was too embarrassed to give me his real name, so he asked if I would make something up, preferably a woman's name. I said, "Why don't I call you Maria?" which pleased him so much that he hugged himself.

"That would be wonderful," he said. Then he rolled his pants legs up to his thighs and showed me that he was wearing panty hose.

"See, don't they look great?" he said. "I shave my legs too."

I knew Cecil was in his office meeting with three big and burly members of the Black Man's Free Store, a storefront in the Western Addition district where goods were collected and given out to the poor. These streetwise guys often helped out at Glide. They felt protective of Cecil and me and the people at Glide, so I wasn't worried about Maria hurting me. But I wouldn't have been anyway. Maria seemed relieved to talk about his secret, which when it came out was simply that he found pleasure wearing his wife's underwear. Then I noticed that Maria had his hand in his pocket and was masturbating.

"You'll have to excuse me a moment, Maria," I said, standing up. I went into Cecil's office and told the men not to be upset, but a person was stimulating himself in my office. All three of the muscular guys stood up instantly, growling to each other and preparing to throw him out.

"No, no, wait," I said. "I can deal with him as long as he doesn't expose himself. He feels he's in a confidential conversation with me, so I'll go back out there. I'll just call you if there's any trouble."

They sat back down reluctantly. Cecil asked me if I was sure about this. I said yes, I just wanted him to know what was going on. When I went back to my office, I resisted saying

"Are you done yet?" to Maria because I wanted to give him privacy. He smiled pleasantly as though he was ready now and said how nice I was to listen to his problem.

"Maria, I think you should talk to a psychiatrist while your needs are bothering you, and I hope you share these desires with your wife. They're not shameful, and I know you'll feel better once things in your marriage are out in the open."

"Well, I really want to thank you for giving me your time," Maria said. "You're lovely in your pregnancy, and I hope to see you again."

So we were as polite to each other as we both felt the occasion warranted. Even the three guys from the Black Man's Free Store were waiting a respectful distance behind Cecil's door as Maria found his way to the exit. I was glad things ended this way; Maria would have felt humiliated if I had broken his trust and asked for intervention from the men. He wanted to feel accepted for his needs.

But that was the way things went at Glide. We were unflappably accepting because we had become so immersed in many different ideas and perceptions and ways of life. The most outrageous, the most vocal, the most expressive and "out" there behaviors kept finding their way to Glide, and we grew more open, more understanding, more knowledgeable, and, I thought, more helpful because of them.

For example, long before sex-reassignment surgery was accepted in medical circles, we met Roxanne, a beautiful MTF (male-to-female) person who didn't mind people coming to her room to look at her body. Roxanne had been one of the first patients to have a sex change—so new at the time that the Stanford University School of Medicine performed it for free. Like many people at Glide, Roxanne had been through bizarre "treatments" before she even guessed who she was in terms of sexual identity. As a teenager, she (then a he) had confessed that he might be gay to his mother. She took him to a doctor who told him to eat nothing but vegetables for a year as a cure against homosexuality. Roxanne had done that and somehow, against the wishes of a disapproving mother, an ignorant doctor, and an unaccepting society, he realized that the problem was neither diet-related nor sexual but gender related. How someone could figure that out all alone, leave her parents behind, then battle the status quo and risk her life having—in fact, insisting on—never-performed surgery made us all proud to know Roxanne. But it wasn't only for her courage. We were proud to know her because she had learned self-acceptance and loved the person she knew herself to be.

Over the years, Cecil and I didn't just stumble on this array of knowledge; in a very real way we sought it. I felt more engaged with life when I was working with gay teens, MTFs, the guys from the Black Man's Free Store, the Black Panthers, and the Marias and Roxannes of the world than I did with conventional ministers and other authorities who promoted conformity with society and never explored true feelings.

Cecil

Very often we were open-minded to the point of inviting chaos, willing to risk almost too much freedom for the sake of breaking free. Life on the edge was worth it to us for the lessons in humanity we could learn along the way. Which brings us to the Invisible Circus.

Like any church, Glide rented out halls and held gatherings for the public. So in 1967 when a group of hippies called the Diggers asked to use the church all weekend for a "happening" that would "bring the tribes together," whatever that meant, there seemed no reason to refuse. They said that Hell's Angels would help with security, so nothing would go wrong. The four of us ministers on senior staff agreed to take eight-hour shifts to keep an eye on whatever things were indeed happening. Because my shift was to begin at midnight on Friday, I was surprised that an urgent call from Glide came to my home around eight P.M. telling me to "get down here right away."

When I arrived, things did not look good. I saw crowds of people bunching up at the entrance, and after I got in, bodies crowding into every room of the church, including the upstairs offices we had cordoned off. I started with these. Desks and chairs had been pushed into corners to make room for oversize pillows on the floor, surrounded by perfumes and lubricants. On the next floor, half the people were naked, and the smell of marijuana nearly lifted the church off its foundation. On the ground floor, rock bands were blaring and strobe lights were pulsing in Freedom Hall, while porno films were showing and belly dancers and women in G-strings danced on the stage in the sanctuary.

An "outlaw media center" in the basement mimeographed "Flash!" bulletins about newsworthy events (one just said "FUCK"), and these were being handed out to very surprised people on the street. I spotted the poet Richard Brautigan going around collecting artwork, poems, announcements, I Ching readings, and transcribed conversations that were given Flash! coverage. He named the media center—typewriters, mimeograph machine, and bowl of Tang laced with LSD—"The John Dillinger Computer Complex" as an homage to the famous '30s gangster and to the age of electronic communication to come.

As I went back upstairs, I could tell that psychedelic drugs were being used because of the mad laughter and angry tears that erupted everywhere, often followed by people slumping to the floor in a stupor. Near disasters cropped up as well. One woman tried to light a cigarette, but her fingertips were apparently coated with lighter fluid because they suddenly burst into flames. When I grabbed her hands to smother the fire, she stared at me. "Where is Jesus?" she said. "Where is Jesus?"

Yeah, I wondered, where was he?

Three of us—Janice, our intern Larry Mamiya, and I—kept calling for paramedics, and when an ambulance finally arrived, a number of semiconscious partygoers had to be helped or carried out. The conscious were not all that much better off, it seemed. So many bodies pressed into "the happening" that walking was impossible. A person had to turn sideways and shimmy between shoulders and backs, which is what I was doing when a prim older woman came into view. She sat on the edge of a bench and reached out to men nearby. "Will you fuck me?" she said to each one. "Please take me home and fuck me." I tried to help her get up, but she pushed my hands away, and before I knew it, the crush of bodies carried me down the hall.

All this time, San Francisco's infamous underground radio (unlicensed FM) was broadcasting reports that the Invisible Circus at Glide had turned into bedlam, with something like eight thousand people packed into the church and more on the way. That's all the other thousands of hippies in the Bay Area needed to hear.

By 6:00 A.M. on Saturday so many people were pushing to get into the "never-ending party" that the police wanted to clear the place out before someone got hurt. If that meant paddy wagons and batons, I realized, we might have a riot on our hands. (Our Hell's Angels security crew had gotten into a fight with some of the partygoers and left.) Yet I refused to just stand there and "let the party self-destruct," as a few jaded officials suggested.

Thanks in part to unusually balmy weather, I asked the Diggers (who had lost their own high long ago and were ready to call it quits) and the SFPD to discuss options for a healthy outcome. There weren't many. Nobody was leaving until the party ended, and those still standing would probably turn violent if the police tried to end it for them.

The responsible act was not to get angry (me) or bash heads (the police) but to see the problem as a public health emergency. We didn't have time to be angry. We had time only to call in the community—the whole village, as it were—and say, *These are our children. We need to move them to a place where their energy can diffuse safely.* The police were remarkably restrained as the decision was made to let the Invisible Circus continue as a movable feast. Like the song by the Animals, this was a "warm San Francisco night" that would be perfect for a beach party at the Pacific Ocean, which was about seven miles away. We got word to the "media center" to start printing directions to a two-mile stretch of dunes along the Great Highway, where police were going to allow partygoers to light bonfires, the rock bands to keep playing, and the dancing, lovemaking, drugs, and naked people to spread out.

Somehow we found enough police vans, squad cars, and Muni buses to haul several thousand to the beach, while the rest walked out of the church under their own steam and peacefully followed the lure of the ocean.

I never knew what the hippies meant by the term "Invisible Circus," but I took it to signify that, when repression is suddenly lifted, people go crazy expressing a freedom they've never had. What was invisible to us in traditional society was magnified hugely "at the Circus." This was liberation at its most primitive, most graphic, most earthy, and most frightening state. I found myself strangely at peace as the events unfolded, having been wary of hippies earlier, and with good reason.

Some months before, one group, a precursor of the Diggers, had nearly burned the church down during a "ritual" in the chapel and refused to take responsibility for it. For this and other reasons I had unconsciously dismissed hippies as too reckless, too white, and too privileged to be trusted. But the Invisible Circus helped me clear away my own tendency to stereotype and see what was now visible: humanity suffering under an oppressive society. I felt more fatherly toward them and sympathetic to what they were trying to express.

I would need that peace of mind, I realized, after waving

good-bye to the last of the vans and turning back to Glide, where I joined members of our staff to begin clearing out the tons of trash and bodily fluids that had landed on everything from the pews to the elevator walls. Starting with the sixth floor, we cleaned and mopped our way down for the next twelve hours—there would be a Celebration that next morning—until the smell of ammonia made us all dizzy. Then, when we got to the basement, one of our janitors showed me to the men's toilet and pointed out a large, boldly scribbled message on the wall above a urinal that said, "FUCK THE CHURCH."

So there it was, I thought, the message for our age. Not "Jesus Saves" or "God Loves You" but a fierce and uncompromising statement that the church needed to consider. How else were we going to understand the true needs of our congregation?

I gave a sermon about it that very Sunday. True, I said, some might say the writer of this graffiti wanted to destroy everything in Glide and left "FUCK THE CHURCH" as a farewell message. But I saw it as a challenge. It said the church needed to stop pimping pretty images of God, blessings, and eternity. It needed to come down from its pedestal to accept the human condition for its foibles and its nobility, its destructiveness and its humanity. And it needed to be impregnated anew to be nurturing again, to be renewing and renewed. Birth is messy, bloody, and chaotic, but lessons grow out of that chaos.

The janitor asked me if he should scrub off the graffiti, but I said, no, not for a long time. I remembered that on my first visit to the Tenderloin, I told the bishop that the only way to save Glide was to turn the church upside down. Now this message from the back of a toilet was saying the same thing, only plainer.

People have asked if there wasn't a lot of grumbling among the staff and from me about the soiling of our beautiful church and the need to hurry and clean it up before services began in the morning. I admit I was not happy with the other ministers who took off when things got wild. But the fact was that I didn't have time to grumble. My concern was to make Glide a place of safety and radical change that people could rely on, no matter what. This Invisible Circus, as disastrous as the literal ton of trash we were carting off by the truckload, was not going to stop Glide from opening the doors on Sunday as we always had. I didn't care what had happened. You could start fires on your own hands, you could write obscenities in the church's toilet, you could damage people's brains with psychedelic drugs. But tomorrow was Sunday, and Glide was going to welcome all the people who wanted to come to our regular Sunday Celebration.

Which we did, with only minutes to spare. The biggest surprise came when the partygoers returned that same morning, floating up the aisles like water lilies, to place around the altar the flowers and seashells they had gathered at the beach. Then they did a "reverse offering" by filling the collection basket with other gifts from the sea and passing it around so that people could take a souvenir if they wished. I don't know if this was an apology or a thank-you, but I loved it that they came back and were genuinely grateful.

So that was the Invisible Circus, and yes, I said to the seminar in St. Louis, people *did* have sex in the aisles and the stairways that weekend. But what could have been an out-and-out catastrophe turned into a lesson in understanding and patience that none of us would ever forget.

12

Nonviolence

Cecil

ONE NIGHT IN 1969, Janice was working late at Glide when a stoned man in an army shirt wandered into the office. He said he was just back from Vietnam and needed money. Janice said she couldn't help him.

"You know," he told her, "I killed twenty of you over there, and I notched my rifle butt after every one."

She understood that the "you" meant twenty Vietnamese people who looked like Janice to him.

"I believe you," Janice said. "But I still can't give you any money." Fortunately, the man wandered out without harming her.

As we say at Glide, you never know who will be the messenger. This man signaled the start of a wave of Vietnam veterans who were drawn to the Tenderloin looking for many things—money, drugs, relief from PTSD (posttraumatic stress disorder), shelter, food, and escape from a pain that no Veterans Administration hospital could provide. Many looked like walking ghosts as they trudged through the halls of Glide. They could not cope with family life, and a lot of domestic violence emerged. For those who still carried army knives that had served them in the jungles of Vietnam, turning to violence was second nature.

But even in the face of potential violence, I hoped that Glide would be seen as a place of love and safe harbor. If we were unconditional in our acceptance and love, we would welcome everyone without judgment. Violence might come into our ranks, but we would not react violently against it. Janice had the gift of being compassionate and tough-minded at the same time, so nobody messed with her. And I must say that most people, especially veterans, respected our work for justice and kept their anger contained.

But during the cultural upheavals of the '60s and '70s, people reacted violently to a lot of things. Hate mail poured in. Someone firebombed Glide's front door after the Hookers' Convention. Bomb threats became a common occurrence, although most were hoaxes. We learned to live with hateful graffiti, too, until after Janice and I married, when the garage of our home got tagged. The worst occurred in the '80s when we were in Atlanta visiting Coretta Scott King to participate in events celebrating Martin Luther King Jr.'s birthday. I had for several years chaired the northern California committee for this occasion, and it might have been that publicity that led to our discovery when we returned of a swastika on the garage of our home with the message "Kill Niggers and Nigger Lovers" underneath. A hate message on the garage was disturbing not only for its hostility. It also meant that somebody knew where we lived.

Church was another matter. During Celebrations, I welcomed the opportunity to work with unfiltered emotion from the congregation and told our monitors not to rush forward if people jumped up on the stage or spontaneously acted out in some other way. One Sunday, I admit my heart skipped a beat when a very excited man leaped onto the stage carrying a big metal bucket and raced toward me, yelling, "I love you so much!" He stopped an inch away and threw a thousand tiny flower petals at my face. I put my arm around his shoulder and said, "Brother, don't ever do that again. You scared the shit out of everybody in the church." The outburst of laughter reflected the relief we all felt, but the message went out: no more pranks on the Rev.

Can you have a revolution without violence? Glide was hardly alone in believing this was possible. We were followers of Mahatma Gandhi and the Reverend Martin Luther King Jr.; we supported Cesar Chavez and other grassroots leaders who believed not in a revolution of violence but a revolution of justice with love. We understood that violence only begets violence and is in itself dehumanizing. But we knew, too, that methods of violence were supported by systems and institutions that had been in place for centuries.

One time, members of a street gang came to my office at Glide after a violent confrontation with another gang in which passersby were shot. They asked me to help them find an attorney to defend them. I looked at the leaders and considered the big step they were taking. These young men grew up immersed in the culture of gang violence and by now hated the establishment. For them even to think of participating in the criminal justice system by hiring a lawyer was tantamount to saying they believed in the American way. So I found them a good defense lawyer who took their case. They were so grateful that they brought cartons and cartons of food into Glide.

That wasn't enough, they decided. "You want someone taken out? You want women? More food?" I had to laugh at how outlandish yet routine were the things they could "get" for me. I said no, I needed nothing from them. I only hoped that one day they would see that Glide stood for the power and the love of community; if you didn't like the status quo, opportunities for nonviolent radical change were everywhere. You just had to keep looking.

A RODNEY KING "RIOT"

A very different way of turning the impulse toward violence into a commitment to peace nearly bowled over my son, Albert, and me during the Rodney King riots of 1992 in Los Angeles.

A bit of background: The year before, white police officers had chased Rodney King, a black parolee, across Los Angeles at dangerous speeds before they caught and beat him senseless while he crawled helplessly on the ground. Fortunately someone videotaped the episode, and soon that tape made its way onto TV news broadcasts across the country. Millions of viewers believed there was no question that the police were guilty of assault. I thought so too. I hoped that technology had caught up with the vision and goals of the civil rights movement, and a new era had arrived in which the police could be held accountable.

So it was no wonder, when the jury surprised the world by acquitting the police, that black folks in South Central Los Angeles could not contain their anger. They began rioting, looting, and setting fires in their own neighborhoods. I hadn't wept since Martin Luther King Jr. was assassinated, but watching the destruction on television, I broke down. The Rodney King verdict sent a message to the world that after decades of civil rights victories, America had not changed. It felt like a huge step backward.

As was true in other cities, the beginnings of a riot flared up in downtown San Francisco, where crowds of people roamed the streets looking for a place to vent their rage. On that night, my son, Albert, then twenty-three years old, and I were standing in front of Glide when we saw hundreds of angry protesters boiling up Nob Hill. These folks had apparently come together on Market Street and were looking for a section of town where they could do some heavy damage, including arson and looting. A few blocks beyond us was Union Square, the upscale shopping area with department stores and big plateglass windows that seemed to be their destination. As the crowd grew closer, a police captain I knew came up to me.

"There aren't enough officers out here to stop that many people," he said. "They're just going to move right through us to Union Square. Can you do something?"

By this time Albert realized the mob was much bigger than

we thought—not just a few hundred but a few thousand. "Dad! Get up on a car!" Albert yelled. "They'll stop for you! Talk to them!"

I wasn't sure anybody could hear me, but I climbed onto the hood of a van just as the first wave of protesters arrived. "Brothers and sisters!" I shouted to them. "You're in a neighborhood where the poor and homeless live! Today can be critical for them if you make your protest known! Come inside and tell us—tell the world!—how you feel."

Some people marched right into Glide, the TV news cameras following them. Others were reluctant but let the crowd carry them in. To me, their attitude said, *Okay, we'll listen, but then we're going to wreck everything in sight.* Fine, I thought. If we could just bundle all this anger into the church, where everybody could look at each other and stay in one place, maybe we could talk about what this violence meant and where it might take us.

By the time I got inside the church, about fifteen hundred enraged people were still crowding into the pews, the window seats, the balcony, and the aisles. They were arguing and shouting at one another as I got onstage.

"Let us be clear," I said. "There is a new kind of shame and pain in the white community! You must know that whatever you do here tonight, you have the capacity to destroy whatever is in front of you"—they started cheering at this—"but no matter what happens, you can't break enough plateglass windows to overcome the heinous crimes that have been committed. What all of us *can* do, right now, is tell the truth. The cameras are rolling. What we *can* do is not hold back. You're in a church sanctuary. Tell the truth! That's what it's for."

One by one the stories came out. People of color were saying, *Racism is getting worse, our kids see cops as the enemy, profiling is out of control,* and white people were saying, *We're all being harassed, that verdict was rigged, law enforcement is out of control.* As the night went on, people realized that we were speaking the same language. Something was very wrong. The question was, what could we *do* about it?

We can organize, people said. *We can stand up to them, we can make a plan.* Gradually, this crowd that had been so bent on destruction started talking about creating something. Why waste time smashing up Union Square when the whole system needed changing? They started to ask doable questions: What could they do right now, when they left Glide, to make things better in their own neighborhoods? What could they teach their kids about this night? By the end of the meeting, it wasn't just that people felt better for having vented their frustrations. They had opened up; they had rejected violence. They were walking out and exchanging phone numbers with every expectation that it was in their power to create a vision for the future.

I learned later that about six hundred people did go on to Union Square, but the police were there to meet them, and only minor incidents of property damage occurred.

As the sun rose the next day, I remember looking at the sanctuary and thinking, *No violence occurred here, either.* Like so many plans that were hatched at Glide over the years, I would not know what happened next for the folks who had met here so passionately all night. But their change of attitude felt historic to me.

THE PEOPLE AND THE PANTHERS

I've never seen the idea of embracing violence tested quite so publicly or profoundly as when the Black Panther Party emerged in the late 1960s and early 1970s. The full name of the group was the Black Panther Party for Self Defense, with emphasis on the last two words. The Panthers were not calling for a violent overthrow of the U.S. government, but they did want it known that the violence embedded in American life was racist to the core—and that African Americans had every right to stand up against it.

I got a glimpse of the Panthers' deep distrust of the white establishment the first time the party contacted me, totally out of the blue. My phone rang at 5:00 A.M. and without introduction, a man said, "Huey's been shot! Can you come right away?" The caller was a member of the Black Panthers and was phoning from a hospital in Oakland where Huey Newton, the party's cofounder, was about to be taken in for surgery. "We need you to watch the operation," the man said, "and make sure they don't kill him." I would have gone, but before I could wonder why they chose me, or why they knew I would come, the phone rang again. "It's all right!" the same voice said. "We got somebody closer." Huey recovered.

To many whites, the Black Panther Party with its "off the pigs" rhetoric could not have been more militaristic or threatening. To many in the black community where police abuse was common, however, the Panthers' resistance to white hypocrisy was a long time coming. In Oakland, the Panthers were known for driving around poor black neighborhoods with law books and shotguns in the car, listening to police radios. When they heard news of an arrest, they would race to the scene, brandishing the guns (which were legal at the time) and using the law books to read suspects their rights.

Compared to the level of violence today, these early confrontations seem mild. From one point of view, the Panthers were lucky that white police didn't shoot them on sight. From another point of view, the white police were lucky they weren't caught brutalizing black suspects as the Panthers approached with shotguns in tow.

The Panthers used the media as their primary weapon. Their most famous photo showed Huey Newton dressed in Panther regalia (beret and black leather jacket), sitting in an exotic wide-backed chair that resembled an African throne. The fact that he was holding an African spear in one hand and a shotgun in the other spoofed white racist fears while sending a message to the world: take us seriously.

What really hit a nerve, however, was the photo of Panthers marching into the California state capitol armed with shotguns and rifles to protest, of all things, antigun legislation. Here again the sight of black warriors in uniform invading all that whiteness, glaring menacingly at every congressional representative who dared look at them and reading a manifesto (their position on the bill) on the front lawn with shotguns at the ready was both an elaborate PR stunt and a declaration of Black Power.

I don't use the term "PR stunt" lightly. Had the Black Panther Party called a press conference to promote its free programs for poor African Americans—breakfasts for children,

health-care clinics, education, legal advice, clothes exchange—
the press would have walked away yawning. It was only when
the party triggered white fears that American media responded
exactly as predicted by plastering Black Panther photos on
every TV screen and front page in the country. The FBI
seemed to be playing a power game of its own when J. Edgar
Hoover made his famous announcement that the greatest
threat to the internal security of the United States was the
Black Panthers' Free Breakfast Program for Children.

The Panthers invited me to speak at Black Power rallies,
sometimes with other clergy, sometimes alone. They liked
the politics and spirituality of Glide and respected our vision
of diversity whether they agreed with it or not. I performed
the marriage service of Huey and his first wife, Gwen, in a
beautiful ceremony at Glide, and Panther leaders David Hill-
iard and Bobby Seale spoke to enthusiastic crowds at Sunday
Celebrations.

Today people want to know how I as a minister who's devoted to nonviolence could have supported the Black Panthers
and their use of guns. I answer that it's easy to get stuck on the
issue of weapons when the larger picture—a world of racism
and violence—is not being addressed at all. I am committed to
unconditional love, which means I respect the reality of others.
In a world where African Americans are more likely than
whites to be profiled as violent, and more likely to be killed,
my focus is the preservation of life.

An instructive story that occurred around this time involves
the Deacons for Defense and Justice, a group of black veterans
from World War II and Korea who created a civilian army in

Louisiana to protect civil rights workers from the Ku Klux Klan. The Deacons provided security for African American activist James Meredith's March Against Fear in Mississippi; they boycotted segregated businesses; they patrolled black neighborhoods using walkie-talkies and citizens band radios; they protected CORE (Congress of Racial Equality) head-quarters; and during a historic battle in Bogalusa, Louisiana, the Deacons fought against the Klan and local police until the federal government sent in troops to enforce the 1964 Civil Rights Act. So in effect, the Deacons won.

One day several carloads of members from the Deacons for Defense arrived at Glide to talk to me about turning their organization into a national movement. They believed that armed self-defense, including retaliatory violence, could be used as tactics to compel the federal government to enforce the law. If this theory worked in the South against the Klan, couldn't it work in the inner city? Couldn't groups like the Deacons, the Panthers, SNCC (Student Nonviolent Coordi-nating Committee, which by then had rejected nonviolence), CORE, Glide, and others make Black Power a real force?

We talked for a long time about the difference between overt hatred of blacks in the South and less visible but just as damaging racism in the North; about the effects of violence in the long run, and whether a coalition of African Ameri-cans with so many different experiences across so many miles could work. I said it would be difficult for people who weren't committed to armed insurgence to join the Deacons. Glide itself was devoted to nonviolence, so people like me and my congregation were out. For us, the way to change the world was to leave every kind of segregation behind and invite all Americans to help us stand up for a just society.

The Deacons stayed a few days and drove back to Louisiana. Their movement did not last very long, but for me it brought up, again, the many disparities in America that rarely surfaced because of racism, which was always simmering underneath so much of society. Most people—most white people—lived under a different set of rules than the gang members to whom I had recommended a defense lawyer; than the Deacons in the South fighting both the Klan and the local police; than the Panthers in any black ghetto in the United States.

These issues cropped up like lighted fuses when in the late '60s the Black Panther Party rented office space for its San Francisco headquarters in the Western Addition, a low-income African American section of town. By this time, police raids of Panther offices all over the country, and shoot-outs with Panthers on the streets of Oakland, had caused so many deaths that tensions were extremely high between any law enforcement agency and the party.

Then one day after they moved in, an explosion occurred at the Panther office in San Francisco, and the SFPD started to mobilize. Nobody knew what caused the explosion or if damage had occurred—no one to my knowledge had been hurt—but the police said they had no choice. There could be a bomb about to explode for all they knew, so they were going to investigate. The Panthers went into high alert and geared up for a huge SWAT attack. Believing the SFPD was using the explosion as an excuse to raid the Panther office for weapons, *they* began to mobilize. The police insisted they were going in, period; they had to protect the safety of the whole Western Addition. The Panthers refused to acknowledge any legal grounds for an SFPD invasion.

Things were escalating fast when Glide members from the Western Addition asked me to see if Glide could help defuse things. Taking a delegation of neighborhood residents and members of the Black Panther Party (about eight in all), I met with the chief of police in his office to talk about all the issues involved, not just the obvious ones.

For one thing, I said, the Western Addition had been a neglected ghetto for years, so the sudden entrance of police to "protect" the area sounded questionable. Second, didn't the police know that marching into the Panther office would be like setting off a powder keg? Talk about explosions—a *lot* of people would get killed. Third, we had information that the police were going to surprise the Panthers by raiding the office that very night. If this was true, they had to call it off.

The chief and his captains listened to this without expression. They seemed to think that just talking about it with us would be losing ground to the enemy.

I proposed that the SFPD hold off until things cooled down. In a few days, if police cleared the way with the Panthers ahead of time and offered to act in partnership with the party, there was a good chance the Panthers would invite them to come. The police looked at my small delegation and saw heads nod. Then the chief conferred with two of his captains and surprised us by agreeing with the idea. The SFPD would wait "until you're ready for us to come out there," he said, looking at the four Panthers in the office. Then he stood up as if to say that was it.

I sat there thinking this sounded too easy. Nothing was

stopping them from launching a raid that night anyway. Orders from the top of the SFPD were countermanded every day and would be again, especially if someone at the scene decided another explosion might be imminent. This was the problem of taking the word of the chief, I had learned. There was never any guarantee to the black community that police wouldn't rush in for any reason.

"On our end, here's what we're going to do," I said. "We're going to have four hundred or five hundred of our people surround the Panther office tonight, and tomorrow night, and however many nights it takes until the Panthers feel comfortable." The chief said nothing for a moment. He couldn't believe we could get that many people out to risk their lives for a cramped office in the middle of a slum. Of course, if we did, it went without question that these people would not be armed, would not fight the police in any way, and would not move from their positions. If a bomb had really been planted and exploded in the night, many of them would be killed. If the police decided to invade the Panther headquarters, they'd have to arrest all five hundred people first, then move in.

The chief nodded as if he understood all that and gave me a card with his direct phone number.

Afterward Janice and I made a few strategic telephone-tree calls (almost as effective as cell-phone and e-mail alerts today) to get the word out and drove to the Panther headquarters, which turned out to be a very small office. It already looked like a combat zone, with sandbags piled around the doors and windows. No one knew what might happen, but support for the Panthers flooded in, not only from Glide and residents of the Western Addition, but from other churches, other neighborhoods, the antiwar movement, and civil rights groups.

As darkness fell, volunteers began to line up in front of the Panther headquarters. More people came, and the crowds swelled into the streets. Soon you couldn't see the Panther office for the mass of people getting deeper and thicker. Still more people came; the police would need a tank to wedge through the hordes (an unfortunate but realistic possibility at the time).

By 1:00 A.M. we had about five hundred people standing quietly waiting, and they were prepared to stand there all night. I had been awake for twenty-four hours, so I went home to get some sleep while Janice stayed on to monitor the effort and make sure nothing went wrong. At 2:00 A.M. she called to say that a police siren had streaked through a nearby street, causing everyone to leap to alert. I called the chief on his direct line and told him that something might have gone awry. "I'll take care of it," he said gruffly and hung up. In a half hour Janice reported that the siren had belonged to a fire engine and that no police threat was present. This was a relief, of course, and things did remain peaceful as the night wore on.

I'm sure the police knew how many people were out there. It must have astounded them that not a single person in that huge throng ever panicked or turned hostile or even uttered a belligerent word. Quite the opposite. The multitudes remained in position until morning, surrounding the Panther office like a human tea cozy in that fog-enshrouded night, and ready to come back the next night if they were called upon, which they were.

Janice

One of Cecil's gifts as minister of Glide was to convince the congregation that unconditional love was the only way to confront violence. We could be firm in seeking justice and in standing up to perpetrators' attempts to engage us physically, but fighting back was not an option. Retaliation would rob us of the humanity we hoped to share with those who were trying to hurt us.

For many years Glide offered training on the eve of massive protest marches against the war in Vietnam to prepare people for agent provocateurs. We didn't know who sent them—the government, ultraconservative groups, the radical fringe—but their job as they saw it was to start fights, bait police, lead the march in the wrong direction, and otherwise disrupt order so that the march would look like a riot on the evening news. Once protesters got the hang of not reacting physically to anything negative, there were few incidents.

In the church, Cecil used the ever-emerging threat of confrontation as a platform to explore the value of nonviolence. One Sunday a woman and three men wearing dirty leather jackets and bandannas walked in late to the 11:00 A.M. Celebration and sauntered down the aisle with a hostile "Try and stop us" attitude while Cecil was delivering his sermon. They had their backs to the church until they got to the front pews, where they turned around so that the whole church could see the big swastikas printed across the front of their bandannas.

People gasped and waited for Cecil's response, but he only nodded at the four as they sat down. He continued preaching but very soon diverted from the sermon he had given at the 9:00 A.M. service. Now he was talking about the fact that we all wear masks because we don't want to reveal who we really are. Masks may be worn to intimidate or anger people, he said, but their real purpose is to keep the world from getting too close. We have to take them off at some point, and only then can we accept ourselves, and accept the love of others.

"There is a force here greater than hatred," he said, clearly referring to the swastikas. "And greater than death. That force is the Spirit inside you that says love is stronger than death." At that point, the four people got up and left.

The next Sunday they came back, still wearing their swastika bandannas. Again, Cecil merely nodded in their direction, but some people in the congregation stood up as if they had had enough of this and wanted a fight.

"Sometimes folks may try to intimidate us," Cecil said, looking everywhere but at the four, "because they want us to do something violent." Then he talked about resisting our own urge to act violently by seeing the humanity in those who want to hurt us. "If we give in to their brute force," Cecil said, "we lose and they lose." And out the door the swastika wearers went again.

On the third Sunday they came back, but this time the men were clean-shaven, and they had all removed their headbands. People spotted them walking down the aisle and started to applaud. Cecil asked the four to stand and greet the audience, which they did, and there was more applause. They were smiling, and so was the congregation. No one begrudged them the ordeal they had put everybody through because we were actually proud of them, and of ourselves and our church.

Afterward they told Cecil that the first two Sundays, they could not believe he had accepted them coming in with their symbols of hate. They had wanted to shock people, but they didn't really hate anybody. They had some vague plan of exposing the church for its hypocrisy, but Glide was different, and anyway, nobody had really wanted to fight. At some point the four had eaten in the food lines and decided to volunteer in the meals program one day.

I think Cecil was the happiest of all of us. We had just gone through an exercise of facing violence with the power of love, and there you had it; we won and they won.

13

Persistence

Cecil

I HAD BEEN minister at Glide for only a few years when members of the congregation suggested that we offer free meals to poor and homeless people who were living in the streets outside our door.

Janice, still relatively new, was fired up by the idea. Even in those early days, I knew if anybody could get a meals program organized, she could. Her skepticism and my idealism were one reason we hit it off so well. I was concerned that the traditional church preached compassion but rarely acted on it, and heaven knows, Janice felt that way too. And I wanted Glide to be different for the same reason she did—when we saw an injustice, we went after it.

Nevertheless, every signpost at Glide told us to wait. We

had no money or staff to feed the hungry. Glide's once pristine dining room had fallen into disrepair. Some of the United Methodist Church ministers with offices upstairs had already objected to unkempt street people coming in for Sunday Celebrations. For me to add lines of hungry folks coming into a part of the church that had never been open to the public would be, to them, unthinkable.

I hoped to get support from Glide's board of trustees but was quickly turned down, as happened so often in those early years. *You should think this food program through,* they said. *Start raising money, create a business plan, calm the UMC ministers, and come back to us. We'll help you get a bank loan to start construction on the dining room. If that works out, handing out sandwiches seems viable, then maybe you could start a soup kitchen.*

So the answer was a resounding no except for one thing—we were going to do it anyway. I didn't care about the money or the UMC ministers or lack of wheelchair access or any of those things—we'd find a way to deal with all of it. What mattered was the community at Glide gaining a sense of itself, of deciding to do something and persisting to the end. Fundamentally, it was a matter of unconditional acceptance. If some of our people were starving, and other people wanted to share the food, we were going to share the food.

Janice found that we had enough volunteers to bring in a mess of potluck dinners to feed maybe fifty people once a week, on Monday nights. That would be a great start. The volunteers, headed by Patsy Harrison and Sam Smith, took on the task of the dinner with fervor and commitment. Janice began organizing schedules, getting equipment, and scheduling repairs to the kitchen in whatever way she could. We would use Freedom Hall for those who required wheelchair access for food. We were on our way.

Granted, on that first Monday night, the place still looked like a bare, hanging-by-a-thread kitchen, but the people who came in for home-cooked meals hardly cared about furniture and wallpaper. There wasn't a lot of food, but you know how it is in a poor family—everyone learns to stretch—and it's not the saving of money that's meaningful but the closeness, the warmth, the sharing. Instead of being a "soup kitchen" with its stigma of charity and assembly lines, Glide made people feel welcome, as though they had been invited to someone's home. Because Glide was their home. That was the ambiance we wanted for Monday night dinners.

More people volunteered, and we began serving dinner two nights a week, then three. At one point, the strain was too much for our rusty plumbing, and after a week of heavy rains, raw sewage flooded the dining room. The stench was so bad that the Health Department asked us to close the program for a while, but we convinced them that leaving people hungry was not an option. After services that Sunday, Janice and I got some wading boots and brooms so we could sweep the water back and disinfect the room all night until dinnertime Monday. That evening, the folks came in as if to say, *What's a little smell among friends?* Our thoughts exactly. The basic thing was not just to care for people but to be courageous in our love, to stand and support those who could not stand and support themselves.

It was up-against-the-wall times like this that Maya Angelou would suddenly show up and insert her magical presence into whatever proceeding she found. By this time, Maya was also a member of the family as far as we were concerned (I addressed her as "Sister," and she called me "Brother"). Whenever we visited her home in North Carolina and happened to mention a favorite dish that we hadn't eaten in years, Maya would spend several hours cooking it for us. Janice loved working in the kitchen with Maya because no shortcuts were allowed. Maya would say, "You have to brown it just like this," or "poach it just like that." Every meal was a feast—of food and of love—with a part of one's soul in every dish. That was how she wrote her poetry, how she took political stands, how she traveled, and how she expressed her love. At a time when we were trying to get our meals program off the ground, Maya's dinners went a long way toward enrichment. Potluck at Glide served up the same kind of love.

Janice began raising money from grants and foundations, as well as from celebrities. Bill Cosby, Marvin Gaye, and Sammy Davis Jr. not only donated money but extended their engagements at the big showrooms in the Bay Area an extra performance or two, for us. In this way, they could give us a whole night's receipts on Saturday night and come by to say hello to the folks at a Celebration on Sunday morning. I think it was Bill Cosby who said that we could make a lot more money if Glide removed the producer's overhead and created its own benefit concerts. Suddenly, Janice—who had been accustomed to bringing in grants of around $1,500 to $3,000—found herself learning the event-planning business from scratch as "a complete neophyte!" as she put it (a bit fearfully) at first. Again, she astounded us all. Producing these events ourselves meant hiring the concert hall, staffing it with union workers, advertising the show, managing the artists (hotel, plane tickets, airport pickup, etc.), and praying that enough people would attend for Glide to clear a profit. People did. The benefits brought in enough money to keep the food program growing.

We often grew close to the celebrities who helped us, because they saw Glide as a spiritual home. For all his travels, Sammy Davis Jr. had never seen anything like the big diverse crowd at Glide clapping to the jazz and gospel music and really getting into the joy of Celebrations. He loved rolling up to Glide in a limousine and talking to people in the food line. He almost always made his donations with a big roll of cash that he would place on my desk and say, "Here, I've brought this for my church," the pronoun *my* meaning everything to him.

In 1972, Sammy was ridiculed by the left for impulsively hugging Richard Nixon at the Republican National Convention. The astonishment and hurt he felt about this could not be expressed to anyone but folks he trusted at his church. I had already made plans to interview Sammy for the taped television program I hosted at the time, so Janice and I flew with a production crew to Harrah's Lake Tahoe, the hotel casino where he was performing. Sammy and I spent several hours alone talking about how ruinous this crisis could be to his career and how deeply hurt he felt by the backlash. He had been in show business since early childhood and panicked at the thought of doing anything else. Many critics said his career was over, but Sammy decided to open up to the people closest to him—the audience that still paid for tickets to see his performance. That night he stopped the show and explained without apology how he felt about the war in Vietnam, the Republican Party, and Richard Nixon. People might not have agreed with his politics, but they were touched by his vulnerability and his trust, and they gave him a standing ovation that went on for a long time.

Sammy and Bill Cosby contributed the proceeds from their performances annually, and this money went a long way to sustain the food program and build its capacity. But we still were without a food budget from the board. We needed to overhaul the dining room at a cost of $150,000. We needed sophisticated refrigeration units instead of the aging rentals we'd used from the beginning. We needed a stockroom, cooling area, elevator, ovens, and grills. We kept persisting, but the board kept refusing. Janice held the program together with baling wire by scheduling more and more volunteers who loaded in food from home.

The turning point came in 1981 when Dianne Feinstein became mayor. She understood the need for more programs to aid the hungry and the poor, and more emergency services. One day she came over to Glide and walked the streets of the Tenderloin with us. She assigned her human services director to help us expand the program to three meals a day, seven days a week. We still had to raise about fifty cents on every dollar the meals cost us, so the city contract was both a dream come true and kind of a nightmare, as Janice learned. The promise of getting paid for meals we had been giving away free was an enormous relief, but like planning the celebrity shows, Janice had to spend a lot of cash up front for equipment, food, and staff, then "wait for an eternity!" as she could be heard saying from time to time, until the city sent a reimbursement check.

The media continued to do heartwarming features on the food program as an example of the little church that could, and this kept bringing in new donors. One of these was Mo Bernstein, an aggressive business owner who threw himself into the renovation and reorganization of staff and volunteers so zealously that we renamed the entire facility "Mo's Kitchen." Mo turned our mom-and-pop operation into a fine-tuned restaurant model with a hiring plan for food servers and preparers from Glide's own population.

Today we use vegetables from the rooftop garden in our "Graze the Roof!" program, and we offer nutrition classes for families and kids. Many of our chefs have come from Glide's population and could make much more money elsewhere, but they always say it's their love of the people that keeps them here. They also thrive on the freedom to upgrade meals so that Glide never loses that combination of high-quality food and down-home family atmosphere.

Today Glide serves about a million meals a year, which means that there's almost always a line of several hundred people around the block three times a day as folks wait for the kitchen to open. The food line at Glide is monitored by our security employees who make certain that entrances to stores and apartments along the way aren't blocked, and that no disruptions occur.

Janice

Cecil has always loved walking through the food line to say hello to the people who are waiting for a meal. When I do this, everyone makes a point of being welcoming and friendly to me. But when Cecil comes through, they are transformed. He says, "Hey, how you doing?" "Good to see you," and they feel his love. The worst disease among the homeless is their invisibility. Everyone needs to be accepted, and Cecil has that rare capacity of making the long dismissed feel seen.

Walking through the food lines also gives us important information. Since the economy started to collapse in 2008, we've found that the working poor—people with jobs that pay minimum wage and lower—are financially stretched to a new limit. They can pay their bills and rent, but they'd go under if groceries were added to their budget, so eating at Glide makes a crucial difference. The downside is that Glide's budget has been negatively affected by the collapse of the economy, too, while the number of people we serve continues to increase. But we learned long ago that calamity teaches you to be persistent, and persistence teaches you to marshal your resources—to become stronger when circumstance could make you weaker. There was a period under one mayor when our food budget got cut in half, and we really had to scramble to keep the program going. That's when we learned to accept help not just from a few dozen but hundreds of volunteers who came through the kitchen hoping to contribute to the Glide experience. Today the food program is serviced by thousands of volunteers who donate about sixty-five thousand hours annually. These are people from rich and poor neighborhoods and countries all over the world who learn the joy of unconditional acceptance with every food tray they handle. It's because of volunteers that Glide has been able to expand and improve the meals program at the same time.

Quite often, people tell us that their happiest memory from childhood is eating regularly with their families at Glide. Cecil beams when he hears this. Cycles of chronic poverty are extremely difficult to break, and homelessness is such a hard fact of survival that we feel if people can go to a warm and friendly place like Glide and get a good meal, life may be a bit more manageable.

Remembering how our meals program grew, I often think of the story in the Bible where Jesus performs a miracle as the son of God by turning a few loaves of bread and a few fish into enough food for thousands of people. With Glide's food program in mind, I interpret the story another way: Jesus, a mortal man, was a prophet and a visionary who could inspire followers to find the answer to any problem by themselves. When he saw that people were starving, he convinced others to share what little food they had, so that everyone would survive. So the few who had something to eat found a way to share it with another few, and they found a way to share their food with still others, and in the end, the people multiplied the food themselves, and kept multiplying the food so that everyone thrived, and that was the miracle.

We often use the phrase *From Fifty to a Million* when we talk about Glide's food program, because that history— starting a Monday night potluck that became an everyday feast—continues to be our miracle.

Cecil

In 2008, for the first time, police reported that drug dealers had been seen sneaking into Glide's food lines to sell dope. Our monitors were surprised to hear this because they watch these lines very closely and can spot a drug dealer from blocks away. Occasionally crime does leak in to Glide, and when it does, we reinforce our training of monitors and deal with it.

This time, however, law enforcement wanted a quicker solution. An SFPD police captain told us to close down the lines and cram everybody waiting for a meal (typically three hundred to four hundred people) into Glide's parking lot, which is a very small space (it holds fifteen cars), where they would have to wait behind a gate until the kitchen opened. Public urination was also blamed on these people, so the police captain ordered Glide to wash off the sidewalks where the folks had been standing. We ordinarily use barriers to separate the food lines from pedestrian traffic; the police wanted more barriers. They wanted undercover agents to sneak into the line. They wanted sting operations.

All this was being played out in the press, so Janice and I took reporters into the parking lot and showed them what it would be like to force several hundred people inside. The experience for them would be worse than caging them, we said—it would feel like slavery, and we would have no part of it. This was another case of society hiding away the poor and the hungry from the eyes of the public. We said no. Under any standard of civil rights and human rights, we wanted our people out of confinement where they could walk around freely.

We tried to explain to the police and media that for several decades, most drug dealers and petty criminals steered clear of *any* of Glide's doings for the simple fact that . . . well, we were Glide! We were the community that accepted everybody, including the "bad guys" of society, because they were all part of the community. (We didn't accept their bad behavior; we accepted—we embraced—their humanity.) However, our monitors learned that drug dealers from the East Bay had been driving through the Tenderloin one day and spotted a bunch of poor people lining up in front of Glide, a church they didn't know. What a golden opportunity, they thought—anywhere that you have poverty and prostitution and people in need, you're going to have drug dealing. Eventually we convinced the police to let our monitors handle the problem (the police did make a few arrests) and to allow the food line to stretch for blocks as it had before. This was the kind of incident where quiet persistence paid off.

Critics and even some theologians will always ask: "Why are you feeding the poor? You're just perpetuating their dependency and creating more problems. They need to grow out of poverty." After fifty years of working with this population, we tell these critics that it's almost impossible for people to "grow" out of poverty in the way that society expects middle- and working-class people to grow. Poverty—the way it grinds people down, the way it damages people's childhood, the way it steals people's futures, the way it drains the economy, the way it shatters hope—is persistent. To do battle with it requires equal persistence, not in winning the war but in loving the people under its power. At Glide, we want to offer a range of life choices that people haven't had before. We don't expect any particular outcome, and we don't judge them for being in the food lines in the first place. We're in for the long haul. We persist in accepting them and loving them without condition because their humanity is our humanity.

14

Resurrection

Dear Bishop Smith,

I feel it is my duty as a Christian and a
Methodist to call your attention to the atrocities
uncovered by Newsweek magazine, Feb 22, 1972,
concerning the conduct of Rev. Cecil Williams of
Glide Memorial Church in San Francisco.

How these heathen mockeries can be condoned
by the hierarchy of the United Methodist Church
has me at a loss for words . . . .

Now, if not enough has already been undone,
this blasphemous hippie, that calls himself
a minister, has been invited to speak at the
Conference in Atlanta. Where will it end; with an
orgy in the Conference room? . . . .

Mr. Williams—

You need to shave off that mess of hair all over
your face and you made your threat you would git
a soap Box if you couldn't git in Pulpit of the fine
Methodist Church here on Peachtree st. that's been
there for years and they are real upright men of
God and don't allow any other kind in their Pulpit.
You better Clean up before coming to Atlanta—we
have Godly White Minister here who revere God
and don't allow just anything in our Pulpit—who
do you think wants to hear you only some of your
kind? You better clean up now—you have created
Hate here beyond awful report you would Preach
on soap box—you may on *Skid Row* some where—
wake up—get Holy Ghost now—you better stay
away from here

Janice

As we moved into the 1970s, the church got even more
crowded each Sunday. Part of the reason was that more celebrities (Roberta Flack, Ralph Abernathy, Johnny Mathis, Joan
Baez, Shirley Chisholm, Linda Ronstadt, Quincy Jones) supported us publicly, spoke at the Celebrations, marched with us
in protests, and volunteered in the kitchen.

Cecil himself was changing. Gone were the stiff minister's
collar, short hair, horn-rimmed glasses, and business suit that
had always felt phony to him. He let his hair and beard grow
out, wore aviator glasses and tank tops, and for Sundays he

donned a pair of dazzling red pants that you couldn't keep your eyes off whenever he left the altar to talk and walk among the pews.

There were, however, times when people couldn't follow what he was saying. One Sunday after the nine o'clock Celebration he asked me how I liked the sermon.

"Like everybody, I loved the way you got so passionate about self-definition," I said, "but that esoteric reference to Kierkegaard got in the way. Unless you connect it to your point, they aren't going to get it." I added that he could probably delete Kierkegaard when he gave the same sermon at the eleven o'clock service.

The look of shock on his face nearly stopped the conversation. Cecil wasn't familiar with criticism. People praised him so much that all he could do was glare at me as if I had thrown paint on the altar. Then he pulled out his notes and removed Kierkegaard.

"And Heidegger too," I said. "Too wordy." More glaring and deleting. After the eleven o'clock, he agreed the sermon was more focused.

After that, we spoke about his sermons regularly between the 9:00 and 11:00 A.M. services.

"I thought you left us on the edge about finding our own relationship to spiritual life," I said one time.

"What? 'Left you on the edge'? Didn't you hear why I wear these red pants?" Of course I did. They were a metaphor for the way each of us can uniquely express our own spiritual path. He just needed to be clearer.

My job on Sundays was to handle the logistics onstage—

not preparing the altar, cross, and flowers as they did in other churches (our cross was gone), but making sure the program flowed smoothly, with plenty of room for spontaneity. Cecil had become so adept at handling whatever craziness might erupt that I could see the audience wishing something would go "wrong"—a person leaping onto the stage, or shouting something abrasive or otherwise acting out.

Cecil loved those moments too. He believed in spontaneity like a jazz musician. "If you know the melody of your life," he would say, "you can create in the moment." The unscripted parts caught you off guard, made you dig into your soul. Many people were surprised when they talked to Cecil during the service because the thoughts they exchanged with him were unfiltered and sometimes crudely expressed. But as a result, for the audience, even the more familiar subjects that came up—love, freedom, courage, passion, justice—felt original and fresh. By the end, it was as though Cecil had struck a tuning fork that hit just the right chord, and then handed it to us, so that we could hear the note our own way. Somehow in that purity of reverberation, change in our own lives could happen.

Cecil

In 1971, the United Methodist Church (UMC) asked five ministers, myself included, to speak during the first week of its General Conference in Atlanta, Georgia. This was a convention of about a thousand delegates who met every four years to set worldwide policy for the church. Although this year's conference would be controversial, with issues of integration and homosexuality to be discussed, the role of the five ministers was to hold services at First Methodist Church, a few blocks away from the convention. It was an honor to be asked, and I looked forward to combining elements of Glide's Celebrations (gospel choir, jazz band) with more traditional services.

Then, however, "all hell broke loose," as Jack Tuell, the bishop who invited me, put it. Word of my participation reached an ultraconservative group in Georgia called Methodist Restoration. This group announced that "Williams is unfit to preach in *any* Methodist church" and accused me of "encouraging booze, nudity, belly dancers, masturbation, and fornication during his services." The media picked up the story, a flood of calls came in, and Janice worked day and night answering queries from church leaders and calls from the press. Before I knew it, the invitation was rescinded until the program commission could hear grievances and vote again. Then Bishop Tuell led the vote to reaffirm the earlier decision, and the invitation stood.

That should have been the end of it, but the leaders of First Methodist Church in Atlanta took their own vote and decided to prohibit me from preaching on the premises. Bishop Tuell refused to accept this move and announced that he was relocating all five of the services to another church. The bishops who were slated to speak at First Methodist Church joined him and said they would withdraw their names as well. Embarrassed by this reaction, First Methodist Church changed its mind, and Bishop Tuell moved the services back.

Bishop Tuell was white and had always stated honestly that one of the five "outstanding preachers" chosen should be a *black* outstanding preacher. Since the other ministers were white, he said it was time for the Methodist church to begin acting with "a mind to inclusiveness." As to the cause of the present controversy, right-wing Christians could blame it on nudity and masturbation at Glide all they wanted, but Bishop Tuell had no illusions that racism played a role. "Whether this storm would have arisen if [Williams] had been a 'radical' instead of a 'black radical' seems unlikely," he wrote later in a memoir.

By this time, the national press picked up the story. *Newsweek,* referring to the "rumors of Sunday-morning debauchery" at Glide, wrote that Celebrations were "no more chummy than many Catholic folk Masses." However, one bishop in Atlanta was quoted as saying that he "wishes Williams had never been invited, but he concedes that black Methodists could turn the controversy into a nasty racial issue if the invitation is rescinded." Now there was a great message—*Watch out when you invite black people. They'll turn an innocent church service into a "nasty racial issue" every time.*

And who had turned this mild midweek service into a "nasty racial issue" to begin with? It was certainly not anyone from Glide. Perhaps if the UMC had been working long and hard to live up to its values, we would by now have a diverse range of perspectives and a truly *United* Methodist Church, not the still-segregated church I had grown up with. Instead of feeling lucky to be tolerated for my "radical left-wing policies" and "heathen mockeries," as one letter writer put it, I felt I had much to contribute to the Methodist church.

People asked me later if I believed a "racist conspiracy" was behind what happened, and my answer was that race, class, gender, and difference of any kind are always a part of everything we do. Having walked into an old-fashioned power game, I had to recognize my weakness (hatred of being rejected by whites) and my strength (Glide's motto, "Rejection inspires action"). Whatever the final decision might be, I was going to Atlanta. If I had to hold a sit-in in front of the convention center or rent the Atlanta football stadium across town, I was going.

And so were a number of supporters, Janice reported. Members of the congregation and a lot of people in the Bay Area who loved Glide—about three hundred fifty in all—got on the plane to Atlanta with me. Our spirits were high because by then, the UMC had formally reextended the invitation to me. True, the controversy had stirred up more death threats and hate mail than usual, but state and local police in Atlanta seemed to be on top of the problem. When they told us they had information that several fundamentalist groups might disrupt the service, I asked them to hold back while I was speaking and let my own security people handle whatever interruptions may happen. They agreed as long as they could protect me out in the open.

We landed, to tumult. Wherever we went, the media in Atlanta swarmed us. On the news that morning, I said, "I am here to make the Methodist church face up to what it means to *live* justice rather than talk it," and that stirred things up a bit more.

As we walked from our motel to the First Methodist Church, a garage door came into view on which someone had painted, "Cecil Williams: We're Out to Get You." Up ahead,

I could see crowds around the church trying to get in. We threaded our way to the back entrance where the fire marshal was telling Bishop Tuell he'd have to cancel the service because the church was too packed. Nobody who got in was going to volunteer to get out, and the crowd outside wanted in. Now a thousand strong, they started chanting, "We want Cecil Williams!"

I made it clear that I was going to speak somewhere, and it would be a good idea if the crowd could hear me. Luckily one of Bishop Tuell's committee members discovered that the main arena of the Atlanta Convention Center, which was two blocks away, would be empty for the next two hours, so he booked it.

"How do we move all these people without provoking a riot?" Bishop Tuell said. Well, that was my job, I thought. I stepped into the sanctuary and took the mike: "Brothers and sisters, welcome to this great celebration! We're going to have a tremendous time together this afternoon!" The audience applauded. "But we have a problem—there are a thousand people outside who can't get in, and we don't want to keep them out, do we?"

"No!" the crowd yelled.

"Okay. We have just made arrangements to move down the hill to the convention center, where everybody can get in and be a part of our celebration. How do you feel? Can we go to the auditorium?"

Everybody applauded and got up to move. We could hear the cheers coming from outside too. By the time we reconvened at the convention center, the audience had swelled to more than six thousand. Backstage I saw that more ministers had arrived, most of them frowning at me as if I were to blame for the controversy. Some of my former professors from Perkins School of Theology were there, I noticed. They looked at my untrimmed beard and nonregulation black velvet shirt, listened to the opening sounds of Soul Exposition, an Atlanta jazz combo that I had asked to play, and gave me their sternest "You're-our-boy-but-put-a-lid-on-it" expression. Throughout it all, Bishop Tuell smiled with the sweetest thumbs-up look I had ever seen.

Minutes before the program began, I learned that Coretta Scott King had arrived and was waiting with Andrew Young, the black congressman in Georgia. I had met Coretta a few times but didn't know her well. When I left backstage to greet her, she looked at me gravely and said, "I want you to know that I am with you." A number of ministers hurried over to introduce themselves to her, but I asked if she would say a few words to the audience first.

And oh, what Coretta Scott King said. "My husband's movement started fifteen and a half years ago," she began. "Although some people don't realize it, his movement was always a movement of the church. As he often said, 'The church should be a headlight pointing the way for the world, not a taillight merely trailing behind.' I am here to participate and support Cecil in the fine work he's doing." She, too, was a resident of Atlanta, and the audience applauded warmly.

A hush settled in the hall after Bishop Tuell introduced me, but no sooner had I taken the microphone when a young white man burst out of the audience and leaped onto the stage, shouting "I've got to speak! I must speak!" He was shaking all over in rage, but the state troopers stayed where they were, as agreed. My security people instantly moved toward him, however—they were used to such behavior in San Francisco, but not at a powder keg like this in Atlanta.

"No, no, he wants to speak," I said. "Let him speak." I turned to the young man and handed him the mike. "Take it, brother," I said. His hands were trembling nearly as much as his voice.

"You are a sinner, you are against God and Jesus," he said. "We want you to know that we don't want you here. You have not accepted Jesus Christ as your savior. You are not a religious person. You should repent. Repent for your sins!"

The audience remained silent.

"My heart is bleeding for the young people of America who are being led to hell by the likes of Cecil Williams!" he said. "I call on you, Brother Cecil Williams, to repent and believe in the Lord Jesus Christ, and to stop your support of the Communist menace!"

He was in tears by that time and still trembling as he left the stage. Usually I liked to talk about matters that so disturbed people when they jumped onstage at Glide, but here all I could do was tell him, "You are welcome to have your say," as he walked toward the exit. Then I turned to the very respectful audience and said, "Now I'm going to have my say." The audience broke out in relieved laughter and applause.

"I haven't come here to scare you to death," I said, looking around the auditorium. "I've come to scare you to life!" People laughed and clapped, and for the next fifty minutes

I addressed this audience of blacks and whites as though we were all at Glide. I used no notes. "Let's walk together," I said, coming down from the stage. "Let's walk in freedom."

I talked about the value of dissent, difference, and diversity. I said that the traditional church had refused for too long to attend to the true needs of the people. Dwindling attendance rates showed this, and if the problem continued, the church would be dead in twenty-five years.

"The reason the church is dying," I said, "is that it has no life. The bones aren't coming together because we as a church have no Spirit. But when we determine to live fully, and to act together, the Spirit will return. These bones are going to walk again!" I declared as people began to stand up, clapping. "These bones are going to fight again!" Now everybody was cheering. "These bones are going to love again!"

It was an exhilarating experience because for just a moment I thought the church could be saved. I thought with six thousand people behind me, the momentum could begin that day for a national movement of new churches—not exactly like Glide, but not like the traditional churches that were driving people away, either. Of course, it was impossible for Glide to lead that momentum at the time (our plate was way too full). And yet, here we are today, forty years later, at a time when many churches have died, many more are hanging on by a thread, congregants are giving up on religion entirely, and people are still searching for spirituality outside the mainstream.

Janice

What an irony, I thought, as I sat in the front of the auditorium watching Cecil hand the mike to that trembling, weeping young man that day. I hoped the ministers who had wanted to stop Cecil from speaking could see this example of unconditional love. Cecil welcomed a stranger who was obviously disturbed and intent on rejecting him. Letting this boy have his say was not only the most Christian thing to do, it demonstrated what any loving church was about—acceptance and compassion.

A greater irony would come later in the 1980s when Susie Buffett, one of our most loving and supportive volunteers, suggested that Glide could be a model for other churches that wanted to open their doors and provide services to everyone, including people in need. She encouraged us to answer the many requests of ministers around the country for Cecil and the Glide team to train them and their church staffs in Glide's ways.

Susie told her husband, Warren, about her love for Glide and one Sunday brought him with her to experience a Celebration. Warren called himself "naturally a little skeptical," which meant he had to see for himself the energy and diversity of Glide's congregation and especially Cecil's love for this work and for the community. Afterward, Warren said, "This is real, and Cecil is real." That was the greater irony, I thought: Warren Buffett "got it" about Cecil more than many of the ministers in Atlanta. And Warren's unique way of supporting Glide was not to write a check but to auction an invitation to lunch with him to the highest bidder. He has done this using eBay once a year since 1998. In recent years, the idea of a private lunch with Warren Buffett has been so enthusiastically pursued by admirers around the world that the closing bid has gone for well over a million dollars. In 2012 it hit a record high of $3,456,789.

By the '80s, Glide had created a series of training programs called the Global Ministry and Empowerment Journey. We conducted sessions and workshops for churches, campus groups, and other nonprofit organizations that asked us to show them in an interactive way the whole range and purpose of Glide's work. Susie became involved and suggested that we take the sessions to churches in their own locations and settings so that entire staffs could participate. She joined us in some of these travels and encouraged us to write a book for other nonprofits about how Glide did what it did—what it took to bring diverse people together in community, to provide caring meals, to adopt recovery programs for specific populations, and to offer an unconditionally loving spiritual home for people whom society had given up on.

Essentially, then, thanks in part to Susie, Glide went on the road. A top priority was to help inner-city churches set up systems and staff that could provide meals, encourage diversity, and reach the people in need. Some churches, concerned about "aging congregations," decided to add contemporary music using guitars or harps that might attract young people with a more "avant-garde" service. The difficult challenge here, we felt, was for churches to learn how to grow their programs from the "bottom up" rather than from the "top down." We explained that our ministry at Glide started by listening to people tell us about their needs, and by engaging those people in creating programs. We believed that the minister and church leaders should not control what they thought people *should* have in their lives. Those affected had to be part of the decision-making process. True leadership, we learned through the years, was about providing opportunities for those who might not consider themselves capable or educated but nevertheless had the passion, street smarts, and commitment to change—to emerge and develop as leaders. People made their own decisions about how much change they wanted; leaders emerged at their own pace and with their own vision and understanding of power.

Fundamental to our experience was that Glide's nitty-gritty, often funky "constituents" required us to reinvent who we were. In the process, we raised challenging questions: Were we trying to control or free the people we worked with? Were we motivated by the needs of our ego or by a responsibility to the larger vision? What was at the front of our minds—getting our way or seeking equality for all? The process was exhausting and exhilarating at the same time.

And it was rife with contradiction.

I remembered teaching high school kids years before about the proletariat (working-class people) going crazy during the French Revolution. These were the outcast and the poor who swarmed into the royal palaces and wrecked everything in sight, leaving their mark—their trash, their blood, their sweat—everywhere. Then they grabbed the king and queen and pulled them on wagons through the streets in a reckless, irresponsible, chaotic way. That was what revolutionary fervor might lead to—freedom so wild and dangerous that it could extinguish whatever vision had fired up the people to begin with.

At Glide, a revolution had occurred, but because of Cecil's vision, what came through the church and continues to this day was organized chaos. People listened when he talked about freedom being meaningful if each of us took personal responsibility for our decisions. The result was that the "proletariat" came through Glide leaving its mark of radical change everywhere, but in ways that would help the church grow. The heart of Glide, for example, grew out of the fact that Cecil was Cecil. He began this ministry with the things he loved and believed in—an authentic African American tradition of gospel music and jazz, principles of liberation theology, and an emphasis on social struggles and social justice. As people started attending Celebrations and expressing their own interests, Glide opened up to many other traditions. That was the "secret" to our diversity—all people were welcome, and all the ideas and things that people believed in were welcome too. And so the congregation kept growing.

Susie was the first to show visitors and trainees the importance of these differences at Glide. And before her death in 2004 she talked about another critical difference at Glide—the emphasis on disclosure. Most traditional churches don't admit, "I've got wrinkles and bumps and pimples and bruises," which are all seen as weaknesses. The reality may peek out once in a while (as we saw in Atlanta), but the institutional church never takes off its clothes. Susie loved it when Glide made mistakes and everybody laughed (or cried) about it, determined to do better next time. She affirmed for us that the world outside really wanted to know the kind of spirituality that distinguished Glide, and the possibilities for change.

15

Trust

Cecil

A FAMOUS NEWSPAPER photo taken in 1970 shows a judge in Marin County, California, walking out of his courtroom with a sawed-off shotgun roped to his body, its gun barrel pointing directly at his neck. Next to him is a Black Panther and three black inmates from San Quentin. They have just kidnapped the judge, an assistant district attorney, and three jurors. The hostages are all white, the kidnappers all black; just outside the photo, a crowd of sheriff's deputies are walking alongside the group with guns drawn.

After more than forty years, it's still hard to look at this picture. We see the terror of the hostages, the desperation of the kidnappers. We know that all of them remained unharmed until they got into a white van that the Black Panther, Jonathan Jackson, planned to use as a getaway car. As soon as the van moved, bullets started flying, and the ensuing shootout left Judge Harold Haley dead, the A.D.A. paralyzed, one juror wounded, and two unharmed. Jonathan Jackson and two of the inmates died. Another, Ruchell Magee, was critically injured.

In the subsequent investigation, police discovered that Ruchell had little or nothing to do with planning the shootout. He had been sitting in the courtroom waiting to testify for another prisoner when Jonathan burst in with a satchel of weapons, tossed him a gun, and told him to free three other convicts from a holding cell.

I've always assumed that Ruchell went along because the court system was a travesty to him. He had been convicted in 1964 of robbery/kidnapping in Los Angeles for what the *New York Times* called "a typical ghetto hassle over a $10 marijuana transaction that ended with guns being pulled." Given an indeterminate sentence of one year to life, he had not been allowed to act as his own attorney because of prison-administered tests that showed an IQ of 78. Nevertheless, Ruchell taught himself law in the San Quentin library and became the kind of jailhouse lawyer whom other prisoners sought for legal advice. As his one-year sentence stretched into seven because of perceived violations that prison guards may have used to keep him under control, Ruchell grew bitter and angry, right up to the moment that Jonathan Jackson tossed him the gun.

After the shootings, it's safe to say that very few inmates were as despised by law enforcement as Ruchell Magee. The

FBI, sheriff's deputies, and local police, embarrassed that security in the Marin courthouse had failed so badly, wanted the world to see what a monster Ruchell was. In his courtroom appearances, he was heavily shackled and escorted on both sides by guards who chained him to tables, chairs, and the floor.

When Ruchell sent word that he wanted me to come see him at San Quentin, his lawyers advised me not to go. He wasn't behaving rationally, and the prison system could not guarantee my safety. I hadn't met him before, but they said he was paranoid and could turn violent at any time. To me, that was all the more reason to see him. I had gone through my own bout with paranoia in childhood and knew how it felt to be driven over the edge. My family and community helped bring me back, but Ruchell was completely isolated. If he wanted to see me, I was going.

I drove out to San Quentin and sat for a long time in the waiting room. It was a large, dim, cold facility filled with African American families. As I sat there, an image came to my mind of Gorée Island in West Africa, a processing center for slaves in the 1700s. I had visited the island during a trip to Africa some years before and remembered walking through concrete bunkers that had acted as holding cells for Africans who had been kidnapped from their villages. Sometimes they waited for months while traders selected the healthiest bodies for transport to America.

The San Quentin waiting room was crowded with women and children, reminding me of the way African girls at Gorée were sent to separate bunkers because virgins got a better price than other women. If the traders raped them and they got pregnant, they were released into the population of free blacks on Gorée Island. This meant that girls as young as eleven and twelve learned how to act like prostitutes as they competed for the attention of the traders. (The women who attend Glide's recovery circles are never surprised at this.)

I sat there thinking of the many ways an evil system like slavery spreads its poison—across oceans, across generations, across race. Ruchell's lawyers warned me that Ruchell was being chained in layers like a Houdini in here. I remembered an exhibit at Gorée Island that displayed the five-kilogram metal balls attached by chains to collars around the Africans' ankles or necks. The people carried this metal ball across the plank that led them to the slave ship. They knew as they looked down at the water that if they attempted to escape, that metal ball would take them to the bottom of the ocean. They carried it during passage, another hell that sometimes took six months. They carried it again to the holding pens where they waited to be auctioned off, and many carried it on the long trip to the plantation whose owner had bought them.

I looked around the waiting room and thought again that slavery never left us. *This is where my brothers and sisters are,* I thought—*in holding cells, on parole, behind bars, in waiting rooms of prisons like this one.*

At the time, Janice and I were working with CUPP (Community United for Political Prisoners) to free unjustly imprisoned black inmates. But no matter how many times I walked through a place like San Quentin—even as the guards took me to visit Ruchell—I was struck by the heavy gates and metal doors clanking shut. This place was my generation's version of Gorée.

The guards left me in a small, bare room with no counter or table—just two chairs separated by a dense glass wall reinforced on the inside with layers of chicken-coop wire. The room felt like a converted prison cell except for a stairway leading up to a balcony where two guards stood on either side of a door. Nothing was said while I sat and waited. Then I heard the rattling of metal, the door above me swung open, and there was Ruchell at the top of the stairs.

I had seen convicts in chains before, but I wasn't prepared for the draping of so much metal in loops and locks pulled tight around the frame of this heavily publicized "monster." Ruchell's body had not only been confined by handcuffs and leg irons, he had manacles on his legs, his arms, and around his waist; he had chains on his wrists, his ankles, his chest, and his neck. The guards were nudging him forward. To get down the stairs, he had to half drag, half hurl his body onto the first stair below him. His wrists were tethered in front of his body so at least he wasn't bent backward, but neither hand could reach far enough to grab hold of the railing, and neither foot could reach as far as the next stair.

The guards stayed up there watching him *thud, thud, thud* his way down, knowing he might topple forward and kill himself at any moment. I stood at the bottom of the stairs watching him too. It struck me that they wanted to humiliate Ruchell, and they wanted the minister visiting Ruchell to witness it. Here was the murderer they made captive for all the world to see, chained up and inching forward like a worm. It was vengeance, and it was inhumane. Ruchell kept sweating his way down the stairs, not daring to look up for fear of stumbling. I wanted to offer something—a prayer, an affirmation, a bit of wisdom, anything—but for once I was speechless.

Ruchell reached the bottom of the stairs and lurched over to the chair on his side of the glass partition. The layers of the chicken-coop wire in the glass were too thick to see through except for tiny circles where the wire didn't mesh. Ruchell somehow got his hands far enough in front of his body to place them palm out on the glass, and as my hands did the same, our fingers searched around and found the circles. In a jolt of electricity, the pads of our skin seemed to touch through the glass.

Ruchell's eyes flooded with tears. "My brother," he said. "My brother, you've come."

"My brother," I said. I could barely see for my own tears. "My brother." We sat like that for a long time. There was just the suggestion of heat from each other's fingers, yet it felt like a blood transfusion.

All of a sudden Ruchell started laughing—a great big laugh that turned into a howl. Just as abruptly he stopped laughing and began talking very fast. I couldn't catch most of it—the glass impeded sound—but a few sentences came through: "Nobody can help me," he said. "I can't even help myself. It's over." Then he slammed the glass angrily, as if to say, *Put all the chains on me you want! I'm not going to let you control me!* The guards rushed forward to end the meeting as they grabbed Ruchell roughly under each arm and half carried, half shoved him up the stairs. Then they returned to take me away.

On the way out, I thought of what the kidnapped Africans saw when they walked through the last gate at Gorée Island, which was known as "The Door of No Return" (literally "the gate of the trip from which no one returned"). As they looked at the slave ship waiting for them, they must have known that conditions were going to be deadly. During the passage, about one in four would die of pestilence. The others had to be watched to prevent them from killing themselves.

As I left San Quentin that day, I felt that my charge as a minister and a citizen was to see things from the slave's point of view in the 1700s and from Ruchell Magee's point of view in 1970. My charge was to think about the American tendency to put black people in chains in many different ways—to enslave them, to incarcerate them, to profile them, to arrest them, to stop them in traffic, to portray them as lazy and stupid. To own them.

Today it's not enough to say that racism is so embedded in American life that we can't see it any longer. Today it's the charge of all of us to recognize racist acts, to spread the word about them, to stop tolerating them, and to never again turn away as if the problem doesn't exist. Statistics now show that more black men are in the prison system today than were slaves before the Civil War. The reason has little to do with crime per se and everything to do with a system of power that imprisons us all.

I drove across the Golden Gate Bridge back to San Francisco, still feeling the heat on my fingertips. At Glide, we say, "You touch one, and one touches one, and one touches one," and so the community expands and binds, in trust and in love. Ruchell and I found a centuries-old sense of community in that gesture, and I hoped it would give him strength. African Americans have it in their blood to live simultaneously in the chains and in this sublime experience. You can't extend that moment for more than five seconds, and yet it is forever.

(Ruchell was sentenced to life in prison in 1975 and as of this writing is currently an inmate at Corcoran State Prison in California. He is seventy-four years old.)

The question of trust weighs heavily on me with every prison visit, but none so much as in 1971, the year following the Marin shootout, when the organizers of "Soul Day" at San Quentin invited me to be the main speaker. Soul Day was planned as a series of talks by African American leaders during Black History Month. About sixteen hundred black inmates would attend. It was not supposed to be rousing entertainment like, say, Johnny Cash's concert at Folsom Prison a few years before. Soul Day was going to be quieter, more thoughtful and controlled.

Or so I gathered as I sat down on the stage with the other speakers. The hall wasn't very big, but it was packed and it was hot. Because the inmates had assigned seats, prison guards paced up and down the aisles, matching numbers on men and chairs, occasionally ordering inmates out of one seat and into another. Once the guards decided everyone was in place, they stood against the walls with arms crossed in their brawny, glowering way, looking not at the stage but at the audience.

I liked the idea of Soul Day, because after all, the soul knows no captivity. No matter what has been taken from you in prison, your soul is with you, deep inside your core and defining you every day. I think that was the kind of thing the organizers thought I would discuss when I got up to the microphone after the other speakers finished. And that's what I thought I was saying when I started to talk.

"All of you know what prison is," I began, "because you are imprisoned here. You know that drugs are easier to come by than books, for example. You know that being locked up can destroy your humanity.

"But let me tell you about the prisons of a lot of other people. The prisons of those who feel no power. Those who feel no love. Those who feel no courage, no pride, no dignity. Those who feel nothing. They have no community, you see. They are not involved with each other. They've given up hope."

I sensed a bit of stirring in the front rows where the associate wardens and unit supervisors were sitting. The guards along the walls had turned toward the stage and, like the inmates, now seemed alert and focused.

"Because you are locked up together, you have a better chance to move beyond the control of others by not letting them fragment you. The prison system wants you fragmented. It puts you in separate cells so you can't meet in community. When you're in the yard, the system watches as you segregate into groups. As long as you are fragmented, you'll never have the power that is yours, the power to be who you must be and do what you must do."

The inmates had been told to sit quietly in their assigned

seats, but some of them started to call out, as black people do in church: "You got that right" or "Tell us, brother." The guards looked dubious, but didn't try to quiet them down.

"People on the outside are always being set up just like you—set up so they must be apart from self, apart from community, apart from the world. They're made to feel isolated, like they can't do anything for themselves. They are 'inside,' too, my brothers. Like you, they know there is no escape. That's why institutions depend on weakness. They can control you when you're weak, fragmented, and isolated. The weaker *you* get, the stronger *they* get."

I could tell by the murmurs in the front rows that this wasn't what the wardens had expected. The inmates whistled and cheered a little more. "Right on, brother," they said. "Say that again."

"But you, each and every one of you, have a different future because you're all in this hole together. And because you're here, now is the time to get *un*fragmented, to get organized. Then your voice will be heard. When you organize, you don't have to put each other down or feel put down. Instead of letting your time here abuse and destroy you, let it give you courage and strength."

The inmates were getting on their feet to applaud. "Courage" was something they hadn't been told they'd feel in prison. The guards let them stand.

"You can start by saying, 'I'm not just going to sit around prison and fight and cuss and fuss and destroy my humanity. I can make my humanity work for me.' When you find your humanity, you've found your courage. When you're courageous together, you have the power to be free inside this institution. I say to you, my brothers, walk your power! Talk your power! Live your pow—!"

And *bam!* the lights went out, and the entire hall plunged into a pitch-black. I couldn't see my own hand in front of me, but I certainly heard the roar of disapproval coming from the inmates.

To me, there was no question the darkness was deliberate. Prison officials must have thought my remarks were incendiary, but hell, I hadn't even started. Maybe they thought I'd be afraid of the darkness and stop preaching so everybody would sit quietly in their numbered seats. Or maybe the prison was looking for an excuse to start something violent. In the blackness, an inmate could throw a fist, and that would do it. The guards would have to hit the crowd with tear gas, clubs, and hoses.

Amid the shouting, I heard inmates calling out to me, "Don't stop!" "Talk to us!" I wasn't going to say, *Take your assigned seats and remain quiet until the lights come up.* Even if that worked, it would give *me* the power, and I wanted them to have it. Somebody to the side yelled, "Get off the stage!" Well, that wasn't even an option. I believed in what I just said—power exists when we find it together.

"Keep talkin' to me!" I appealed to them. "Keep tellin' me! Walk with me. Stay with me!" When there is no escape, you have to trust each other or risk a riot. So they did. They called out to say, "Talk to us, brother"—and I was ready.

"Man, it's dark in here," I shouted into the noise. "And you can say 'Amen.'"

"Amen."

"I said, *it's dark in here!*"

"Amen!"

"But you know what? That doesn't bother me because we're going to walk in the darkness together. And we're going to talk in the darkness and move in the darkness and do what's right in the darkness. No, that don't bother me."

"We hear you, Rev."

"Because real struggle comes out of the darkness, do you know that? It comes out of the pain and hurt you all have gone through. That's when you can be free men, no matter where you are."

"Right on."

"You know the truth better than anybody—not from prison, not from darkness—because you've had to face whatever confines you. Not only face it but explore it, embrace it, find your humanness. When we do, we are free. No matter where we are, inside or outside."

"Keep on, man."

"And here's the *good* thing about darkness," I said. "When they turn the lights out, you can whisper your plans to each other, because in prison you're so close. You sleep close together. You eat close together. You *engage* each other in closeness. In the darkness, power grows when it's shared. They can't fragment you here! We're standing in the darkness together."

And now this hall, where sixteen hundred infuriated inmates had been close to erupting against the guards and one another only moments ago, was silent as a tomb. They not only had the potential to act as a single unit, they had become that one body. They knew how to exchange information secretly. The prison authorities might have believed that turning off those lights would keep them under control. But from where I was standing, the reverse was true—*they* were in control. So I kept talking.

"I said before that it's easier to get drugs smuggled into prison than to find books in the prison library. Did you ever wonder why that is? Maybe it's because you're not allowed to read anything too 'radical.' Reading keeps you free, while dope keeps you caged. Ideas keep you free. Thinking for yourself keeps you free."

Everybody applauded at that, and while they were applauding, the lights came back on! Then the inmates really started cheering, not because they had "won" but because they had felt it, the power of a freedom they could control, whether they were imprisoned like animals or free to walk away. And I knew they were thinking about the power of organizing. What it would mean to break down controls—in the dark, in the yard, in the food lines, from one cell to the other. What it would mean to be truly free deep inside the prison.

Standing there, looking at the inmates, I thought about how people wonder why young men join gangs. The answer is simple. They join not just for the power but for the trust. The longer they face threats and hardships, the more they depend on each other, and the closer they become. The ties grow stronger, belief in each other develops, and perhaps for the first time, they feel love. It's like a family, but in a larger sense, when that kind of love is nourished and deepened, community develops, and the isolation they used to feel, the loneliness, the anger, has a chance to fade away.

Just about every prison movie I've seen shows the murderous power of ethnic gangs behind bars, but rarely do we see why gangs came together in the first place—the need for protection and (brutally negotiated) trust. The prison system has learned to manipulate ethnic gangs to maintain control, and the result is more inhumanity, unnecessary deaths, and living hell. The kind of community I was talking about does not mean you're obligated for life. It's not permanent or eternal. People who trust one another can create community again and again whether they're locked up or they can walk away.

At Glide, not only in deference to our parolee population, we keep the church doors open so people can come in *and* can go out. On the outside of prison, this precious freedom is what causes people to build trust in one another.

16

Fame

Janice

SOMETHING DANGEROUS HAPPENED to Glide in the 1970s and 1980s that in a sense continues to this day. It began when we were discovered by the media and became the exciting new fashion of the era.

It was not unusual for TV crews and writers from all over the world (*National Geographic, Ebony, AsianWeek, The New Yorker, Playboy*) to report on Glide, but soon interviews with Cecil got splashier and sillier, and many focused on the same superficial story: A "daring new church" in San Francisco had this "happening, hip, contemporary culture" where people of all races and lifestyles could be seen rocking, dancing, clapping, and cheering to a "live rock 'n' roll band that replaced the traditional church organ." Leading Glide was Rev. Cecil

Williams, the "controversial minister of jive," who hoped to convert the "tomb" of the traditional church into a celebration of life.

Nothing about this image was untrue. It was just that it skimmed the surface and mostly ignored Glide's commitment to the poor, its stands against racism and injustice, and its attempt to establish long-term, separately funded, and compassionate programs. These were dull to the media but essential to helping people find jobs, go back to school, learn a trade, recover from addiction, see a doctor, open a bank account, take a parenting class, ask the advice of a lawyer, and so much more. Much more dazzling to the press was Cecil dancing onstage, with John Turk (the gifted jazz musician who led the Glide band) egging him on.

In his own way, Cecil tried to balance this surface popularity with his weekly television show, *Vibrations for a New People,* a taped public service program that appeared on the local San Francisco CBS affiliate. The show ran for many years and drew a surprisingly large audience for early Sunday morning, probably because Cecil was so good at conducting in-depth interviews with local and nationally famous people (Angela Davis, Pete Seeger, Dennis Banks, Sammy Davis Jr., Bill Cosby). The programs were serious, but there was always room for humor. Cecil once referred to Angela's membership in the Communist Party and remembered her first visit to a Glide Celebration. Watching the clapping, singing, diverse audience, she said (referring to Karl Marx's famous statement about religion), "Why, Cecil! This *isn't* the opiate of the people!"

Being fashionable was fun for a while, because we both got

into it. Cecil took to wearing an African dashiki that made him handsome and vibrant when he sang with the Glide Ensemble while the congregation cheered him on. Outside the church he wore leather jackets with fringe on the arms and bell-bottom pants or studded jeans that were the height of cool. He got on trucks and toured neighborhoods with a bullhorn, calling on people to vote for Democrats like Willie Brown and John Burton. Many people recognized him and cheered as they would a movie star.

At the same time, my poems were being anthologized and published as collections (*Shedding Silence, We the Dangerous*). Maya Angelou had become a powerful advocate of my work, paving the way for me as a guest poet at an international literary festival in Wales. She was always present for us when we needed her most. After my mother died, Maya telephoned from North Carolina to ask how I was doing.

"I feel really off balance," I told her. "I haven't been able to cry about it."

She paused for a moment. "That's because now there is no one between you and *It*," she said.

I thought, *Well, of course that's why I'm off balance.* Mortality is very much in your face when you're a parent. My mother had been standing between me and *It* for a long time, and now I was the one who stood between my daughter and her mortality. I hung up the phone and found myself weeping. Maya's comment had been such a wise and comforting thing to say, but that was typical of her. When Cecil was in trouble—with the church, police, racists, and homophobes—she would talk to him as though an angel had just landed on his shoulder.

Facing hostility was a known thing to Maya: "I step into it," she would say. "I open my mouth, and—" Then her hand would make a graceful arc from her lips to the sky, as though God came forth from her throat.

My work at Glide—securing corporate partners, organizing schedules, raising funds—brought me into the city's political and philanthropic fast lanes. I went to meetings and power lunches in a teased mane of hair that could barely get through the door and long pants sinking into brown leather boots that actually made me feel tall.

On Sundays, Cecil was always tinkering with that tricky business of being relevant and timeless at the same time. He knew how to incorporate the newsy and the trendy into his sermons by being playful with the congregation. "Hey man, let's get *down*," he would say. "We gonna boogie here! We gonna celebrate life!"

He had the gift of tossing out tricky, complicated thoughts that made you listen closely even while you were chuckling:

What people are really saying is, "I don't want to do much of anything." And do you know one thing? There are so many people who are programmed to not do much of anything till they don't do much of anything. And that not-much-of-anything never lets them become *what they have to* become *at the time that they gotta be coming.*

Or he would catch us off guard with something personal and emotionally moving:

Now my brothers and my sisters, there's a state of emergency that has to do with who's going to have control. That's the state of emergency. The emergency is that some time ago, and every day, I decided that I'm not going to let others control me. I'm going to control the destiny of my life. That's the state of emergency that I face every day. If I control my life, then I know who I am. I feel, I do, I act who I am. I define who I am!

People were stunned by him, by the music, the light show, the diversity, the causes, the insistence on personal freedom, acceptance without judgment, and unconditional love. They left Celebrations dazzled and with their heads abuzz, wondering, "What just happened?" and for the rest of the week, Cecil's more substantive message sank in. Then they couldn't wait to come back.

If the sanctuary seemed crowded before, it now was jammed to its windowsills from the balcony to the exit aisles. So many children sat on the stairs to the stage that every time Cecil raced down to the pews and back, the audience leaned forward to make sure no little fingers got stepped on. But Cecil was a master at that too—with lightness and fluidity he danced up and down the stage and never touched a thing in his way.

A wave of new celebrities came through that kept Cecil hopping as he appeared in photographs with an astounding range of people—Willie Mays, Diahann Carol, Ashford and Simpson, Cicely Tyson, Bishop Desmond Tutu, Danny Glover, Carlos Santana, Bobby McFerrin, Bonnie Raitt, the Dalai

Lama, and Sharon Stone. Harvey Milk and George Moscone spoke to the congregation, as did other local politicians—Jerry Brown, Nancy Pelosi, Barbara Boxer, and Dianne Feinstein—who continue to support Glide today.

Coretta Scott King became a dear friend after her appearance in support of Cecil at the Atlanta speech. And Maya Angelou always celebrated Cecil's achievements in her unique way. Cecil was in the midst of receiving an honorary doctorate at Southern Methodist University when presenters stopped the ceremony to welcome Maya, who flew to Dallas and grabbed a taxi without telling anyone so that she could say a few rousing words in praise of Cecil. This was also her gracious way of letting this institution know it was about time.

On Sundays, so many celebrities showed up that people began asking, "Who's coming next week?" Or they'd call ahead as if it wasn't worth going to church if a celebrity hadn't been booked in advance. We were startled by this trend and asked the staff to give a scripted answer. When somebody asked, "Who famous will be here Sunday?" we'd say, "Cecil Williams!" with great pride, at which the person might laugh and say, "Uh-huh, great. But who really famous is coming?"

Cecil kept cranking up his sermons to stay on top of this new kind of attention. He used newspaper headlines, black dialect, movies, songs, and books to prick up people's ears as he zeroed in on the deeper message. Eventually, though, I began to wonder if the depth to his convictions was fading. Cecil told everyone to be "cool" about what was "down," but the sermon itself wouldn't really "get down." He'd talk about things that were "in" rather than challenge people to examine what they believed. He knew there was a line between being fiery and titillating, but that was easy to forget when he was riffing on B. B. King and Chaka Khan.

"Is it truth you're going after, or entertainment?" I'd ask after the nine o'clock service.

"Hey, you know what I do," he'd say. "This stuff is good."

"As a lead-in, sure, but it's becoming the whole thing."

"Well, it starts with me, it builds with me, the door opens, and they get it. Just let me handle it."

I worried that when Cecil's controlling side showed—*I'm the one, I've got it covered*—he pushed aside his skill as a minister to transform and instead gave us instant gratification. People left the church on a big high as always, but not a provocative high, not a "What just happened?" high to think about all week. More of a "That was fun—let's go have pancakes" high.

Soon Glide's Celebrations were turning into shows, with Cecil Williams as show master. His knack for getting the easy laugh, the easy applause, was turning addictive.

"Where was that transition from thinking about injustice to doing something about it?" I asked after one nine o'clock Celebration.

"It's implied. It's in the part about finding a path to Spirit."

"It doesn't feel like the path to Spirit. It feels like the path to power, which people think is vicariously available through you."

Sometimes he'd change the message for the eleven o'clock, sometimes not. When he did, it wasn't with much conviction.

The hardest part was watching Cecil throw out flippant answers to glib questions he himself had raised. "People play games all the time, don't they?" he would say. "Yeah, man, we play games because we're programmed to, aren't we?"

"What did that mean?" I would ask. "Programmed in what way?"

"You know that bestseller called *Games People Play*. That's what it means."

"But what does it mean in your—"

"Just leave it."

But the minute someone in the congregation seemed to be in trouble, Cecil got back on track. One Sunday in the middle of Cecil's sermon, a very large man, clearly upset, stood up in the pew and trudged angrily into the aisle. He had a three-pronged artificial hand that was made of gleaming metal, and he waved it like a club at Cecil, who stopped preaching and walked down the stairs. As he came near, Cecil opened his arms to embrace the man, who very heavily placed his clawlike hand on the side of Cecil's neck. From the stage I could see the sharp tip of one of the prongs right next to Cecil's jugular. Cecil must have felt it there but did not draw back. He continued the embrace, and that was apparently what was needed. The man must have been so tired of people being afraid of him that when Cecil's arms stayed wrapped around his body, he put his cheek on Cecil's shoulder and started to cry. The two stood like that for several minutes, and nobody in the entire church said a thing. When the man stopped crying, he allowed Cecil to escort him back to his seat.

It was this quality in Cecil—this openness to humanity that inspired us all to face the things that scared us and take a step toward transformation—that I worried was in danger of being displaced by fame. One Sunday he got so mad at my questions about his sermon that he stormed out of the office. I went after him.

"You know what? I don't care what you say," I said. "You're losing yourself to this stuff. Glide isn't for all the people anymore. It's for the hangers-on. It's for the fans. It's for the adoration of you." He walked away.

I felt there was a smaller and smaller space for God, for Spirit, for the people's experience, for the magic of Glide—until finally there was only space for Cecil and that damned ego. His compassion, his vision, his humanity hadn't disappeared or faded, exactly. You just couldn't see them for the glare.

But I was in danger too. I felt crowded out. Cecil had the answers while I still believed in the search. We couldn't seem to create together in the same way. Everything we were building at Glide, this daily uphill march of Sisyphus that we thought of as our ecstatic work, this calling of Cecil's that was also a vision I shared, all of it seemed to be losing ground.

"You can't dance around up there and say things that aren't very meaningful," I said. "That isn't you. That isn't Glide."

"It's the new Glide," he said. "We adjust to change. We are change. We lead the change."

I knew he was under other pressures. There were conflicts with members of his family who wanted him to be a more "acceptable" minister. Theological objections remained in the conservative African American religious community about Glide's relationship to the gay and lesbian community, the transgender community, the prostitute community, and the "IV community," as San Francisco's public health director once characterized drug addicts. Photo after photo of Cecil in the news, with Hollywood stars, with politicos and with gay couples he had just married, mystified a lot of people.

Then, too, there were the women. They called for counseling appointments with Cecil; they knocked on his office door hour after hour. Men would call too, straight and gay. When you're charismatic to begin with, *and* you become famous, *and* you lead campaigns against injustice, *and* you're a powerful influence in politics, *and* you're single (Cecil and his wife separated in 1975), people want to be close to your power.

"It doesn't feel right," I would say. "This could endanger us." We had agreed a long time ago that people of color who become leaders, especially religious leaders, were under greater scrutiny about two things—sex and money—than anybody else. At the beginning there were critics who actually said that Cecil and I should be watched or he'd spend contributions on a Cadillac and I on bejeweled clothes. Moneywise, we couldn't have had a cleaner operation, but on the other front . . .

"Wait, are *you* threatened by all this?" Cecil would answer, and I had to ask myself if jealousy did play a part. Of course it did. Cecil was incredibly caring about my needs as an incest survivor and had for many years stood back like a loving brother, giving me all the space I needed. We had become so close as friends that we could talk about sexual attraction as something we had placed on the shelf until (and if) I felt more comfortable. Lately, I had to admit to myself that I didn't think of Cecil as a father figure or counselor any longer. I was probably falling in love with him—not sexually, I thought, at least not now—so yes, jealousy was a part of it, but mostly because I was making a lot of decisions and wanted to be Cecil's center at Glide. So I leveled with him.

"I expect anyone as famous as you are to have an entourage, and a private life. But allowing all these women around is scary. It puts you at risk," I said.

"The community is us. We are the community," he answered. "People get to hang out. We should be grateful that they do."

I saw what he meant. People came and went, but few got personally involved. The famous Cecil might have been flattered and distracted by the attention, but the real Cecil was still helping people—was still counseling mothers who sold sex for drugs, still finding homeless people who slept under the freeways, still talking to drunks camping in doorways, and still reaching out to women who sought shelter in those inhumane hotels where they were raped and robbed of their stockings and blankets. This work he did so far away from the cameras and so often in the dead of night was a calling he could never say no to. It could not satisfy him because it was never-ending, but it enriched him and deepened him all the same.

And these two sides—the famous and the private—of an already filled-to-the-brim day were beginning to exhaust him. We both worked long hours and often joked that Glide "always ran on a quarter tank," meaning we never had enough money or time to fill our reserves more than a quarter full. What did that matter, we would say, when the gas in our tank was love, the thing that powered us was Spirit, the fire inside us was the promise of a just society? Fame, on the other hand, was not fuel, and Cecil, it seemed, was running on fumes. The harder he worked to keep Glide timely and famous, the more that "screaming loneliness" seemed to return, and the emptier he seemed to feel.

Fame was also taking its toll on many self-empowerment communities in San Francisco at the time. Three of them—the groundbreaking drug rehabilitation program known as Synanon; transformational workshops called Erhard Seminars Training, or "est"; and another religious group devoted to the poor, the Peoples Temple—had also been hit by a tsunami of acclaim. To the public, as Cecil noted, there was one big difference between these other groups and Glide: their leaders were white. While the media often assumed that controversial and outspoken African Americans like Cecil could not handle the responsibility of a growing church like Glide, leaders like Werner Erhard were given a wide berth.

That imbalance was on our minds as word got out that, allegedly, Jim Jones of the Peoples Temple and Chuck Dederich of Synanon were sexually abusing women and men of all ages, yet nothing was said about this in the media for a long time. Cecil had come to know Chuck as a colleague earlier when the two formed a partnership in which Synanon donated surplus packaged foods from its corporate sponsors, and Glide distributed these foods to the poor. The Peoples Temple with its congregation of minority and disenfranchised people was often listed along with Glide as a supporter of political causes. Jim could get a letter-writing campaign going in minutes and show up at a political demonstration with hundreds of people. His power meant a great deal to political candidates and incumbents alike, and they said so publicly, as did many others, at dinners and fund-raisers.

The Peoples Temple cadre often marched in the same political demonstrations as Glide, but they didn't stay long. Members would file in from the sides for a few blocks as Jim shook hands with civic leaders and had his picture taken. After a few blocks, they would file out again.

Only when Jim spoke at Glide did Cecil and I witness his alarming need for control. A sizable entourage from the Peoples Temple attended the Celebration, and whenever Jim raised his arms a certain way, his people reacted on cue—they applauded, laughed, stood up, or sat down as directed. By contrast, when Cecil spoke at the Peoples Temple, the audience remained polite and attentive, but not to him—it was Jim who sent out signals from the stage telling everyone how to react. Cecil was not fazed by this. He never took a position for or against any other ministry or social organization, nor did he judge the behavior of other leaders or their followers. His concern was Glide.

Over the years, the crowds, the fame, and the money faded for these other groups, and their leaders sought out Cecil for advice. Werner Erhard of est invited us to dinner at his home one night with a dozen of his workshop leaders and supporters. They talked about how people should be "trained" to accept that they were "estholes" and laughed at Werner's jokes until he gave them the signal to be quiet.

"How do you at Glide keep 'making it happen' for people?" he asked Cecil. "What do you do to increase participation?"

We knew that est trainings involved rigorous and lengthy meetings with confrontational trainers who kept the doors locked until people "got it" (the meaning of life, we assumed), and that few meals and bathroom breaks were allowed. At Glide, Cecil told Werner, "We always keep the door open," meaning people had the freedom to stay away if they wanted. When they *chose* to come back, the Celebration was more meaningful. "And they can use the toilet," he added.

Werner didn't like this answer. It seemed clear that he didn't care about Glide—he wanted Cecil to publicly endorse est. To be polite, he turned to me.

"What do you think of est?" he asked.

"Well, all that control sounds like cultural genocide to me," I said. I was about to explain that when people at the top believed they had the answer to ways that people at the bottom should live, fascist elements surfaced. Before I could get into that, however, we were leaving. (Est ceased operations in 1981.)

We learned more about control issues when Chuck Dederich invited us to spend a night at Synanon's compound in Badger, California, near Fresno. Synanon had started out as a compelling new approach to drug addiction at the time. Addicts lived together as an alternative community while helping each other through various stages of rehabilitation. However, Chuck grew increasingly unstable after the death of his wife, and now, it was rumored, ran the compound like a dictator.

This seemed to be the case when we walked into the dining room and realized that all the staff members wore guns, and the women were sitting at separate tables from the men. Microphones hung over the tables to record our conversations. Cecil noticed when he sat down next to Chuck that everyone at the head table was waiting for Chuck to speak. When he did, the subject was marriage. Chuck, who later took several wives, decided that married couples at Synanon should switch partners as a way of finding their souls. He didn't really want to know why Glide succeeded; he wanted to incorporate some of Glide's "spiritual focus" into Synanon's organization. Later as we went to a guest cottage, which we were pretty sure was bugged, Cecil whispered, "This is nuts. They want to control *everyone*."

The media sometimes compared Cecil and Jim Jones because both were leaders of racially diverse spiritual communities that carried a lot of political clout. In 1977, when Jim realized his empire was collapsing, he called Cecil to say he was taking his congregation to Guyana that night because people were "after him" in San Francisco.

"Don't do it, Jim," Cecil said. "Stay and face this, whatever it is. Don't run." But Jim took the congregation to Guyana and orchestrated the infamous mass suicide involving himself and nearly a thousand followers in 1978.

After a while, it appeared that Glide would be one of the few self-empowerment groups to survive that long era of sexual/political/religious freedom that stretched from the 1960s to the 1980s. One reason was that Cecil understood the paradox of freedom. His sermons often centered on the idea that most of us want to be free but are afraid of freedom at the same time. Looking to somebody charismatic and wise to lead us was a very human thing to do. We might feel liberated for a while, but we might also become dependent on that person to make our decisions for us. Cecil refused to be that kind of leader. God—the Spirit inside us—wants us to be free, he would say. We are born with the ability to make our own decisions, and when we learn to manifest that power, we liberate ourselves. No minister or leader is more powerful than we ourselves are.

That was one of those truths that Cecil was trying to get at when he used the lyrics of popular songs to get the audience's attention. He would sing out about freedom as the Isley Brothers did: "It's your thing! Do what you want to do!" In the wild and stormy '60s and '70s, being hip and sending a message was enough. But as Glide moved into the '80s, Cecil wanted to get beyond the flashy and the trendy. He started to explain all the meanings he saw packed into the song's lyrics (freedom, self-definition, difference). He even introduced Kierkegaard in an understandable way as he got deeper into the philosophic thinking that he hoped would follow the listeners out the door.

I could tell that Cecil was getting securely back on track one Sunday when he talked about the effects of fame. "People ask me all sorts of questions, like, 'Who is God?' and 'What is courage?' and 'How can I be free?'

"Well, don't you get it, brothers and sisters? *You* are the answer to your own question. You've been carrying that answer inside you all this time. You were born with it, and you're living it now. The next time you wonder, 'Why can't I be as powerful as I want to be?' remember that. You are the answer."

Nobody was laughing now. They just stood up and applauded.

When the nine o'clock Celebration ended, I ran down the stairs to Cecil's office. "Well, you don't need me anymore," I told him. "You just said it all."

"Feels good," he said, looking exhausted. What a contradiction he was, I thought: that which seduced him made him great. He would always struggle with God over being the center of the world, *and* he would always feel the power of God inside himself. He knew who he was, and now *whose* he was.

I lingered for a moment. A few days before, Cecil had revealed to me that he was worried about his upcoming divorce and was suffering at the thought of losing his children in a custody battle. He looked so vulnerable and on the verge of tears that I found myself wanting to hold him close.

Now I remembered that rich baritone voice during the sermon. I smiled. "You are the answer," I whispered, on the edge of tears myself. As I walked toward him, he looked up at me, his dark eyes glistening, his hands reaching out to take hold of mine. I remembered those hands, the way they invited the congregation into this sanctified place of love, the way they held up pieces of the fallen cross to reveal a new beginning. It was a new beginning for us as well.

And speaking of radical change: From then on, when people asked, "Hey, who famous is going to be at Glide next Sunday?" we would say, "*You* are!" You are the center of the stage. You are the answer. You contain the light that you are searching for.

Sometime later I knew that peace had come to Cecil when we were walking down the street and someone yelled from a passing bus, "Cecil, we love you!" As the bus pulled into its stop, Cecil yelled back, "Love the people on the bus!"

17

Recovery: The Beginning

Janice

A YEAR AFTER we were married, in 1983, Cecil asked if I would talk to the congregation about being a survivor of incest.

I had no idea this had been on his mind. Opening up to him about the abuse—even though I had trusted him completely; even though he helped me save my own life—had been so excruciating that I couldn't imagine the whole congregation knowing about it.

At Glide we say that everyone is in recovery from something. You needn't be addicted to want to cover up emotional pain that's been buried for a long time. "For you to gain recovery," Cecil told our first recovery circles in the 1980s, "you've got to go back to the beginning of your pain and come forward again. You've got to tell the truth, your whole story."

Breaking one's silence to tell the whole story had become a mantra at Glide and a life goal for me. Japanese Americans of my mother's generation were called "the silent minority" in part because most families didn't speak about life as internees during World War II. They so completely adopted the idea of "moving on" and "not dwelling on the past" that often the first time their kids heard about it was in school. When my family was released from the internment camp in Rohwer, Arkansas, I was four years old and retained no memory of the camp itself. I did grow up wondering how much of a "threat to national security" almost 120,000 Americans of Japanese ancestry could have been when most of the people interned were American citizens by birth, and almost half were children. The silence about the internment in my family was filled in by repeated statements from my mother about white people seeing us as inferior. Overt racism directed toward us after the war caused me to grow up ashamed of my Japanese ancestry.

Then I came to Glide.

Like many people there, I learned the power of telling our stories openly and without apology. Already active in civil rights with Cecil and others, I was drawn with increasing passion to the Japanese American redress movement. This was a national effort aimed at compelling the federal government to acknowledge the injustice of the internment and to provide reparations to internees. It thrilled me that an important force in the redress movement was the Sansei (third-generation Japanese Americans), most of whom had been born *after* their parents' release from the camps. They recognized that the United States could not grow as a nation until the government confronted the unconstitutionality of the internment. The more I followed the redress movement, the more I realized that, between my mother's continuing silence and my own commitment to radical change, the shame I felt growing up was forcing its way to the surface.

About this time I began working with other Japanese Americans to publish an anthology of writings and visual art— many created in the camps—that spanned four generations of Japanese experience in America. While gathering and editing these historic pieces, I met an Issei (first-generation Japanese American) peace activist and artist, Mitsu Yashima. Before our meetings and over tea, she told me about her prison experience in Japan as a pregnant young woman. Mitsu had been visiting relatives there in 1940 when she was arrested for her "antiwar politics" and placed with eight to ten other women and men in a cagelike cell no bigger than a small pantry. The cell had no toilet, and Mitsu felt she was causing further suffering to the others because of her pregnancy and her frequent need to urinate. This indignity was the worst part for her. She could not bear causing discomfort to others and asked to be removed from the cell. After taking her out, the Japanese soldiers beat her so badly that she suffered a miscarriage and nearly died.

Mitsu's story brought tears to my eyes. She was a longtime activist whom everyone in the Japanese American community admired, but none more than I. Her gentle yet fervent dedication to the cause of peace and justice was something I wished my family felt. She reminded me of my maternal grandmother: unconditionally loving and always compassionate toward the pain of others, even those who remained silent.

After I told her how frustrated I was over my mother's silence, Mitsu without introduction simply began to tell me stories of what people faced in American internment camps—the mothers giving birth to babies who were stillborn and disabled (as my cousin was); young mothers (like mine) who lost their teeth for lack of calcium in the camp diet; rampant dysentery, chronic depression, alcoholism, and suicide. She spoke with compassion and understanding—"*Everyone* suffered," she would say—and gradually I realized, in each moment of Mitsu's gentle revelations, why my mother had avoided my constant questioning about the camps. It wasn't that she felt I did not deserve to know; it was that she was too hurt and humiliated to recall and tell. (This is really how change happens, I realized; it does not happen with a finger in the face.)

I began to understand that my mother—and even I, a cynic and skeptic—had internalized the Japanese sense of *gambatte*, the quality of straightening your spine, swallowing your suffering, moving on and not imposing it on others. To the activist side of me, no amount of "moving on" and "not dwelling on the past" was going to keep the internment from resurfacing. As history reminded us, racism continued long past the war, and so did the consequences on our own negative self-perceptions.

These feelings inspired in me a passion similar to Cecil's for civil rights. I discovered that instead of turning the rage against myself, I could make my voice and others' heard; I could fight for justice from the perspective of the marginalized, the profiled, the stereotyped, and the discriminated against. American society did not expect Japanese Americans to fight for redress—one presidential administration after another assumed the camp experience would fade from history books and not be discussed in American classrooms. This assumption was the worst kind of precedent that could happen in a democracy—if it could happen to us, it could happen to any group.

Nevertheless, in their own spirit of *gambatte*, former internees who had been jailed for challenging Executive Order 9066, President Franklin Roosevelt's directive to intern Americans of Japanese descent, kept the battle active in the courts. These Nisei (second-generation Japanese Americans)—Fred Korematsu, Minoru Yasui, and Gordon Hirabayashi—were heroes to me for challenging the government's authority to incarcerate Americans without trial and for no offense. They consequently endured tremendous public hostility after the United States Supreme Court ruled against them in 1943 and 1944, upholding their criminal convictions and the legality of the internment. But heroes, too, were the determined Sansei lawyers (one of whom, Don Tamaki, now serves on Glide's board of trustees), who in the 1980s brought the now famous "coram nobis" petitions, which succeeded in reopening the Korematsu, Hirabayashi, and Yasui cases and nullifying their 1940s criminal convictions.

The pressures brought by national coalitions for redress led Congress to create the Commission on Wartime Relocation and Internment of Civilians (CWRIC), a formal fact-finding body that conducted hearings in nine cities for former internees to testify about their internment experience. For the first time, the United States officially considered making reparations to those who had lost so much (property, savings, jobs, education, health, and even life) while incarcerated in the camps. This development held out a promise of justice that many Japanese Americans thought they would never see.

For the first time, my mother was so overwhelmed with anger at what happened in the camps that she decided to testify at the commission hearings in Los Angeles. I didn't hear about her decision until afterward when she wrote me a letter and included her testimony in the envelope. I never imagined that my mother would break her silence, especially publicly, and the panel of commissioners hadn't made it easy. In the midst of reading her statement, my mother was interrupted by an impatient commissioner who said her time was up and to go sit down. After three and a half years behind barbed wires that had cruelly disrupted her life, she remained standing before the commission and continued reading until she was done.

Holding that handwritten statement in my hand, I stood in my living room weeping for many minutes as I read and reread her testimony. I still couldn't believe it—my mother hadn't said a word about those camps for forty years, and now this. I called her on the phone and asked what made her decide to testify.

"I just got so mad!" she said. "Thinking about those years wasted, and having to live in the same barracks with my mother-in-law . . ." Through my tears, I couldn't help laughing. Mother's dislike of my paternal grandmother had always been at the top of all her grievances.

But perhaps it was that combination of laughter and tears that helped me begin a new search for a true family history. For most of those years that I had asked my mother to tell me about the camps, I was also asking her to protect me from my stepfather and other men. When she refused to talk about either reality, I concluded that if my mother wouldn't save me, and if (as I had learned at age twelve through unsuccessful prayers to Jesus) God wouldn't save me, how could anyone on the outcast fringe depend on the U.S. government to save us? In other words, the principle to believe in was not "justice for all" but "justice for some" in our democracy, and that formed the basis of much of my cynicism. And yet if that loss of fair treatment was the case, as Cecil would say, do you give up? Do you decide you're not worthy of equal treatment? Or do you fight for what's right in the world? Do you give up on your mother or do you learn to love her for the imperfect person she is (and we all are)?

Finding my mother all over again would be a lifelong act of recovery, and one thing that contributed to it was the second reason my mother insisted on telling her whole story before the commission. "I didn't want them to get away with doing this to another group," she said. That was an astounding big-picture reference coming from my mother, and so true. She was one of hundreds who appeared at the commission hearings, and the impact of their collective voice was felt very deeply in subsequent crises—during the AIDS hysteria of the 1980s, for example, when calls went out to quarantine gay men "just in case"; and after 9/11, when hate crimes and violence against Muslims led to fringe groups calling for internment.

After my mother testified, I wrote "Breaking Silence," a poem addressed to "Mr. Commissioner," in which I hoped to glimpse a slice of the anger that made my mother insist on telling the whole story.

> *. . . So when you tell me I must limit testimony,*
> *when you tell me my time is up,*
> *I tell you this:*
> *Pride has kept my lips*
> *pinned by nails*
> *my rage coffined.*
> *But I exhume my past*
> *to claim this time.*
> *Words are better than tears,*
> *so I spill them.*
> *I kill this, the silence . . .*

My mother had remained silent not only about the years of being interned, but also about the molestation I endured from my stepfather and other men for eleven years. We so rarely spoke of it that I, too, ended up silenced because I felt she didn't believe me. When she turned a blind eye, I internalized the shame. This is one reason why Glide was so life-altering for me from the very beginning. Anger that I didn't know had been building up became an organizing principle in my life. The rage that came out in my poems and political activism helped me to finally face the shame. My voice felt powerful when I shouted out in anger against injustice. I began to sense that until I looked underneath all that anger, the wounds would continue to fester. This was where Cecil opened these wounds in that excruciating yet healing way. I really did not understand what it meant to be loved until he listened and believed in me.

This is one of those emotional minefields where Glide performs its magic. The love I thought I was incapable of feeling started to surface, slowly as a stream at first, when I began developing Glide's recovery programs with addicts and survivors of abuse and violence. I sat in and participated in the first recovery circles in which women told horrific stories about the way crack cocaine made them willing to do anything for the drug, such as sell their bodies and even their children for a hit of crack. In these circles, I was shocked to learn that nearly all the survivors had been abused or raped in childhood.

These courageous women became my mirrors. I saw myself in their guilt, their powerlessness, their self-destruction, but also their hope. And here, too, in this circle presided the enormous power of love. Each time my turn came to speak, the women protected me, they held me, they listened to me, and they loved me. Telling Cecil had been painful but renewing. Telling these women was like discovering family for the first time.

So I told Cecil yes, I would talk publicly at Glide about being an incest survivor, though it took a while and a lot of soul-searching for me to reach this decision. Finally the Sunday came when I stood before the congregation. I announced that I had been invited to tell my story of childhood sexual abuse. I said that the memory made me feel like a butterfly pinned on a slab of paraffin, my wings stilled, my screams silenced by shame. I had grown up believing that my telling the truth was a potential killer of my mother and would surely destroy the people around me. Saying out loud what actually happened would disgrace the family and all my ancestors. What had kept me silent, I told the congregation, was believing that I had caused the abuse, that I was guilty of what my stepfather portrayed as the worst of crimes, my need for affection and acceptance.

In the midst of this testimony, I struggled against tears to say that first my grandmother's love and then Cecil's unconditional acceptance had saved my life, and so had the support of the women and men in Glide's recovery circles. My worst fear coming to this podium, I said, was that I would be judged, reviled, and rejected if I told the congregation about this dark brokenness in my life—me, the minister's wife, the director of Glide's programs—and especially if I spoke of it in church.

The audience, which had been silent all this time, spontaneously stood up and applauded for a long while. I felt lighter than air because of their reaction. A great weight was being lifted off my shoulders.

Cecil hugged me for a long moment, then stepped to the microphone. "Let me ask *you* now," he said. "Are there others who experienced sexual abuse? Would you tell your story?" We were surprised to see more than a hundred people—mostly women, some men—stand up and raise their hands. Many of them had tears in their eyes, and they looked up at us as if to say, *Where else but in church can we finally tell the truth?* It was the beginning of Glide's survivors' circles for women and men, not only about incest and chemical addiction but domestic violence, anger, and problems with food, sex, and gambling.

Love, I learned, is the antidote for holding on to the anger of the past. Recovery is a perpetual journey. It requires learning to love oneself, to forgive oneself and then others, and to stay alert for every moment that your heart opens.

Another of those miraculous moments happened to me in 1992, when I was invited to speak and read my poetry during a Day of Remembrance at Sacramento State (California State University, Sacramento). The occasion commemorated the fiftieth anniversary of the beginning of the Japanese American internment. As I drove through Sacramento, I remembered that my paternal grandparents' store in Stockton, the town of my birthplace about fifty miles south, had been confiscated by the government during the war, and all their family heirlooms were lost.

Or so our family thought. Somehow, my grandmother's beautiful, fragile teacups and bowls—stuffed into a cardboard box with the name "Mirikitani" hastily printed on its side— had been stored by a kindly white neighbor, who had given it to a Japanese American family, who in turn had brought it with them when they moved to Sacramento. One day that family's grown children, who had read my books of poetry, came upon the box and recognized the name.

I was onstage concluding my presentation when a delegation brought this mysterious box to me and explained where it came from. Speechless and choked up before everyone, I opened the ancient flaps and pulled out the precious remnants of my family's history. Soon the audience was on its feet.

Thanks to Cecil, and thanks to Glide, I had felt the power

of love, but at this moment, the power of recovery took on a greater dimension. I was struck by the incredible kindness of people I didn't know who had preserved what would be invaluable to me forever—not only a sense of history but the practical things (property, jobs, human rights, money) that had been lost. I did not lose the rage I felt over the atrocity of the camps and the racism at their core. But I found in these delicate cups and sturdy bowls a way to tell my own daughter and her generation that we must remember the love, endurance, and capacity for forgiveness in human beings. In "Letter to My Daughter" I remember my mother and grandmother, who in their own way taught us lessons of pride and self-definition.

> Daughter, I want to tell you
> > That my grandmother would fill cups
> > With tea after a day's work,
> > Tell me how my eyes contained light
> > And illumined possibilities.
> > > It matters not what others say about us,
> > > All that comes before us dwells within us.
> > > All that comes hereafter is our legacy.
> > We are rekindled by memory,
> > The movement around us, the stirring for justice.
> > Remember the stories we write on our skin,
> > > Again and again.
> > Remember this:
> > To love in yourself what the spirit has gifted.
> > All that comes before, all that comes hereafter . . .
> > > All of it. All of it.

18

Recovery: The Journey

Janice

WE ARE ALL in recovery, yet we are never "recovered." If we keep working on it, recovery frees us from past behaviors and leads us to discover who we are and what we can become.

Glide's recovery circles had been meeting for a few years when in the late 1980s the nation was hit by a new drug epidemic. Cecil believed this latest crisis was so catastrophic that it could cause "the death of the African American race."

The drug was crack cocaine. Cecil and I knew nothing about it until young men from the Tenderloin mentioned a powerful new "rock" that was knocking everybody out. Cecil suggested they all go over to the Haight Ashbury Free Clinics and schedule some sessions with the founder, Dr. David Smith, but the guys said no. "The bus from Glide goes past the projects in Hayes Valley," one young man said. "If I even make it to the clinic, I've jumped off the bus at least once to get a hit."

Cecil and I drove across the Bay Bridge that week to attend a class on drugs and crack cocaine at the University of California at Berkeley. We learned that crack was so powerful, one hit could get you addicted, and that when it came to options for treatment, there were practically none. Crack was cheap, it was prevalent, and as Cecil learned when he asked African American drug dealers themselves, it was being targeted to poor black neighborhoods.

"The illegal-drug industry sends it to the population that's most desperate and suffering, but it's not just black people," Cecil said. "It's black *women*. The crack dealers say that if you get to the women, you get to the children, and then you get to the men," he added.

In 1988, we began to hold open-mike meetings that turned into breakout groups where people could talk to each other more intimately. These precursors of recovery circles soon evolved into a different approach to addiction that was unique to Glide. For one thing, we discovered that black addicts didn't do well at meetings of Alcoholics Anonymous or Narcotics Anonymous because most 12-Step meetings did not factor in racial identity. You could not tell African Americans to "Give yourself up to a higher power" without someone thinking you meant that higher power to be white society.

We discovered, too, that AA and NA were too middle class for Glide's population. For people trying to find shelter for the night or worrying about getting their children back from foster-care homes, conducting a "fearless moral inventory" on oneself seemed glib and simplistic. Our population needed culturally relevant programs in which sexism, classism, and racism were acknowledged as factors in people's attitudes and behaviors.

Cecil kept encouraging everyone to be more and more inventive. Since the 12 Steps didn't work for African Americans, Glide's recovery population wrote its own, matter-of-fact "Terms of Faith and Resistance." They included such notions as "1. Gain control over my life, 2. Tell my story to the world, and 3. Stop lying."

Glide also developed its own drug program called "Facts on Crack," in which groups of fifteen to twenty-five addicts met daily for seventeen weeks. Since Glide had no budget for "experts" (and Cecil and I were not sure that anyone in the crack cocaine epidemic was an expert; to us the people themselves were experts), participants in recovery circles learned to rely on one another without facilitators.

Each subsequent group after the seventeenth week ended was counted as a "generation." Meanwhile, a "placenta group" of nonusers grew around the users to support them. At the end of their seventeen weeks, the recovering addicts made two-year career plans and practiced job interviews and filling out applications. Glide's housing and meal services helped them get on their feet. By the time the thirteenth generation met in 1992, Glide was also offering classes on everything from traditional African clothing to literacy, computer use, and cultural history.

Yet for all this, the crack cocaine problem continued to sweep through the Tenderloin like a hurricane. What used to be vibrant, raw energy on the streets was turning into a zombieland, with strung-out moms holding the hands of dispirited kids and unemployed adults looking for crack hits on every corner.

Cecil wrote a blistering op-ed piece for the *New York Times* in which he railed at President George H. W. Bush for attending a six-hour drug "summit" in Colombia but doing nothing about the crack cocaine epidemic at home. The subject and title for the column were bold: "Crack Is Genocide, 1990s Style."

"Genocide is not only the extermination of a people through systematic mass murder," Cecil wrote. Genocide happens "when the spirit of a people is destroyed, when the culture of a people is eradicated, when basic human relationships are ripped apart, when large numbers of people are killed because of drug-related crimes and overdoses."

A glimmer of hope appeared when the Bush administration's new drug czar, William Bennett, invited Cecil to fly to Washington, D.C., to meet with civic leaders and drug treatment experts to help formulate a solution. He flew to the capital thinking that the only way for African Americans to fight this thing was through massive programs of treatment and recovery, especially in the inner-city ghettos. With Bennett at the lead, he hoped the federal government would find the money for the effort.

But the feds already had a plan, a much different one.

"They don't care about helping people get off crack," he told me on the phone. "All they care about is more money for more prisons, more cops, and more guns." He said he had stood up in Bennett's office shaking his fist. "You are interested in a policy of enforcement!" he shouted. "We are interested in a *public health policy* that puts the priority on recovery and treatment programs!"

By the third day in Washington, Cecil called a press conference about crack cocaine as genocide in the black community. "I'm blaming first and foremost the [George H. W. Bush] administration," he said. "Secondly, I'm blaming our social apathy. We're lackadaisical. People don't care. The reason they don't care is because it's not hitting their families and their neighborhoods. When it does, you will change your minds."

The administration did nothing except implement more force, but—typical of Cecil when he's been denied action—he came home fired up with a new plan. "To hell with the feds," he said. "We'll fight our own war against drugs, but we'll arrest the drugs, not our kids."

It took an enormous effort to pull this off, but in April of 1989, close to two thousand people—including ministers, social workers, doctors, cops, defense attorneys, civic leaders, teachers, detox/rehab counselors, former dealers, recovering addicts from all over the country, and many people from the federal government who heard Cecil in D.C. and agreed with him—arrived in San Francisco for a two-day conference sponsored by Glide. It was called *The Death of a Race: The Black Family/Community and Crack Cocaine National Conference*. Coretta Scott King and Maya Angelou served as speakers.

Cecil was on fire again when he gave the opening-day welcome and quoted drug czar William Bennett who had said, "Some neighborhoods are so infested with drugs that children should be removed from them and placed in orphanages."

Cecil read this out loud and aimed his response directly at

the TV cameras in front of him. "Let me tell you, Mr. Bennett, you are not going to get our children. We gon' keep 'em! They belong to us!"

Cecil added that African Americans had been through so many horrors throughout history that they were now "sanctified and blessed" to resolve the problem themselves. But it was not only their problem, he said, and they were not alone.

"We are now moving as a people! We've got white brothers and sisters. Asian American brothers and sisters. Latino-Hispanic brothers and sisters. Native American brothers and sisters. And we are coming home together."

The massive information exchange at the conference proved so valuable that Glide sponsored a second conference in 1990 and a third in 1992. The stories that came out led to a variety of humane and effective treatment programs that helped prevent drug-related crime and imprisonment.

Then one morning, Cecil and I were driving to a conference on drugs and recovery, held in an Oakland hotel, when a reporter on the radio made a staggering announcement. "Kim Williams, daughter of Rev. Cecil Williams, has been arrested for possession." Kim, we knew, had privately been fighting a drug problem, as were many other teenagers at the time.

We were stunned, horrified, and very worried about Kim. Because the news did not mention who had arrested her or in what city, we couldn't help her until she was allowed to make a phone call, and that could take hours. We decided to go on to the hotel, where Cecil would give his keynote speech, alert our lawyer, and wait for Kim to reach us.

The ballroom of the hotel was packed with perhaps a thousand participants, many of them in recovery themselves. Waiting for Cecil had pushed the energy level so high that they were clapping and singing as we came in. Cecil was introduced glowingly, but I could see he was still in shock about Kim and struggling with his emotions. We were miles from Glide, but to Cecil at this moment, his community—his family—was here.

In his address, he spoke passionately about the importance of treatment and recovery, then paused and looked in the faces of the audience for a long moment.

"Recovery begins when you tell the whole truth, no matter how painful," he said. "I want to say to you I'm really low this morning. I came in with a heavy heart, but the Spirit has touched me. My daughter was arrested just hours ago, and I'm sure it had to do with drugs. I—I . . ."

He never got to finish. The crowd burst into applause for his honesty and openness. He was a nationally celebrated expert in the "drug wars," as they were called, but at this moment he was a parent facing heartbreaking news like so many in his room. Hundreds of people came up to the stage, thanking him for his courage in telling the truth. I was grabbed by friends who hugged me tightly. It seemed the entire ballroom was weeping. Everyone knew that few other speakers in Cecil's position would have made this disclosure, but he had to. His own recovery depended on it. When he told his own truth, he bonded with everyone in the room.

Our journey with Kim through her addiction and recovery has been difficult, humorous, painful, and now joyous. Kim is a new person, immersed in her recovery and self-discovery and a hardworking mother of her own daughter as well.

After our first crack conference in 1989, Cecil received a visit from a group of residents at Valencia Gardens, a notoriously run-down federal housing project in San Francisco's Mission District. They told Cecil that crack cocaine had not only taken over life at the project but had a special appeal to the children living there. Kids knew at age eight that they could make more money by acting as lookouts and runners for drug dealers than most adults in legitimate jobs.

The usual approach to a place like Valencia Gardens by the criminal justice system was to "clean out the criminal element" with police raids. Glide's goal was to keep people in the community. In a crisis like this, as Cecil later told reporters, "the pusher needs recovery, the user needs recovery, the residents need recovery, the housing project needs recovery." Stop thinking punishment, prison, segregation, control, judgment, he would add; start thinking love, help, treatment, acceptance, compassion, patience, recovery.

Valencia Gardens did have a loosely built Tenants Association led by a dignified and loving elderly woman named Carlene Williams. We helped her group connect with key elements downtown, such as the San Francisco Housing Authority, the police department, the Substance Abuse Referral unit, the parole system, social workers, and a medical clinic. After the success of our first crack conference, we believed more than ever that the only way to stop the drug problem was to embrace everyone connected with it from the ground up.

So one Saturday with Cecil in the lead, about eight hundred of us from Glide traveled two miles, mostly on public transportation, to Valencia Gardens with banners and posters that declared, "It's Recovery Time!" Carlene and the Tenants Association had alerted residents that this Saturday was going to be a Celebration, so we made it a family picnic and concert combined. We brought a flatbed truck with a stage, our Sunday band, and the Glide Ensemble choir, and this was followed by a couple of vans loaded with fried chicken, potato salad, beans, and rice. We walked into the courtyard singing "Amazing Grace" and laid out the food.

"This isn't judgment time," Cecil said on a bullhorn. "It's recovery time. We're not here to run anybody out. We're your church, your family. Come and enjoy this fine fried chicken and meet us in the courtyard."

I could see people looking out from behind windows but not leaving their apartments, even when Cecil called up to them a few more times. So he got off the truck and went up to the top floor to knock on doors. People tried to argue, but there was no refusing the Rev.

And he had help. None of us knew until later that a resident of Valencia Gardens named Alex, a former inmate who'd been confronting his own struggles staying out of trouble, was worried that nobody would come out to meet us, so he actually paid residents to leave their rooms and take part. Cecil had met and liked this young man a week before, when Alex came to Glide asking if he could help with the Valencia Gardens recovery project. Alex had recently become a father and wanted people to "get it" about Glide. So here was Cecil going door-to-door convincing people to come out, while Alex was doing some of his own convincing with wads of cash.

Later in the day, Alex brought some kids over to ask me, "Can we listen to some of your music now?" Members of the

Glide Ensemble immediately got up on the truck and rocked the place with gospel music that could be heard at least a block down Mission Street.

At the end of the day, it was Alex who pointed to the graffiti and garbage and said, "You know, if *we* start cleaning it up, we'll feel pride in this place." What a great idea, we said.

Two weeks later, Cecil led the contingent of eight hundred on a return trip, this time with paintbrushes and rollers, and the residents really got into it. Rolling a thick layer of paint over graffiti you've hated for years can be emancipating.

Glide's partnership with the Valencia Gardens Tenants Association carried on long after we painted over the graffiti. Alex found a more creative path for his life, beginning with a yearlong job at Glide and later testifying for us at the second and third crack cocaine conferences.

Recovery is a complex issue. Part of it is systemic, involving lifestyle, the economy, available resources (very few if you're poor), and that element of "dependency" that can be passed from one generation to another.

But the most important factor is self-esteem. Wanting to change—to never again be dependent on a chemical or a system (like welfare)—is a positive thing. But believing you have the power to change can be transformative. At Glide, our first step to recovery is access to the wisdom of each other. Whenever you create community, we learned at the very beginning, you create hope.

19

Diversity

Janice

GLIDE HURTLED INTO the 1990s growing so fast that twenty or thirty people were always waiting for us with an urgent problem when we came to work each morning. Cecil hated the kind of crisis mentality that kept him putting out fires all day so that he couldn't create anything new, but we had no choice. Every problem had to do with Glide's core values—diversity, Spirit, love, justice, acceptance. How could it be, we wondered, that the things we found so uplifting might actually bring us down?

Diversity was a prime example. It was such a simple idea: put a bunch of people of mixed races together, give them a mission they believed in, and let them learn to work things out. That was the theory, and it held up as long as Glide stayed small with, say, ten or fifteen employees. But as we grew, we kept hiring—as much as possible from our own population (street people) and budget (limited)—and perhaps inevitably, conflicts and arguments broke out everywhere. Street monitors yelled at people in the food lines, volunteers burst into tears in the kitchen, accusations broke up one meeting after another, and resentments exploded in recovery circles, tutorials, and choir practice. Cecil and I kept rushing back to work or rushing out of meetings or rushing to end a phone call so we could talk with men about sexism, people of color about homophobia, gays about bigotry, whites about racism, young people about ageism, able people about disability, and on and on it went.

We wanted to reinforce the fact that Cecil really meant it about unconditional acceptance. He meant that Glide not only welcomed everybody, but also didn't give up on anyone. To department heads, we would say, "Being in charge doesn't mean you can fire somebody for calling a white man a 'motherfucking racist.' You have to think about other options, like maybe the person should go into counseling or join a recovery circle to confront his anger. Getting fired is the easy answer, and at Glide we don't take the easy way out. We think about other people's experience and we find a way that will work for everybody."

It helped some people when we asked them, "How would *you* like to be referred to as a 'bitch' or a 'baby' or a 'motherfucker' or a 'racist'?" But it did not help to say this to big, brawny ex-convicts, because in prison they were called names like that all the time. The key was *our* compassion and *our* trust. I would say to an employee in trouble, "We don't tolerate that language at Glide, but we don't want you to go back on the street and have to rob somebody and end up in jail, either. We know that you're a good worker. We know that you want to make it, but you're going to have to change your attitude."

What we were talking about is now called "anger management," but when that phrase crept into general usage, many people (Cecil and I included) cringed. Glide did not want people to "manage" their feelings or "control" their behavior so they would strip themselves of their own uniqueness and conform to the status quo. Following Cecil's model of liberation theology, Glide offered a safe place for people to find their own freedom and make their own choices. Instead of anger management, we offered recovery training in which all of us—department heads, street monitors, addicts, survivors of violence, Cecil, and myself—had the opportunity to recover the power of self-definition that might have been lost over years of being beaten up, lost, dismissed, and written off as worthless by society. At Glide, our only chance for survival was to *keep* all that was unique about each of us. If we didn't seek recovery to protect our differences, as Cecil said, we would be just like *them*, the ones who kept tight control on a status quo that to us was getting more totalitarian by the day.

Of all the people I talked to about recovery, a lot of men on the staff, especially the big guys who had just been released from prison, couldn't hear this from me. I was a small, thin Asian American woman who had no power, as far as they were concerned. They related only to Cecil, and whenever I sensed this, my own demons leaped up to say, *You're no good, men are more powerful, be quiet,* and all I'd want to do was disappear. What an irony: here I was proclaiming the importance of everyone, especially women, getting a seat at the table, but I myself didn't feel I deserved to be there. I even resented Cecil for always being the most powerful person in the room.

This reality was why recovery was so important. I certainly did not want Cecil to say, "Okay, guys, listen to Jan!" That would have been patronizing, and I would have hated it. On the other hand, I'd be in a meeting and my brain would go dead because I was sure no one would listen to me. It did no good when I told Cecil how I felt, because he only got frustrated, "Stand up to them," he would say. "Just be more present." Finally in the midst of a recovery circle discussion, the truth hit: I could rage and shout and take my clothes off to get people to pay attention, but if I myself did not believe that I was worthy of being heard, I would not be heard.

Cecil

It was important to sit down with folks and just say flat out that diversity was hard, and it had to be. Diversity helped us go deep into our own self-definition. You couldn't change your attitude if you didn't know who you were in the first place.

So what was it that kept triggering various blowups at Glide? I'd ask. If the answer was "white racism," I'd think, good—let's get into it.

When you grew up under the thumb of the white power structure, as most of the folks at Glide did, the idea of being equal in the world—of having just as much power as any white person—was not easy. We lived under a system that gave white people privilege and entitlement. It was an unjust system that caused uncountable problems, and it could destroy us. But it was the reality of this country, and the question was: Would we help it destroy us by losing our tempers and lashing out? Or could we embrace the system and use it as a mirror, to hold up and find the power within ourselves?

I'd add that people of color (and Janice would add: women of all races) were going to feel put down until we learned how power worked. We had to trust our own intelligence, our own strengths, and our own history to figure this out. Remember the plantation owners of the South before the Civil War? I would ask. They were taught from birth that they owned the world, so they didn't have to imagine a different world. They just ruled what they saw, and that's why black folks became the most inventive people in the world. Slaves created a hidden alternative culture, right down to a different language that could say the opposite of what those in power thought they heard.

That was the lesson I wanted Glide to bring to all of us: the way to combat the wrongdoing of power, even when the wrongdoers were wagging their finger in your face, was not to strike out with your fist but to work on yourself. The path to a just society was to find your own freedom, because, my sister and my brother, you are already free. You are free to know that you are different, and that you can be proud of that difference. You are free to know that you have choices, and that you can take responsibility for those choices. Seek out that freedom, and no one can ever lord it over you again.

And as to the system running things today, I would add, it might have the power, but look at the mistakes it made. This was the system that took us to war, that profiled us, that discriminated against us. It fouled the environment, it ruined the economy, and worst of all, it used its power against humanity.

That left us with an inhumane world until some group, some community said, *We're going to break loose and live differently. We're going to make things happen that lift us up. We're going to take on a privilege of our own so that we can share it.* That was what Glide's community was doing, I'd say. We were standing up to all that privilege because we were different; we worked together; we stood up as one, but we conformed for no one.

That was the promise of diversity. Working with people you'd been raised to distrust and be scared of was exactly what we all needed. We wouldn't be able to connect with the humanity we shared otherwise, or find that power inside we didn't know we had.

Janice

Glide dealt with diversity on multiple levels. The first was self-definition, and that meant everybody, Cecil and myself included. I was like the teacher who had to believe in that person inside with something important to say; Cecil was like the father who had to know his authority and his charisma could only do so much. Everyone loved the benefits of recovery, but we all had to learn that recovery was a discipline—it had to be practiced daily over the long haul.

Sometimes it helped to act out the parts. Instead of yelling, "You arrogant white bitch!" we learned to be patient and firm.

"Your manner does not feel appropriate to me," we might say. "It sounds like you think you know more than I do, and it feels like you're not listening to me. I need to be heard, too, so let's start over." It wasn't the message that made a difference so much as the I-deserve-this-seat-at-the-table tone, this I-believe-in-me tone.

Cecil

The second level of embracing diversity was the connection to our own relationship. Janice and I *required* each other to change, and we did so in a blunt way that neither of us would allow anybody else to use. Nobody could have come up to me and said, "You are a pompous, arrogant, egotistical ass," as Janice did. Most of the time she didn't say it that way, but that's what she meant. And I would admit it: By now Janice was Glide's executive director—if I countermanded a decision she made, *of course* she would be mad. But if I felt (as I usually did) that circumstances left me no choice, I got mad at her, too, and then we were on.

"Why do you feel so powerless?" I would say.

"Because you undermine me."

"Nobody can undermine you but yourself."

"You're doing it again!"

Janice

From that perspective, I understood the point of view of staff people who were so angry they felt they had to raise their voices and get in somebody's face. It was because they felt unseen to begin with, just as I did. Many Glide workers had been so beaten down in their lives that they didn't believe in the value of their own voice. That was a huge part of recovery training, but as with so many other things, it was easier to say than to put into practice.

Cecil, after all, was the most powerful person at Glide. From the beginning, his vision had transformed Glide. He made the decisions, and other people carried them out. I was the opposite—I wanted everybody's viewpoint before a decision was made. My own creativity was stimulated when I heard other people's reactions and ideas. This was why, as Glide grew, I brought in management consultants to help us build the infrastructure. After all, Cecil and I didn't know about organizational framework. We wanted everybody on staff to be encouraged and supported, but team building was hardly our forte.

Cecil agreed in theory that Glide could not keep growing unless we learned to delegate authority. He wanted department heads to take the initiative, to feel they were in control. But where, how, and when to hand over authority to them?

Cecil

The pressures of growth, of spectacular growth, were getting to us. One day I found Janice on her knees examining banisters and those little strips of nonskid carpet on the stairs. She told me that OSHA (Occupational Health and Safety Administration) inspectors could pop in at any time now that we were receiving federal grants. We had to make sure Glide was in compliance, she said. I looked around with her eyes and saw safety hazards in every window sash and doorknob in the place. A hundred things had to be checked. I tried to calm us both down.

"Nobody's going to trip on the—"

"We have to check the heating vents today. The electrical sockets are sixty years old. The light globes haven't been—"

"Fine, we'll get the guys in maintenance to—"

"They're busy checking baby cribs! They've got to fix the leaky faucets! We'll lose the contract if the stairs aren't—"

"You don't have any tacks—"

"Honey! Get some duct tape. There are only nine floors—we'll just take it one stair at a time."

I agreed with Janice that organizationally, the infrastructure of Glide also needed a complete overhaul, but I disagreed mightily with her on how to do it. These were the years (late 1980s to the early 2000s) when the number of volunteers coming through Glide annually grew into the hundreds and then thousands and then *tens* of thousands (today it's twenty-five thousand), and the number of employees climbed to over a hundred (today it's 175).

Seeing this, I kept working as I always had—from the gut—only harder and faster. I authorized payments, started projects, called and canceled meetings, and arranged my calendar not just to put out fires but to keep Glide moving ahead of the whirlwind, to keep it creative and fresh instead of reactive and predictable. Along the way, sometimes I got ahead of what Janice was doing, and that's when things really exploded, the two of us arguing in the office and then in the car and then at home. We had a tall Formica counter in the kitchen, and every night we'd end up standing on either side, pounding on the top of it, yelling things we told our staff weren't "appropriate."

"You're not listening."

"You're out of your mind."

"You're insecure!"

"You're an egomaniac!"

Finally we both had to say, "Look: I don't want to yell, and I don't want to see that side of anger from you." Janice would admit, "I am really hurt," and that would stop me. I didn't like hurting Janice, or anybody—I didn't like hurting the cat. We'd look at each other and agree that we were losing our souls; we'd destroy each other if we went on like this.

All this was happening at a time when our home life felt increasingly shaky. Following our marriage in 1982, we had been trying to merge two households—Janice and her daughter, Tianne; me and my two kids, Kim and Albert. All three kids were in their early teens and had supported the idea of our getting married, but the actual fact of it, and of all five of us moving into a new house together, was not so easy. My ex-wife had recently died suddenly of an aneurysm, and in their grief, Kim and Albert needed to be given a long leash, I felt. This brought up a long-running disagreement with Janice. She thought I was too permissive as a parent, and I thought she was too strict with Tianne.

We didn't get much help from our relatives at this time because they hadn't exactly embraced biracial marriage to begin with. When Janice went home to announce that we were getting married, her mother said, "You've just killed me," and went to bed. Some members of my family hoped I'd marry a striking black woman who would help me amass a power base and become a national civil rights leader. They could not believe I was going to marry this beautiful Asian American poet and still be taken seriously.

Happily, Janice's mother eventually became a dear friend, as did her younger brother Layne, who walked Janice down the aisle when her biological father refused to attend the wedding. My relatives came to love Janice as a member of the family, all of which reinforced my belief that diversity does work at home, when you really make an effort.

For the kids, things took a while. It was hard for Albert and Kim (and me), who were raised on deep-fried soul food not to feel cautious about raw fish and pickled vegetables. Janice, dreaming of happy family dinners with everyone sharing many kinds of food, started cooking three different meals every day. That stopped after the children proved they could be self-sufficient about getting their own food, but the upshot was that everybody started retreating to separate corners instead of celebrating our differences and coming together as a family.

Disagreements at work and at home got to be so painful that Janice and I decided to seek couples counseling. This was a last-ditch effort, and we might not have made the appointment at all if a friend hadn't found the "perfect couples therapy couple"—an African American man and an Asian American woman who worked as a team. Our friend said these two psychiatrists were compassionate and discreet. They would keep the pressures of Glide out of counseling sessions so that Janice and I could get to the truth of our problems and not worry about people at work panicking about our future. But when we sat down for our first appointment, as soon as I said, "We're on the verge of splitting up," the black psychiatrist nearly jumped out of his chair.

"*What?*" he said. "Not *you* two! Why, that can't happen—what would everyone say?" By "everyone" I figured he meant the congregation at Glide, but it didn't matter. Janice and I started laughing and couldn't quite contain ourselves—not on the way to the car, not when we got home, and not for the next thirty-plus years. What we had to do was affirm to each other exactly how much this love meant to us.

I had to learn that affirming our love meant practicing a discipline I had never really considered before, and this was *mutuality.* As much as I believed in Janice as my life partner, as much as I respected her as the cofounder of Glide, as much as I admired the infrastructure she was building that would keep Glide rock-solid long after we were gone, I tended to fall back on the old "man of the house" mentality I had been raised to believe.

In 1930s Texas, no matter what side of the race or class divide you lived on, men ran things and women supported them. When I played Church with my family and made sure all the races of the world were represented, it never occurred to me that my sister could be "the Rev." At Perkins, during the civil rights movement, at mobilizations against the wars in Vietnam, Iraq, and Afghanistan, I didn't notice an imbalance of gender. The last thing I ever wanted to do at Glide was to take advantage of Janice's love. But I had to ask myself: from our first protest together to our monthly meetings with the board of trustees and every event in between, had I expected her to back me up, follow my lead, take care of all the phone calls and paperwork? I certainly supported Janice, and I never asked her to get me coffee. In that regard, I told myself, I was a feminist man. At home I did half the shopping.

I did notice that when we went to black-tie receptions, people's racial and gender biases were extreme. They would ask Janice if she were the caterer for the event, or the flower arranger, or even my chauffeur. At Glide, if visitors came to my office and saw a photograph of Janice and me with African Americans in the background, they'd very often point to one of the black women and say, "Is this the minister's wife?" I would turn them around and say, "No, this is my wife, Janice, whom you just met." Some people from foreign countries were careful to correct Janice when she told them that she was the minister's wife. "Oh no," they would say. "It's not possible."

Experiences like that seldom happen today, and when they do, we tend to laugh them off. Some time ago I realized that letting go of power in the management of Glide made me more spiritually balanced than I ever thought I could be. Mutuality with Janice allowed me to respect our differences and explore the spirit flowing through Glide in different ways than I had before. Janice and I had always reinspired each other every day; increasingly we became like two sides of the same coin.

I began to refer to what Janice and I had together as "this love," this precious thing we shared. In life, love was everywhere; at Glide, we had the chance to love unconditionally; but "*this* love" I had with Janice was intimate, profound, and daring. We were a very public couple whom tourists could love from afar because our different races naturally made us the poster couple for Glide in all its diversity. And we were an intensely private couple whose love was nourished by the soul of the people we served. If we fought over the possibility that Glide could have a future after we were gone, then fine—we would fight with the kind of ardor and purpose that this love had given us. But if we fought the "wrong" way, with bitterness and recrimination and unexplored resentments, we'd not only go under as a couple—we'd bring Glide down with us.

Janice

So that was the third level in our campaign to make diversity work. When people saw a black man and an Asian woman onstage during Celebrations joking around about their marriage and their kids and driving each other to distraction at work, the normalcy of "this love" felt so uncontained that all the old restrictions seemed to lift. This was how we wanted our employees to feel as they let go of negative stereotypes and got past short-term anger and remembered why they came to Glide in the first place, and why they stayed: they came because they believed in the mission, the magic, the mojo of an inclusive community. They stayed because Glide was here to do good—to bring a sense of justice and love to the world. And they stayed because knowing deep down that they were building something larger than themselves had changed them profoundly.

Cecil

The final level was about making sure you could see the diversity of our population in the diversity of our staff. If you grew up hating gay people, or thought you did, but discovered this lesbian or that transgendered man at work was as capable and inventive as you, why, you began to change. It was not an easy change, but it could usher in a new perception. At Celebrations, for example, when our outrageously, flamboyantly gay retail representative dramatically showed the audience the Glide products they could buy—caps, T-shirts, aprons, fans (especially the fans)—everybody laughed and applauded warmly because here was a funny person who was good at spoofing gender, and because suddenly all one thousand of us in that sanctuary felt like family. It wasn't that everyone's preconceptions disappeared but rather that in the face of the love for this man that swept over us, the old stuff we were taught about hatred and judgment didn't seem to matter.

Janice

Glide now has eleven thousand members and is still one of the fastest-growing churches in the international United Methodist Church community. We never want to be passive about this membership. Whenever we're about to call for a decision, conduct a meeting, or call for job applications, we make a point of asking, "Is everybody at the table?" This is intentional diversity. If the answer is no, we go out and find whoever is missing, and we do this for the health of Glide as much as for the inclusion of "minorities" (all groups at Glide are minorities). If we truly practice unconditional acceptance, we don't give up on anyone, and we don't leave out anyone. Diversity has taught us that we're stronger for all our differences when we remember that our humanity connects us all.

Cecil

I'm always learning how complicated these principles can be, and yet how simple. Making sure everybody is at the table truly means *everybody*, especially those closest to you. It was in that spirit that on a recent Father's Day I had to tell the truth about something very difficult. I had to tell it at home first to my intimate family—my son and daughter—and then I had to talk about it to my Glide family that Sunday.

Janice had arranged a Father's Day reunion for my adult children, Kim and Al, and my grandson Al, who lived in Southern California, to come and stay with us. I hadn't seen them for a long time, and I hoped we would open up to each other as honestly and easily as I thought we always had. But soon after they arrived, I noticed that my own kids were being careful and polite, as though I was a kind of minister you respect and defer to rather than your old dad whom you love and joke around with and can say anything to. What had happened? Of course the kids loved me. But had I, not they, been the distant one? With each exchange, I could feel that we weren't exactly coming alive with each other—we were visiting, but our hearts weren't present.

Sometimes when people ask, "How do you make Glide work?" my answer is that you have to participate in every moment. You cannot avoid the hard stuff—the differences, the conflicts, the arguments, the anger, the mistakes—any longer. You have to recognize over and over that facing, confronting, resolving, accepting, and discussing every concern, no matter how small, is the only way to prove your love, to show you really mean it.

This is what my kids and I shared at home that weekend. For my Father's Day sermon, when they were in the audience, I told the biblical story of the Prodigal Son, in which a young man leaves home and squanders the effects (money, inheritance) of his father's love. When he sees his son coming home, however, the father is so joyful that he stretches out his arms to embrace him.

The other son asks, "Why do you welcome him, he who has been absent for so long? I have been with you and obeyed you all these years, yet you favor him."

"This is my son also," the father responds. "He has been dead, but now he is alive. I rejoice that he has returned. By coming home he is no longer lost. He is found."

I told the congregation that I thought of this story as a lesson in compassion. The son gave up part of his identity each time he acted wastefully. He got so wrapped up in his own desires that he lost his heart, his ability to feel. The father understood this. The act of returning home, no matter how many years had passed, provided both of them with that rarest of all things, the power to come back from the dead—not just to renew their love but to be fully present to each other, to be honest, open, and revealing at every moment.

Thinking of that parable, and noting there were such things

in the world as Prodigal Fathers, I asked my kids to forgive me. I told them that I had done the best I could, but I made many mistakes. I tried to provide the love and support they deserved, but I wasn't present enough for them. I gave too much to Glide and not enough to my family. I got so caught up in building my vision of a beloved community that I lost my way as a father.

Another lesson of the story, I said, is how easy it is to veer off your own life path. Much of our "job" in life is to stay vigilant, to find that corrective force inside that keeps affirming who we are and the love we feel for our parents and our kids. I said that I had lost my way as a father but I hoped that now I was found. At eighty-two, I still felt driven by Glide's vision, and I would certainly make more mistakes as their father, but I was coming home.

It was curious. How many times had I as a minister counseled fathers to remain close, to stay in the moment with their children, to affirm their love over and over? I remembered the surprise on Randolph Hearst's face when I asked him to tell his daughter Patty that he loved her. This was in 1974 when Randy, one of the most powerful newspaper tycoons in America, was about to go on television and plead to a group of terrorist kidnappers to keep his daughter safe. "If Patty's alive, she may be watching," I said. "Help her be strong." Randy didn't want to say something so personal and private to banks of microphones and television cameras. "I think what you're really worried about is that she won't believe you," I said. "But this is the moment she needs to hear you say it the most." Randy nearly choked up with tears when he went before the cameras, but he did it—he told his daughter he loved her. I thought then, as I did on this Father's Day, that sometimes it takes a crisis for a parent and child to confirm their love for each other. (Patty Hearst did survive the kidnapping and went on to raise a family of her own.)

So both stories—the Prodigal Son and the Patty Hearst kidnapping—had the same message for me. I had to tell myself that it wasn't too late, that I could trust my children's compassion and their love for me as their dad. By the end of the sermon, I saw the spark of affirmation in my children's eyes. They now had kids of their own, and their smiles took on that understanding that perhaps only parents can know. They were coming home also.

Janice

There was not a dry eye in the house that day. Every father knew what Cecil meant, of course, but so did anyone who remembered how it felt to be the child of a flawed parent, and that was all of us. Cecil's kids didn't need to forgive him— they accepted their father as the imperfect and vulnerable man trying so hard to give them his love—and so they gave him their own.

20

The Beloved Community

Cecil

As we moved through the 1990s and into the 2000s, Janice and I began to draw on the power of the true beloved community—not only the poor and disenfranchised to whom we had always been committed and who gave back so much love, but also the city and world around us that had a lot of love to give.

Janice, for instance, had been worrying about conditions in homeless shelters for as long as I had known her. When she first came to the Tenderloin in the early 1960s, all we had were flophouses that catered to men. Janice formed and joined a number of coalitions that created a better kind of shelter for the homeless with protections for women and children. But there was only so much that could be done. Reports continued about dead rats in the pipes, cockroach excrement that had to be wiped off the mouths and faces of children when they woke up, walls so thin that beatings could be heard day and night. For Janice the hardest part was working with kids who had been sexually traumatized in the shelters because (for one thing) predators routinely removed light globes from hallway lamps and hid in the darkness waiting for women and children to find their way to the bathroom. Rapes, robberies, and molestations were so common that many families took their chances and slept in doorways outside.

About that time (the mid-1960s), a Glide volunteer named Joyce Hayes mentioned to Janice that many children who lived in the Tenderloin were hanging out in the streets after school and needed a place to go. With their own money, Joyce and other volunteers bought school supplies, opened up a small room on Glide's second floor, and started a tutoring program with about fifteen kids. The volunteers began by teaching them to read better, gave them art projects and recreational activities, built shelves and cubicles, and created play areas.

We discovered that a number of children were truant from school because they weren't dressed properly, and they smelled. Part of the reason kids drop out of school is loss of self-esteem because they're caught up in a cycle of poverty that never stops. They don't learn because they don't go to school; they don't go to school because they don't have self-esteem; they don't have self-esteem because other kids tease and bully them about their clothes and their smell. In addition, parents who were addicts often sold their children's books and shoes for drugs like crack cocaine. In spite of their circumstances, these kids wanted their families to remain intact and protected their parents fiercely, so they never told us what happened to their stuff.

This was when we all fell in love with Joyce Hayes. She had an amazing ability to bring her love to children, both as a teacher and a foster mother (she personally fostered more than eighty children during the four decades we worked with her). The kids at Glide knew they could trust Joyce even when she scolded them. "I don't know what happened to these books, but you're not coming back to the program until you return them." Within twenty-four hours they would be standing at the door with the books in hand. Not being in the after-school program at Glide was so awful for them that they'd do anything to get back in.

The children's program took over the whole second floor as the first fifteen kids turned into a hundred, and parents and volunteers increased their involvement. We began to apply for grants from private foundations as well as city and federal programs, and these helped us to hire staff and expand our scope of services. But the prospect of turning away children because we didn't have room and always operated on a shoestring proved exhausting. When homeless mothers told Janice about what they needed to keep their kids safe, they not only talked about an after-school program and shelters that were protected and clean, they wished also for a place the whole family could go during the day. This would be a warm and welcoming site where there might be an actual kitchen with a working stove and refrigerator and nutritious food; where the bathrooms were safe, and where licensed counselors and teachers provided creative activities for the kids. In other words, they dreamed not just of more rooms for the children's program but their own building.

That idea had been simmering in Janice's mind after our friend Jeff Mori, a youth director who worked with Mayor Willie Brown, told us about a former cigarette warehouse a block away from Glide that had been taken over by questionable interests (gambling, sex traffic). When she learned that the city wanted to clean out the warehouse and sell it, Janice's eyes got so wide they seemed to shoot off sparks. Every other day we walked up Ellis Street to look at the "bad cigarette warehouse." She could not stop talking about what an opportunity of a lifetime it would be for Glide to purchase a building that would not only get kids off the street but help families create their own center.

Janice researched every aspect of buying Glide's first outside property and worked with parents, staff, and our board of trustees chair, Amy Errett. She found donors, government agencies, and foundations to contribute $3 million, more than any amount she had raised before, to purchase the building, gut it, redesign it, and staff it. By this time Joyce Hayes, now director of the children's program, joined Janice in working with the architect and interior designer to create both a day-care center with a magnificent rooftop playground for younger kids, and an after-school program with tutors, classes (cooking, computers, gardening, reading, ESL, creative arts), sports, and field trips for older kids. Janice and Joyce knew that the essence of a family center was to provide a second home for parents as well as children. So they included adult programs that would provide parenting classes, counseling, and support groups as well as access to all the other programs at Glide.

The Janice Mirikitani Family, Youth, and Childcare Center (JMFYCC) opened in 1998 and became a model for drop-in programs of education and support for children and families in a distressed inner-urban location. From the fifteen kids who came to a fledgling program in the late 1960s to more than five hundred parents and children who take advantage of the complete center today, the aim has been to provide a safe and welcoming place that nourishes and celebrates, very much like Glide.

But the JMFYCC was only part of what would become Janice's own vision of holistic care. She was also aiming for a health and social services center inside Glide that would provide wraparound care to people who had little or no medical care before. This was a huge need in an impoverished section of the city because it not only required health-care professionals in an actual health-care center, it called for the kind of loving and conscientious care that would provide the poor and homeless with actual medical histories and continuing physical, mental, and drug therapy. I don't think even Janice knew that something this big was in her sights—at Glide we never had a strategic plan—because for many years, it was all our volunteers could do to help people on a need-by-need basis.

Back in the 1970s, for example, Janice was surprised to discover that many women in the streets believed mammograms were harmful. They couldn't afford the procedure anyway, and they heard, too, that it was painful, so they didn't consider having it done at all. Janice went to the American Red

Cross, which had mobile mammography vans going around the city, and asked if a van could spend a "Breast Health Day" in Glide's parking lot offering mammograms for free. The Red Cross said it couldn't provide the service for less than $40 per person, so Janice spoke to Glide's congregation one Sunday and described what Breast Health Day could do for women if she could raise enough money. The offering basket went around a second time and collected an astonishing $1,200, enough for thirty women to have a mammogram, if they would take advantage of the service in the first place.

I never knew how Janice got fearful folks like these women even to step into the parking lot, let alone the Red Cross van. She said the relationships they had formed with recovery program counselors and volunteers (Ntombi Howell, Jackie Freeman, Edna Watts) were the main reason, and that the combination of free things—a raffle, popcorn, bags of donated groceries that she gave away—was another. But it was more than that. The women came because they trusted Janice and they trusted Glide. All day long, the Red Cross staff tirelessly explained the importance and the slight discomfort of mammography while Janice made jokes ("Okay, it's like being run over by a truck, but think of the benefits"). By the end of the day, of the thirty women who had the procedure, six were informed that they needed further tests. The possibility that these six women might have had cancer, and that a mammogram might have caught it in time and led to treatment that could save lives, sent word out to Glide's population that mammograms were worth the trouble. Breast Health Day probably saved the reputation of mammograms for a lot of women of all ages, including teens. And it also said to Janice that health services are valued by the public, even when they're scary.

The success of this event led to the success of another. Janice created a partnership with Planned Parenthood, which was researching poor populations at the time and testing for STDs. This opportunity prompted her and the women on Glide's staff to hold health fairs in which gynecologists, pharmacologists, psychologists, gerontologists, and others talked about the full range of health challenges facing women, as well as STDs, birth control, and options available to them for healthier choices.

It was during these educational forums and discussions that several women asked: "What about domestic violence? Isn't that a health issue too?" Janice remembers standing there shocked, saying yes, of course it was. That was the beginning of another series of programs, including two we still have today called "Women Overcoming Violence" in our Women's Center and "Men Unlearning Violence" in our "Men in Progress" groups.

Neither Janice nor I could imagine then how those simple beginnings would by 2008 become the licensed primary and mental health clinic we now call Glide Health Services. GHS is one of the country's leading models of patient-centered holistic health and healing, and it's managed entirely by nurse practitioners who provide primary internal medicine as well as training to nursing students. Along with our Walk-In Center that provides shelter reservations and rental assistance, GHS has expanded mightily to two floors of Glide in a creative partnership with Dignity Health (formerly Catholic Healthcare

West), St. Francis Hospital, and the University of California, San Francisco School of Nursing.

Glide's increasingly overlapping services began to remind Janice of a lumpy, bumpy, multilayered, do-it-yourself tapestry. Work on this magical community effort started back in the 1960s with a single, fragile thread (say, our potluck for fifty), and another thread (the first children's program). As each service grew and connected with others, a unique kind of tensile strength developed that withstood setbacks in the economy and our own always-growing, sometimes two-steps-back-for-every-step-forward internal management. I like to extend the tapestry metaphor by putting Janice at the loom day after day as she weaves the stories of individual lives into the enormously multifaceted and always growing community that is Glide.

As the first team of founders and program directors, Janice and I continue the team leadership paradigm with two co-executive directors, Rita Shimmin and Kristen Growney Yamamoto, a Ministry Team that includes Pastor Karen Oliveto, and our many committed directors, managers, and staff. We also continue to build what is now called the Glide brand: "A radically inclusive, just and loving community mobilized to alleviate suffering and break the cycles of poverty and marginalization." That's quite a mouthful because we're committed not just to a center with its incredible range of services but to a spiritual community of volunteers, board members, congregation, and staff who hold the values of justice, unconditional love, and acceptance.

Janice says that because of our management and infrastructure reorganization in the 1990s, a lot more people work at the loom providing the one thing that most poor people never receive in their lives—access to a compassionate and organized system that provides quality holistic care. Glide also provides electronically shared case histories that can follow the homeless wherever they go.

Today Janice's long-term reorganization at Glide is responsible for an annual budget of $16 million; a mostly full-time staff of 175 employees; Glide Health Services, which itself serves people from our Meals and Walk-In programs to our Women's Center; and 95 fully staffed programs that cover an enormous range of services and needs. That she was appointed San Francisco's second poet laureate (in 2000) by Mayor Willie Brown while in the midst of restructuring Glide both energized and nearly killed Janice, even as she inspired and worked with hundreds of young writers in the schools, at Glide, and other youth poetry groups (like Youth Speaks) at poetry performances around the city.

Janice

The key to Glide's expansion lies in the unique network of coalitions and partnerships that Cecil began building a half century ago. But the culmination of his vision for the beloved community became evident in 1998, when he proposed an idea that was considered so outrageous that even Glide's most ardent supporters couldn't imagine it. I have to admit it was so big and so "out there" that I grew fearful of it too.

Cecil's idea was to build a beautiful nine-story apartment house (not a housing project) for low-income and homeless people. Most of the residents would be recovering addicts, homeless people with multiple diagnoses including mental illness, and low-income families with children. To help them make the transition from the streets to apartment life, the building would include support services and personnel such as social workers, counselors, support groups, legal advocates, and health-care practitioners.

Like other programs that had become essential to Glide's services, Cecil's idea of "dignified housing" began without funding or a business plan. Glide owned the property next door, a parking lot (not the one on our other side that we used for various events, even parking) that we had leased to a rental-car company for many years. That lease was about to run out, and Cecil wanted Glide's new apartment house to be built at that location, which happened to be across the street from the Hilton Hotel. He liked to imagine guests looking out their window at an aesthetically pleasing apartment house designed by poor people themselves. Cecil also envisioned interiors that would be equally inspiring—decks, gardens, terraces, a community entertainment room, an infant care center, and space in the lobby for a farmers' market on the weekends. Living there would not be charity, Cecil made clear. This building would be subsidized, affordable housing in which residents would contribute a percentage of whatever income they had.

Critics derided the idea as far too costly and elaborate for what should have been, they felt, a cheaply built housing project. The building Cecil had in mind would cost a fortune, they said. The mix of diverse populations with horrendous health-care and mental-health needs would create chaos, discord, even violence. If he insisted on building it, they said, at least he could save money by splitting up the renters according to category (AIDS patients here, seniors there, mentally ill elsewhere) and save on health-care costs. But this was the kind of top-down decision—made for efficiency, not love—that Cecil would never support.

There would be no splitting up, he said. "Glide is a diverse and inclusive community for a reason," he told the critics. "We work together and make our decisions together. If we start segregating the people in any way, everyone loses. The residents of this building will come from our own ranks. They'll live together, create their own tenants association, make their own rules, and monitor their own activities."

"Street people running their own building?" the critics exclaimed. "The place will end up full of graffiti and trash in three months," some said. "It'll turn into a [drug users'] shooting gallery in six."

Cecil believed that was the kind of negative assumption that turned so many housing projects into prisons of the poor. At Glide, if you accepted people unconditionally, you did more than empathize—you treated them like family. You recognized that generations of homelessness and despair created cycles of chronic poverty that we, today, working with new and different partners could break. And you thought instead of assuming the worst, it was time to give people from the streets a fighting chance at changing their lives.

So when the question came up—Who could afford the costs of creating such services?—the answer, as Cecil said in his sermons, was all of us. All of us could afford to help people in trouble; for too long, we just didn't know how. All of us wanted to correct the social injustice of people suffering when help was nearby. Here was one way to do it.

Considering the enormity of the idea, it was surprising how quickly Cecil convinced the people who made decisions that they, too, were part of the beloved community. Everyone got it. They took pride in their part in it. People from the private sector who had never spoken with people from the public sector got their heads together like long-lost friends. Lawyers, donors, architects, contractors, bankers, the mayor's office, brokers, investors, developers, and builders helped Glide with everything from tax credits and realty advisers to construction lenders and redevelopment agencies. In the end they raised a building that was valued at $12.3 million on completion.

Key to the effort was our own board of trustees, which in the early decades (1960s–1980s) had routinely denied funding for programs that today are considered basic to Glide's vision (meals, job training, recovery, etc.). Over the years, the board changed dramatically as shortsighted trustees departed and a diverse membership of lawyers, health professionals, educators, financial planners, and investment experts came on. The board's president, Amy Errett, a Jewish lesbian venture capitalist, had begun attending Glide in the 1990s. For the first eighteen months that she attended Celebrations, Amy later told us, she was so overcome by the diversity and energy of the congregation that she "used to hide out in the balcony in tears." When we asked Amy to join the board, she led our organizational renovation campaign into the twenty-first century where it continues to be a model of nonprofit growth.

When we got to the design phase of Cecil's building, I asked homeless people in the Tenderloin what the word *home* meant to them. One person who could not conceive of living in an apartment said that "home meant a locker with a lock." One little girl told her mother that the bedroom closet in a soon-to-be-completed apartment was larger than the room they lived in now. People gave us all sorts of tips about placement of light, space for stoves, size of bathrooms, and so on. During construction, a merging of visions took place when the construction company made a point of hiring workers from the Tenderloin.

In 1999, only a year and a half after he proposed the idea, the Cecil Williams Glide Community House (CW House) opened its beautiful facilities, including fifty-two apartments, at 333 Taylor Street. The residents then and today are a mixture of people from the streets: most are diagnosed with multiple physical illnesses, mental conditions, and addictions. Some have AIDS; many are low-income families with children. All who move in say they want to make positive changes in their lives and take responsibility for the continued maintenance and beautification of CW House. Social workers, youth advocates, counselors, tutors, nurse practitioners (from Glide's health-care clinic), and financial consultants either maintain offices on the ground floor or are on call around the clock.

CW House became a model of supportive services for low-income residents, and the dream for affordable and dignified housing grew. Since then Glide has opened two other apartment buildings, each with its own development team and its own character, thanks to the inventiveness of real estate developer Paula Collins and the creative business vision of Mel Carriere. Deborah Whittle, director of our housing programs, helped design (and now oversees) the support services our residents require. The housing teams created a separate 501(c)3 nonprofit company (the Glide Economic Development Corporation) with its own staff and board. The two buildings are located on the same property:

125 Mason Street, which opened in 2009, is a fourteen-story building with eighty-one apartments for working poor families. 125 includes an outdoor courtyard/play space for children, a landscaped terrace where residents can cultivate their own gardens, indoor exercise facilities, and community spaces that can be used for classrooms, receptions, meetings, and meals.

125 Mason gave us a chance to discover and express publicly the incredible emotions that surge into anyone's consciousness when poor and working-class families move from the streets to their own apartments. To help artist Mildred Howard design the façade for 125 Mason, I again walked around the Tenderloin asking people, "What does home mean to you?" This time the answers rained down on my notepad like this:

safety, warmth, meals that are hot, loving, from the hands of mom.
community. love, clean, a haven from the elements like wind and rain and cold.
compassion of a good parent,
change. housing that does not regiment time, safety from rip-offs and rape

> *home: curtains, furnishings that were bright; safe toilets*
> *and bathrooms*
> *cook whenever I want,*
> *privacy   people to talk to that aren't trying to sell me drugs*
> *or rape my body*
> *community.*

Mildred and I looked at this flood of words and saw something like a Japanese haiku poem in the making that would reflect themes of grace and hope. Mildred wanted the words to look like they were being absorbed into the façade of the building like rain at the same time that they stood out from the surface. As I arranged the people's words into a poem, Mildred selected different fonts for different letters. The effect when you're looking up at the words from the sidewalk, especially when it rains, is to feel the "village"—all those homeless people who otherwise have so little visibility—speaking in a single voice.

> *community gathers*
> *   warmth*
> *   a safe place*
> *our world.*
> *And miracles appear*
> *in the trees*
> *we find the way*
> *like water*
> *like rain*
> *enters earth*

grace flows like water
like music
harmony
spirit
kindness
grace
Grace pours
like compassion,
like rain.
Dreams we hold
in our hearts . . .
our dream
Justice like waterfalls
tumbles into rivers
amazing grace
wakes us
to the beauty of
this home.

149 Mason Street, which opened in 2011, is an eight-story building of fifty-six furnished studio apartments for homeless people moving from the worst living conditions on the streets to state-of-the-art studio living, complete with a satellite health clinic on the premises to assist tenants with medical and psychiatric services. The 149 building is a far cry from the giant neon woman's leg doing a can-can kick in front of the LIVE NUDE GIRLS sign on the former house of burlesque that occupied this property before. I often wondered if the money was easier to raise for 149 Mason because a newspaper article headlined "Minister Buys Porno House" ran a photo of Cecil standing in front of that kicking neon leg.

Today what home means to the people in Glide's three buildings is such a cherished thing that it's difficult to describe. An aura of gratitude and sanctuary fills the halls when you walk from one apartment to another, and the sense of the community growing around you is palpable. In the dozen years since CW House opened, not a single mark of graffiti or piece of trash has appeared in any building. The residents' associations have all kept a fine balance ensuring both privacy and safety for all tenants. Of course there have been problems, but when you work with a support team that cares both personally and professionally for clients, and residents who learn how to trust themselves and others, solutions are always found, as Cecil says. Always.

People often ask what we do when tenants violate the rules of the apartment house, the laws of the city, or the expectations of Glide as a family. Here a comparison is helpful: in other buildings, the worst thing that can happen to tenants is a visit from the police. In Glide's buildings, the worst thing that can happen is for a tenant to be told, "Cecil will be disappointed when he hears what you did."

Enough time has passed since CW House opened that we are beginning to see long-term results. A single mother remarked recently that she's starting to "breathe easy" knowing that both her kids will graduate from college soon. Breathing easy probably means she will work two jobs for the rest of her life to pay for it, but her feelings of achievement and peace of mind are priceless.

One long-term result we never anticipated came from two families who wanted to move out of 125 Mason Street. It almost never happens that tenants leave any of our apartment houses. You can imagine the joy we felt on discovering that both families had saved enough money after they moved in to buy their own homes.

I have always believed that Glide is about creating a beautiful city where all people are welcome. Today as ghettos become gentrified, fewer and fewer people can afford to live in safe neighborhoods, so poor people are being run out. But they are never going away, and we shouldn't want them to. When a family hits hard times, everybody needs to come to the table.

People who have watched our new buildings going up like to say that Glide has changed the look of the Tenderloin, and of the city. They may sense that it wasn't easy, but how I wish they could see Cecil as I remember him in 1997, standing at the edge of the world, calling out, "City! Corporations! Nonprofits! We can build this! It may sound crazy, and there isn't enough money, but this is the beloved community! Our reality is beyond the possible!"

21

Affirmation

SOUL FOOD

by Janice Mirikitani
for Cecil, 1987

We prepare
the meal together.
I complain,
hurt, reduced to fury
again by their
subtle insults
insinuations
because I am married to you.
Impossible autonomy, no mind
of my own.

• • •

You like your fish
crisp, coated with cornmeal,
fried deep,
sliced mangos to sweeten
the tang of lemons.
My fish is raw,
on shredded lettuce,
lemon slices thin as skin,
wasabi burning like green fire.
You bake the cornbread flat
and dip it in
the thick soup
I've brewed from
turkey carcass, rice gruel,
sesame oil and chervil.
We laugh over watermelon
and bubbling cobbler.

You say, there are few men
who can stand
to have a woman equal,
upright.

This meal,
unsurpassed.

Cecil

The key to living a full life is to affirm, affirm, affirm. When things are good, affirm who you are and what makes life so good. When things are tough, affirm the values, the principles, the beliefs that have made you strong and are waiting to support you now. Notice what is happening to you every day and affirm your love whenever you can. Affirm what makes you different from everyone else—that is your power. Affirm the humanity of other people, especially when you don't like them. Affirm that something larger, that Spirit that is the life force in all of us.

Today most travel guides list Glide as a must-see activity for tourists who visit San Francisco. Traditional churches may say it's unseemly to be recommended as a tourist attraction, but for us, the joy of looking out from the stage at intrigued and earnest faces from Russia, from Nigeria, from Japan, from Indianapolis, from Australia, from China, from France, from Vietnam, from Spain, from the Czech Republic, from San Francisco, and elsewhere has made our belief in diversity and our Celebrations of life all the more—well, celebrated.

Tourists may not quite understand spoken English at Glide, but what they hear is untranslatable in any language, because it is spiritual. Everybody in the audience is no mere observer or onlooker but a participant in one big affirmation of life. The program is not just a show or a concert but a true Celebration of life and of the different languages we speak.

I think this is why visitors to Glide feel so much emotion when they attend a Celebration. They're struck by the diversity of people clapping and singing and sharing all that high energy coming at them from the stage. It's not that life is easy—more often than not, hard work and crises hit us every day. Rather what you sense at Celebrations is the will to fight back, to find and affirm the person you know yourself to be. And most of all, as our friend Warren Buffett so often says he learned from his late wife, Susie, who used to say she learned it at Glide, you feel overwhelmed by the possibility of unconditional love as if for the first time. People stand up and tell us what's happening to them in Glide's programs—how they're learning to forgive others (and themselves) for incidents too horrible to believe. Others recount, as I sometimes do in my sermons, despicable events in the news that we as citizens of the world must confront and understand. Gradually all the differences in the room are both celebrated and set aside, and all that is felt is our humanity, our soul, our hope for a just world. Often I see tears in people's eyes when I sum up my own feelings:

> At last. At last. It's taken so long, so many years, so much time, so much waste. We've wasted so much. Time after time, love after love, experience after experience have all brought us here, and now we know. Once we were lost, but now we are found. We are different and we are the same. Our strength lies in each other. We have come home at last.

Janice

One of the few times I felt the world coming to a similar revelation occurred when Cecil and I attended Bill Clinton's inauguration and listened to Maya Angelou read her poem "On the Pulse of Morning." To me, this was one of those rare works that seemed to reflect the vastness of the universe yet was so specific that it touched every detail of my own life. That's what great poetry does, I've always thought. It relates to a single drop of water as well as to the sea. Maya and Cecil are similar in that way—they have the gift of saying things that soar high above yet somehow connect us all.

One Sunday, in the middle of a sermon by Glide pastor Karen Oliveto, a disheveled woman in the second pew began screaming. I had noticed earlier that she was moving around restlessly and making comments while other people spoke. But now she was standing up, shouting profanities and accusations.

The congregation knew that it wasn't unusual for people to jump on the stage and interrupt the service—Cecil usually gave them the microphone and turned whatever they had to say into a sermon. But this woman was shrieking and weeping in such agony that even the efforts of our sensitive ushers and security staff could not calm her.

Cecil walked across the stage and asked Karen to "hold up" while he went down the stairs to see about the woman. People in the pews got out of his way so that he could stand next to her and talk to her, even though she couldn't hear him over her screams. He kept his head near hers, however, whispering to her and patting her on the shoulder. That seemed to give her some comfort, although she kept yelling.

"I've been out in the streets for over seven days!" she cried. "Without a place to sleep or shower or rest! No one listens to me! I've been wearing the same clothes for over a week! I can't bear to smell myself!" At this, several of us left the stage, too, so we could be with her and put our hands on her shoulders along with Cecil's. This quieted her a little, though her screams continued. Cecil signaled to members of the Glide Ensemble, and they began singing a beautiful gospel song, "Keep Your Loving Arms Around Me," very softly, while moving to the risers. Those words of protection and peace— "Keep me in Your care, / Let me know You're there"—seemed to slow the heaving and shuddering of the woman's shoulders as she turned her weeping eyes to Cecil.

"I've been so alone!" she told him, and just saying it out loud to Cecil's compassionate face seemed to be enough. He kept patting and whispering to her for several minutes, until finally she said, "I'm finishing up now. I'm done."

By this time the whole ensemble—more than eighty people—had taken its place on the risers, and a dozen of us from the stage had circled around the woman, soothing and gently touching her as Cecil kept whispering and the sanctuary filled with song—"Whatever comes, just keep Your arms around me." When it seemed that she was going to be all right, Cecil went back to the stage, Karen continued her sermon, and everyone else in the church, myself included, sat there transfixed by what had just happened.

After the service a man said to me, "That was the most incredible enactment of unconditional love I've ever seen." After all my years at Glide, I could hardly believe it either. Here was a distressed woman who felt sheltered enough to express immense suffering, and as a result, because this was Glide, we all were blessed in return. We were all part of the beloved community that Cecil had envisioned from the start. When the Celebration ended, each of us walked out of the church feeling those loving arms around us as well.

I asked Cecil later what he had been thinking when the woman started screaming and he got up to help. "I didn't plan anything," he said. "I just let the Spirit lead me." It occurred to me then, as it has many times, why people from all walks of life trust Cecil Williams. It's because he treats everyone the same. Whether it's a former inmate or a movie star or the mayor or a homeless addict, Cecil relates to people's humanity, and he does so without assumption or judgment. Watching him do this inspires all of us to do the same, the next time we encounter someone who seems threatening or foreign.

This is one reason why Cecil is so loved in our SpeakOut sessions, which we hold every week at Glide for anyone who wants to speak at the microphone in front of whatever group happens to congregate. Usually about seventy-five to one hundred people attend, most of them from the street and many of them homeless. I'm always grateful that anybody shows up, because these are mostly people who don't ordinarily relate to others, let alone venture into a church or other enclosure where they may feel trapped, especially by the attention of others.

Cecil is so happy at SpeakOut that I wonder if this wasn't what his days of playing Church were like when he was a kid. He doesn't run the show so much as bask in the delight people take in each other's disclosures. I also love this anything-goes session because the testimony is raw and biting yet capable of the most incredible tenderness, humor, and dignity. Everybody gets to speak for two minutes about whatever they want—some people sing, some play musical instruments—and over the years, we've seen an astonishing change among the regulars.

Magnolia, for as long as she lived, was an example. Here was a person who came to Glide at age sixteen, having survived everything from rape and incest to homelessness and prostitution. She spoke publicly about growing up and about battling her way through self-destructive habits (drugs, anger, homelessness), and just as she began to find strength in her identity during her thirties, doctors told her she had breast cancer. At first, Magnolia expressed her rage at SpeakOut—rage against the medical system, against the pain, against chemotherapy—but she never lost hope. Even in her moments of despair and physical challenges, she would show up at Glide, volunteer at the Walk-In Center where we find shelter and other ways to help the homeless, and attend every SpeakOut and Sunday Celebration. Magnolia rechanneled her emotions against the violence that faces children every day by writing poetry and offering whatever services she could provide. Our affirmation of her voice, her feelings, and her gift meant everything to her. She carried around a notebook as a safe place to put her truths. But she had the ability to keep most of her poems in her head and recite them so vividly at SpeakOut—not just a stanza or two but lengthy and complicated rhymed verse with a little bit of rap that she performed quickly and matter-of-factly—that no one in the audience moved a muscle. Magnolia began to work with other breast cancer survivors during writing workshops and even mustered up the nerve to recite her most difficult poem at Springalicious!—the drag-queen extravaganza in the Castro (San Francisco's gay district)—and quieted the raucous audience down to complete silence.

It would be an understatement to say that Magnolia found unconditional love at Glide. She was transformed by this love, and by the persistent acceptance and encouragement by Cecil and me and the community. Her body might have grown weaker once she was restricted to a wheelchair, then bedridden, but her presence, her sense of self, her ability to grow and her belief in affirming who she was got stronger until the day she died.

Unconditional love thrives in the chaos of life, as Cecil says, and we often see this in the circus atmosphere at SpeakOut. One man will sing incoherently into the microphone without any sense of time or space, so that when his two minutes are over—and our host Angela Coleman, no stranger to recovery, is clapping and yelling "Thank you! That was great!" and three other women join her to pull the microphone from him—we're all cheering because his singing turns into a moan because everybody gets it that he's really moaning for life.

One young woman came to SpeakOut with two different colored wigs, one black and one red, which she didn't put on because her hair was bleach streaked anyway. In the middle of SpeakOut she sat down in the aisle talking and giggling to herself, with her legs so far apart that people could see up her skirt. Respect is the name of the game at SpeakOut, and some of the wildest, scariest men here, who in other circumstances might have chased her down an alleyway and attacked her,

looked away out of respect and listened to what she was trying
to say.

Another regular whom Cecil and I have nicknamed the
Calculator Man usually brings a cell phone and calculator to
the microphone and speaks mostly in numbers. He explains
that he's publishing a magazine that will make Glide a million dollars in a month, and he calculates that if we sell 60,000
magazines at 25 cents, it will earn us $100,000 in a day, and
$250,000 in a month, multiplied times 12 to net us a million
dollars a year times 6,000 for a total of $59 trillion. Nobody can
keep up with his figures and nobody wants to—the Calculator
is so certain of his projections that we can all celebrate getting
Glide *and* America free and clear from financial trouble at last.

One woman named Lucy came to SpeakOut week after
week saying nothing but "Jesus! Jesus! Jesus!" while other
people were speaking. She sat over on the side trying to keep
this inner presence from bursting out of her so loudly. But
every time Lucy tried to lower her voice, a few "Jesus! Jesus!"
exclamations would come out on their own. Later she came
over and apologized.

"I don't mean to interrupt people's microphone time,"
she said. "If you don't want me to come here, it's okay. I
understand."

"Lucy, no," I said. "We not only want you to come, we *need*
you here. If you don't come, SpeakOut won't work."

It works because it humbles, it warms, it tickles the funny
bone, and it makes you grateful. It works because when Speak-
Out ends and Cecil tells everyone how much he loves them,
people absorb that love and take it with them and give it to each

other. It works because Cecil congratulates us all for telling the truth, and he reminds us why we do this week after week.

"Because the truth . . ." he begins.

"MAKES US FREE," everyone calls out, and we remember that the stories told that night go to the heart of what Glide is all about. The truth does set us free—from self-loathing, from judgment, from hopelessness—to be who we really are. Because each one of us is different, and celebrating our difference gives us our power.

That is the miracle of the beloved community as seen through SpeakOut. Many of these people have been labeled "crazy," "disturbed," "irrational," or simply "not normal." Some feel claustrophobic indoors, or are afraid of conspiracies against them, or are driven by voices in their head. Yet week after week, they choose to come in from the streets and sit quietly—or mostly quietly—in this room so they can listen to someone else's truth. After spending their days being wary and distant and suspicious of other people, they cheer and applaud strangers at SpeakOut who for a little while feel like family. To me—the cynic, the skeptic, the doubter—that is the Spirit that Cecil always talks about, made visible at last.

Cecil

In SpeakOut I've learned the value of staying open to life. Transformation can occur at any time you are ready. This is something I've always admired about any disenfranchised group trying to change society. Just by making an effort to change the status quo, people change themselves. They are walking with the Spirit, and they are bringing the world forward. When African Americans sing "We Shall Overcome," they have already overcome. They have gone beyond what others believe is possible.

This was why, many years ago, Janice and I changed the lyrics of this song from "some day" to "today" so that Glide's congregation could affirm its message as justice-in-the-making.

Oh, deep in my heart, I do believe,
We shall overcome today.

That is being spiritual. If God wants us to be free, God wants us to be responsible. "It's spiritual," I say to the congregation. Then I draw it out—"It's Spirit, y'all!"—and people smile. That's the one they'll remember.

The key to Glide's first fifty years, as Janice and I have always thought, is that you cannot *make* a loving community. You have to leave that responsibility to the people. It's like a jigsaw puzzle that's always about to come together yet is never unformed. If you seek justice, you must love; if you love, you must accept; if you are accepting, you know Spirit; if you are spiritual, you are free; if you are free, you understand difference; if you are different, you can imagine; when you imagine, you can act; when you act, you understand recovery; when you seek recovery, you share in humanity; when you feel humanity, you seek justice. The inseparable nature of those qualities is the love story for us all. Loving what is different about yourself, and affirming that love every day, starts the whole puzzle coming together again.

APPENDIX

I wanted to write a new poem for the International Poetry Festi-
val at Wales in 1993. Maya Angelou, who had recommended me
as a presenter, would be sitting in the audience with Cecil, my
muse. Cecil and I had been married for ten years by that time,
and the issues of sexual abuse we had discussed continued to come
up in moments of intimacy. His patience and wisdom helped me
understand that the warring in my mind existed as well in my
own body.

Cecil and I explored Wales whenever we could, astounded by
the rolling green countryside, so quiet you could hear the baaing
of lambs, and by the Festival itself, which encouraged people to
borrow books freely from outdoor exhibits. I was a runner at the
time, and early one morning I took off on a road so narrow that
if I spread my arms, I could feel the tall grass brushing my hands
on both sides. It was dangerous running here because this was the
only road that cars could use to reach the Festival.

I had been worrying all night that "War of the Body" might
be too controversial for the Festival, and then all of a sudden
I reached the top of a hill. The stunning view of lush Welsh

farmlands—even more beautiful at that moment because the sunrise had just broken through—moved me so deeply that I burst into tears. I remember hearing myself saying "Thank you" over and over.

The poem was well received that day and became part of a book collection released by Virago Press, a British house that Maya had encouraged to become my publisher. She has always been generous in this way. Like Cecil, she uses her celebrity to empower the voices of others.

Maya was the featured poet at the Festival and the only woman invited to sing with the Welsh Men's Choir. She then led these rich and eloquent male voices in the singing of "Amazing Grace." It was magic.

—Janice Mirikitani

War of the Body

by Janice Mirikitani
for Cecil, 1993

I had hoped for a truce
not believing it possible,
this protracted war with my body,
so long waged, hating my breasts
that stung to the touch,
this flat body, frigid as a bivouac.
I had feared no marriage
could survive my demolition.

From her childhood,
the invasions of male artillery without warning
at night when stars were hidden,
excavated, scudmissiled her.
Like a prisoner of war, she crept into
sweet, unchallenging silence
where she could escape,
leave from the village of her body
and watch it burn from a distance.
She wished the mothers
would rescue the children at least,
clutch them to their backs,
and carry them to safety.
But he quickly scattered them like a fallen nest,
broken eggshells, twigs, feathers,
crushed by his heavy bootheel.
He grinds the child into the soft wood
of her cage, until her back
is a wall of slivers.

> *He captures chickens, rubs his fingers into them,*
> *molests the kittens, dogs in heat, as they hiss, howl,*
> *often die. He laughs, knowing that the child sees.*

I tell you these memories,
yielding my silence like a weapon,
as we vault through minefields of marriage,
my rage meaner than mortar,
thoughtless as prison food.
My body, like a burn victim
is cauterized shut.
I tell you in the warm sunlight of morning,

your eyes swarming like bees.
You say the dead can spring from our throats.
You have laid your face into burnt soil,
seen leaves rotting like flesh,
but from the bones sprout lavender,
henna, elm.
You whisper Isaiah to me, *"Rain does not return*
to heaven until it waters earth."
                    Everything is useful.
                    Come, you say,
bring your slivered wall,
your burned village,
your amputated sex, the prisons of silence,
your torn bird
to my sanctuary.
                    No secret is too shameful.
Place your soiled breasts
into the nest of my hands.
Truth is not punished here
in this demilitarized zone
where you are not a segregated woman
but an integrity of light.
                              My body
                              in the forest of your arms,
                              becomes unseparated,
                              as I pull your mouth
                              to my throat
                              so that I may have two tongues.
                              I breathe with your breathing.
                              My flesh opens, unstitched.

Hair flows the length of sheets,
and the oils of our skin
blend like two streams joining.

This river is clean.
On the shore at this moment
the child is clutched on my back,
being carried to safety.

Wales